OFF-WHITE HOLLYWOOD

'An undoubtedly important book. With its analysis of the historical transformation in the cultural understanding of gender and ethnicity in film, *Off-White Hollywood* fills a gap in both whiteness studies and cinema studies. Negra is to be congratulated!'
Jon Stratton, *Curtin University of Technology*

'Diane Negra's smart, savvy, imaginative exploration brings to the surface cultural changes – from the turn of the twentieth century to the present – in the invisible racial and ethnic assumptions that underlie the allure of filmic glamour and sex appeal. Perhaps Negra's most startling effect is to break the silence with which the culture industry typically embalms stars who once seemed to rule Hollywood but were ultimately casually discarded by a system that regards women as commodities, ethnicity as artificial flavoring, and whiteness as a norm.'
Martha P. Nochimson, *Mercy College*

Off-White Hollywood investigates how the 'ethnicity' of white European-American actresses has played a key role in the mythology of American identity and nation-building. Embodying national fantasies and 'assimilation myths', ethnic female film stars symbolised the promise of American multiculturalism and proved the desirability and reliability of the American Dream.

Through case studies of stars spanning cinema's history, Diane Negra examines Hollywood films and promotional material as a vehicle through which American culture expresses and negotiates gender and ethnic identities. Negra focuses on key stars of the silent (Colleen Moore and Pola Negri), classical (Sonja Henie and Hedy Lamarr) and post-classical eras (Marisa Tomei and Cher) to demonstrate how each star illuminates aspects of ethnicity, gender, consumerism and class at work in American culture. Tracing processes of transformation, containment and resistance, from the assimilation imperatives of the early twentieth century to the current ethnic revival, *Off-White Hollywood* shows how star personae have reflected the changing meaning of whiteness in US culture.

Diane Negra is Assistant Professor in the Department of Radio, TV and Film at the University of North Texas. She is the co-editor of *A Feminist Reader in Early Cinema* (2002).

OFF-WHITE HOLLYWOOD

American culture and ethnic female stardom

Diane Negra

London and New York

First published 2001
by Routledge
11 New Fetter Lane, London EC4P 4EE

Simultaneously published in the USA and Canada
by Routledge
29 West 35th Street, New York, NY 10001

Routledge is an imprint of the Taylor & Francis Group

Typeset in 9.5/12pt Galliard
by Graphicraft Limited, Hong Kong
Printed and bound in Great Britain by
Biddles Ltd, Guildford and King's Lynn

British Library Cataloguing in Publication Data
A catalogue record for this book is available from the British Library

Library of Congress Cataloging in Publication Data
Negra, Diane, 1966–
Off-white Hollywood : American culture and ethnic female stardom/
Diane Negra. p. cm.
Includes bibliographical references and index.
1. Minorities in motion pictures. 2. Women in motion pictures.
3. European Americans—Ethnic identity.
4. Actresses—United States—Biography. I. Title.
PN1995.9.M56 N44 2001
791.43′652042—dc21   2001019928

ISBN 0-415-21677-X (hbk) ISBN 0-415-21678-8 (pbk)

CONTENTS

ILLUSTRATIONS

ACKNOWLEDGEMENTS

Off-White Hollywood was conceptualized and written as I lived and worked in a number of different locations during the last five years including Texas, New York, Ireland and Poland. It has struck me from time to time that my own geographical and cultural mobility has facilitated my interest in and understanding of the lives of the women I discuss in this project, many of whom negotiated significant national, cultural and linguistic borders in their lifetimes. I hope that my discussion of their work proves the more illuminating for the travels I have been fortunate to undertake.

There are a number of people whose exemplary behavior as teachers and scholars has influenced and inspired me and in this capacity I want to thank Robert Allen, Sabrina Barton, Jennifer Bean, Mia Carter, Natasha Casey, Mary Desjardins, Luke Gibbons, Susan McLeland, Mary McGlynn, Walter Metz, Anne Morey, Marcy Paul, Tom Schatz and Justin Wyatt.

I wish particularly to thank the participants in my Ethnicity and American Film seminars at the University of North Texas and the University of Gdansk for their intellectual curiosity, enthusiasm and energy. I am also indebted to the members of the Women's Writing Group formed at the University of North Texas in 1998. Diana York Blaine, Francesca Morgan, and Claire Sahlin provided evenings of rich conversation that helped to further this project. Other UNT colleagues past and present especially Harry Benshoff, Olaf Hoerschelmann, and Shanti Kumar have provided timely advice, support, and humor. Elizabeth Butler-Cullingford, Steven Cohan, John Hartigan and Sean Griffin offered perceptive readings of chapters in progress. In 1998, Jeff Chown and Bob Self kindly invited me to share in the rewards of directing the Media and Culture in Ireland Summer School in Dublin each summer, and my understanding of the dynamics of ethnicity and European heritage has been furthered by working with American students studying abroad.

I wish to thank Dean Warren Burggren and Kathryn Cullivan of the College of Arts and Sciences at the University of North Texas for their help in facilitating my leave on a Fulbright Lectureship to Poland during the last year of my work on this project. At the University of Gdansk Andrzej Ceynowa, Beata Williamson, and Cheryl Malcolm offered generous and collegial support for which I am very grateful. Thank you also to my friends in Gdansk including Homa Firouzbakheh, Ove Bergerson, Soren Rasmussen, Andrew Shacklock and Susan Pearce.

My research assistants, Shelley McGinnis, Ashley Smith, and Manasi Sapre, were of great help in preparing the various chapters of this project. Shelley, in particular, provided me with indispensable assistance; her ready understanding of the goals of this project made it possible for me to rely on her for research details that support the chapters. During the research and writing of this book, I also had the pleasure of working with other fine graduate students who displayed a commendable dedication and rigor in their scholarship including Hyon Joo Murphree, Andrew McIntosh, Owen Pillion, Przemek Budziszewski and Kasia Chmielewska. Energizing interaction with these students has fueled this project in many ways. Audiences at the Society for Cinema Studies annual meetings, the Console-ing Passions Conference, and at Marie Curie-Sklodowska University and the University of Wroclaw provided useful feedback on chapters in progress. Bill Luhr graciously extended an invitation to present material from this project at the Columbia University Seminar on Cinema and Interdisciplinary Interpretation and I benefited from the insights of that knowledgeable audience. At Routledge, Rebecca Barden has been a strong source of support and encouragement in regard to this project. Alistair Daniel has been a most helpful guide through the editorial process.

The College of Arts and Sciences at the University of North Texas has generously supported this project. I am very grateful for this institutional assistance which took concrete shape in the form of two Junior Faculty Research Grants in 1999. An Irish-American Cultural Institute Grant was provided to me at a highly opportune moment in 1996, enabling me to make research trips to archives that were indispensable in the research for Chapter 2. A University Film and Video Association Research Grant facilitated the research and writing of the dissertation out of which this book emerged.

At a very early stage of this project my grandfather Peter Negra (a descendent of Italian immigrants from Genoa) passed away, and just shortly before it was completed my grandfather Gerard McDonald (whose family were from Co. Antrim and Co. Sligo in Ireland) died after a long illness. I hope that this book honors their memory.

1

HOLLYWOOD FILM AND THE NARRATIVIZATION OF ETHNIC FEMININITY

For the tourist in Hollywood who sets out to follow the legendary inscriptions on the Walk of Fame, the logical place to begin is at the corner of La Brea and Hollywood Boulevard. At this intersection stands a monument entitled 'The Gateway to Hollywood,' composed of four silver caryatids modeled to resemble the actresses Dorothy Dandridge, Mae West, Dolores Del Rio and Anna May Wong. The monument is intended to commemorate these actresses, whose different ethnic and racial identities are to symbolize the diversity of Hollywood itself. For others, however, it may have a very different import, serving as a less sanguine reminder of Hollywood's tendency to absorb and commodify female ethnicity.

In general, we may observe how monuments such as this one participate in the perpetuation and consolidation of received accounts of history. They seek to educate us by telling us what we ought to believe, or reassure us by telling us again what it is we already believe.[1] Monuments such as 'Gateway to Hollywood' thus work to obscure what they overtly commemorate. The notion of a 'gateway' implicitly references immigration history, and posits a connection between the absorptive capacities of Hollywood and America itself. In memorializing four (dead) actresses of differing races and ethnicities, the monument taps into national myths about diversity while at the same time relegating such questions to Hollywood's past. Consequently, Dandridge, West, Del Rio and Wong are rendered as blank icons so that, as a travel writer in *The New York Times* observed, 'the sculpture looks like a batch of oversized hood ornaments.'[2] 'Gateway to Hollywood,' while a seeming tribute to actresses positioned to embody some version of ethnic femininity, reduces their meaning to superficialities. The sculpture acknowledges the contributions of ethnic women in film but simultaneously contains and heavily proscribes that contribution.

Part of the impetus for this book is to disturb such complacent understandings of Hollywood's deployment of tropes of ethnic femininity. Rather than accept the memorializing impulse behind 'Gateway to Hollywood' as a phenomenon sui generis, I argue that it is, in fact, fully expressive of the character of ethnic femininity as it is constructed in the Hollywood representational system. In this book, I consider the place of ethnic femininity in that system in fuller detail and in a clearer context, investigating Hollywood film texts and promotional discourses as means by which American culture expresses and negotiates gender and ethnic identities. To do this, I set out to examine the ways in which one of the most consistent representational tropes in Hollywood history – that of ethnic femininity – has been put into narrative. In both film narratives and in larger, overarching narratives of celebrity, I document processes of transformation, containment and resistance germane both to new accounts of Hollywood history and to the formulation of an evolutionary perspective on contemporary questions of gender and its relationship to ethnicity. In so doing, I hope to elucidate the discursive power of female stardom and the complex ways in which stars delight and trouble the national imagination.

The case studies introduced in this book include silent era stars Colleen Moore and Pola Negri, studio-era stars Sonja Henie and Hedy Lamarr, and contemporary stars Marisa Tomei and Cher. It will be evident that this study has opted to limit its focus in several important respects. In order to attain a sufficiently rich level of analysis, I consider the stardom of ethnic actresses in selected historical periods, rather than attempting to fully encompass the entire silent, classical and post-classical eras. That sort of overly generalized strategy would entail the neglect of key details and trenchant patterns of evolution and contradiction in star personae, in favor of a more sweeping argument that I do not seek to make. Further, I do not select examples of stars whose most prominent affiliation is with other national cinemas. The ethnicities scrutinized in this project reflect not so much any possible diversity as they do the kinds of ethnicities most frequently relied upon by Hollywood to stage assimilation myths. In exploring the relationship between ethnicity and whiteness throughout this book, I treat ethnicity and nationality as very close categories, in large part because this is often the way they are formulated in public discourse.

Secondly, while the 'Gateway to Hollywood' monument makes plain that Hollywood has incorporated and commodified a variety of female types, some of these have already been well analyzed. There are, for instance, numerous studies of Hollywood and racial difference. Gina Marchetti has provided insightful critique of Asian ethnicity in Hollywood representation.[3] A number of scholars have studied Latino and Latina representation in American film and television.[4] Donald Bogle has assessed the history of stereotypes of African-American representation in American film, and his work been fruitfully updated by Ed Guerrero and Mark Winokur.[5] The stars discussed here have been substantially neglected, with the exception of Jeanine Basinger's study which profiles silent-era figures including Pola Negri and Colleen Moore, although she does not consider the ethnic features of their stardom.[6]

My interest in white ethnicity and the Euro-American hyphenate in particular necessitates some discussion at the outset. This book chiefly examines Euro-American constructions of whiteness, rather than Latina or African-American or Asian American identities (which deserve analytical attention in their own right, but sustain, I think, a very different relationship to assimilation ideologies than do Euro-American ones). White ethnicities have consistently emerged as representationally useful in defusing social tensions by activating assimilation myths. These ethnicities are perhaps most in need of fresh analysis, for they have tended to be both literally and figuratively 'naturalized.' Furthermore, white Americans of mixed European ancestry have been almost uniquely positioned to claim or disclaim aspects of their heritage at will, often electing one ethnicity based on social definitions of what it implies. Since the advent of nationalist ideology in the United States in the mid-eighteenth century, 'American' has often, to some degree or another, connoted 'Euro-American.' Yet in sharp contrast to the valuable, abundant bodies of work that address representation and African-American, Asian and Latino identity, Film Studies has been relatively slow to attend to the significant numbers of films and film roles which articulate European and Euro-American ethnicity. The few studies that exist (apart from a few recent notable exceptions cited throughout) tend to focus on stereotype analysis. In this project I take up a question that has been too seldom posed in film studies: What functions has Europe been made to serve in the American cinematic imaginary?

The US is a nation that prides itself on the coherence and orderliness of its internal differences and invests deeply in the mythology of a variety of different ethnic groups in peaceful co-existence. These tenets of American social life have long been validated and perpetuated through popular culture. As female embodiments of national fantasies, ethnic female film stars have symbolized the promise of American pluralism and proved the desirability and reliability of the American Dream (sometimes in triumphant success narratives, sometimes in negative object lessons). The biographical narratives of these female stars propose in various ways the conditions under which American success can be achieved. The 'Americanization' of such stars (whether confidently or uneasily enacted) reflects many of the ideological cornerstones of American life. Accordingly, their success entails discourses on hard work and sacrifice that reinvigorate myths of meritocracy. Repressed (as in the case of stars like Hedy Lamarr) or exuberantly performed (as in the case of Cher), star labor is often a labor of the body and nearly all of the stars under discussion can be seen as adherent to dominant disciplinary practices of femininity.

I will argue that it is insufficient to consider the ethnic woman as a mere stereotype, despite the fact that she has so often been represented as excessive, hypersexual, primitive, animalistic or exotic. In fact, the ideological/cultural work she has performed has been complex and variable. In much of the work of film history, cursory assessments (or none at all) are made of the place of the 'foreign woman.' Incarnations of the type are seldom connected, and when one discusses the role of the foreign, female 'Other,' we tend to think only of canonized actresses such as Greta Garbo, Marlene Dietrich or Ingrid Bergman. One of the foundational assumptions for this project is that when we look beyond the canon, we discover that discourses of gender and ethnicity have played a prominent part in the packaging of many Hollywood actresses, whose careers, even when they are not well-remembered today, were by no means inconsequential. I envision this project as part of an ongoing effort by feminist film theorists and historians to understand women's representational history, and thus it is deliberately centered around actresses whom traditional film histories have tended to overlook or dismiss. I challenge the implication in a number of film histories that while female stars occupy a place in Hollywood history, their meanings are prosaic and their reception straightforward.

In fact, throughout most of Hollywood's history the construction of an American feminine ideal has taken place in contradistinction to a shifting ethnic other embodied through stardom. On some occasions female stars remain as counter-ideals; more frequently their biographies and film roles reflect efforts at transformation in accordance with ideological requirements. Most recently, in an era in which 'white ethnicity emerges as a trope of empowerment,'[7] ethnic identity is valued for its own sake in opposition to a whiteness deemed sterile. In all of these instances the constructions of female star personae manageably reproduce broader cultural processes, enabling us to trace their dynamics more precisely. Examining female stars promoted in terms of their ethnicity will ultimately help us to trace the ephemeral discourses of white, patriarchal hegemony, and thereby contribute to a better understanding of women's positionality in culture.

Arguing that Hollywood distills complex processes of social incorporation, I consider the ways in which the careers of certain actresses instantiate a 'crisis of assimilation' where Hollywood and its audience undertake the roles of benign host and sponsor to the foreign 'Other.' Through readings of their stardom, I illustrate that Hollywood models the domestication of white feminine ethnicity as a means of maintaining crucial cultural myths about American assimilative capacities.

Whiteness and its border spaces

The literature theorizing and historicizing whiteness has increased many times over since this project was first conceived. At this writing, that body of work continues to rapidly expand, with 'whiteness' itself taking up the place of a critical keyword in many branches of humanities scholarship. While I cannot summarize all of the theoretical developments in this growing area, I would like to selectively discuss some of the work that is most influential upon my own.[8]

This project adheres to the agenda shared by much of the scholarship on whiteness, which 'focuses largely on the critical project of unveiling the rhetorical, political, cultural, and social mechanisms through which whiteness is both invented and used to mask its power and privilege.'[9] In *White* Richard Dyer convincingly establishes that whiteness has long been a relational category in Western culture, often visible only in relation to the signifying capacities of color. In other words, we should note that in many important respects whiteness takes its definition from non-white and not-fully white others.[10] It is certainly true, as Sharon Willis observes, that in American film as in our culture at large, 'whiteness has had a hard time seeing *itself* at all,'[11] but we have seldom examined the work of 'border agents' such as white ethnic stars whose qualified whiteness can trouble the security of a white identity whose power has historically derived from its status as the normative unnamed. As Ann duCille succinctly puts it, 'a silence about itself is the primary prerogative of whiteness.'[12]

With whiteness normalized to the point that it often becomes invisible, ethnicity can serve as a marker of disruption, drawing attention to the precarious cultural power associated with whiteness. Indeed, Dyer himself suggests this in a brief section of his book entitled 'the colourless sources of racial colour,' where he recounts makeup techniques used to soften the Slavic looks of stars such as Dietrich, Claudette Colbert and Hedy Lamarr.[13] Although white, these European-born stars were, apparently, not white enough. If (as in Dyer's account) orderliness, civilization, rationality, modernity and industry are all figured as white, then color signifies the oppositional attributes of disorder, primitivism, and recidivism. Ethnicity within whiteness threatens to erase the comfortable distance between whiteness and color. Dyer's discussion of whiteness as essentially undefined except in opposition to color is generalizable to ethnicities that in some sense, signify the threat of 'color' within whiteness. This recognition of internal hierarchies within whiteness is integral to my study. Historian Matthew Frye Jacobson rightly notes that 'The contest over whiteness – its definition, its internal hierarchies, its proper boundaries, and its rightful claimants – has been critical to American culture throughout the nation's history, and it has been a fairly untidy affair.'[14] From Jacobson's *Whiteness of a Different Color: European Immigrants and the Alchemy of Race* I borrow the concept of 'probationary' whiteness. Jacobson draws attention to the insecurity of whiteness for assimilating Americans, and provides a vocabulary for identifying those whose European ethnicities (particularly those linked to New Immigration in the early twentieth century) conferred upon them a brand of whiteness that was always contingent, seldom as secure as those whose racial credentials were rooted in the Anglo-Saxon 'old stock.'

Lauren Berlant's work on the cultural politics of nationalized images of the normal also informs this study, particularly its latter chapters on contemporary stars whose nostalgic and free-floating ethnic identities speak to/from an emergent panic over national identity in the late twentieth and early twenty-first centuries.[15] Additionally, George Lipsitz maps out in precise and compassionate terms the material and ideological investments that Euro-Americans hold in defining Americanness as whiteness. Rather than a racial truth, he notes, 'whiteness is, however, a social fact, an identity created and continued with all-too-real consequences for the distribution of wealth, prestige and opportunity.'[16] For this reason, whiteness can adeptly re-fashion its boundaries to adjust to new circumstances, and such changes have been both reflected and consolidated through elements of the representational sphere. Lipsitz observes:

> 'Whiteness' emerged as a relevant category in US life and culture largely as a result of slavery and segregation, Native American policy

and immigration restrictions, conquest and colonialism. Economics and politics relegated various racial groups to unequal access to property and citizenship, while cultural practices institutionalized racism in everyday life by uniting diverse European American subjects into an imagined community called into being through appeals to white supremacy. Wild West shows, minstrel shows, Hollywood films, and commercial advertising have not merely reflected the racism that exists in social relations but have helped produce a unified white racial identity through the shared experience of spectatorship.[17]

Drawing from Lipsitz's arguments thus enables me to begin with the notion of whiteness as an identity rubric around which social and economic power has been consolidated.

John Hartigan's work on white racialness represents another way of examining the operations of whiteness in a bordered context. His ethnographic study of present-day Detroit examines a site that represents 'a shift in the architectonics of whiteness, from a time when it was stabilized in the city through a host of social and political operations to a moment when it became construed as "out of place."'[18] Many of Hartigan's interviewees are descendents of Southern white 'hillbillies' who migrated to Detroit seeking employment. This group of marginal whites represented exactly the kinds of threats once associated with the New Immigrants of Southern and Eastern Europe – an undeniable physical whiteness, yet a failure to conform to the unstated social norms associated with that category.[19] Whites in these kinds of 'border spaces' often threateningly disconfirm the inevitability and desirability of whiteness as a form of social capital.

Part of the significance of this study lies in its challenge to conventional wisdom that the vast majority of white ethnic stars suppressed their ethnic affiliations. Certainly many did so; yet, as I demonstrate, the fictionalization of ethnic identity could also work in reverse and many stars retained, exaggerated or invented altogether a profitable ethnic persona. Unlike such stars as Rita Hayworth (the former Margarita Cansino), Doris Day (Doris von Kappelhoff), Paulette Goddard (Pauline Levy), and Natalie Wood (Natasha Zacharenko-Gurdin), whose manufacture involved the suppression of ethnic nomenclature in favor of less problematically white identities, the name-based personae of the stars in *Off-White Hollywood* reflect decisively ethnic white identities. These modes of ethnic performance suggest that a simple renunciation model of ethnic identity does not enable us to account for the diverse white ethnicities of mainstream stars playing a wide variety of roles throughout Hollywood history. This book documents modes of ethnic 'passing' that could not be accounted for under a monolithic model of whiteness. In the majority of case studies, it directs attention to the modes of response that come up through stardom toward a changing view of Europe, an 'Old World' site that is alternately decrepit and vibrant in the American imagination.

Ruth Frankenberg's study of the way in which white women are implicated in racism is also germane to my project. Frankenberg's telling interviews with white women subjects about their own race histories leads her to consider the contradiction between the nebulousness of whiteness, and its continuing association with the monopolization of cultural power. She writes that:

> Within the dualistic discourse on culture, whiteness can by definition have no meaning: as a normative space it is constructed precisely by the way in which it positions others at its borders. To put it another way, within that discourse, 'whiteness' is indeed a space defined only by reference to those named cultures it has flung out to its perimeter. Whiteness is in this sense fundamentally a relational category.
>
> However, whiteness *does* have content inasmuch as it generates norms, ways of understanding history, ways of thinking about self and other, and even ways of thinking about the notion of culture itself. Thus whiteness needs to be examined and historicized. We need to look more closely at the content of the normative and attempt to analyze both its history and its consequences.[20]

Like Frankenberg, I address the social construction of whiteness, and a focus on Hollywood film stars will allow me to explore the way in which stars occupy a unique place at the intersection of cinema, ethnicity and social discourse. By complicating the category of whiteness with respect to Hollywood female stardom from the silent cinema to the present, we can see how stars work in particular ways to organize social discourse on ethnicity. My project of complicating the whiteness of certain stars thus represents an effort to use star personae as material sites of analysis for more nebulous cultural phenomena. Frankenberg has noted that:

> To speak of 'the social construction of whiteness' asserts that there are locations, discourses and material relations to which the term 'whiteness' applies. I argue in this book that whiteness refers to a set of locations that are historically, socially, politically, and culturally produced, and, moreover, are intrinsically linked to unfolding relations of domination.[21]

Star personae, I would argue, are especially suitable sites for analysis given their precise locations within a social geography of gender and ethnicity.

In considering what relations obtain between a star persona and the social and political context of its popularization, it is important to look at both specific historical events and broader, more nebulous patterns of popular feeling. In considering the representational trajectories of ethnic star personae in the context of social history, I hope to be able to more precisely locate shifts in the incorporation and excorporation of particular ethnicities into the white ideal.

To consider whiteness and femininity together further entails recognition of the fact that both identity positions take their definition as negative terms. (To be gendered female is to be non-male, to be white is to be not black). White femininity means, therefore, only in relation to a double negative – that is to say, it means only in terms of what it is not, and twice over. For this reason, these two categories are both internally reliant on forms of representational absence. The crucial difference, of course, is that whereas whiteness connotes privilege that conceals itself by a seeming invisibility, femininity signifies disenfranchisement from cultural power. It is important to note that the ethnic woman is doubly transgressive under white patriarchy for her sexuality constitutes a threat and her whiteness is often not completely secure. (As a non-Anglo-Saxon, she troubles the facile assumption that whiteness and color are self-evident and mutually exclusive categories). Being twice excluded from the ideal category of white masculinity, the ethnic feminine might be cast into a representational void for she possesses neither of the operative defining traits: color as a negative value and masculinity as a positive value. From this apparent paradox at the heart of ethnic femininity, we may glean some understanding of the intense ambivalence with which the figure of the ethnic feminine has been representationally rendered. Although Hollywood films generally depict women in terms of dualistic constructs, ethnic women seem even more likely to be positioned as purely virtuous or innately evil. (Although I replicate that construct here, I hope to critically challenge it as well). The ethnic female star is a figure of great potential ideological disruption, for she threatens to expose the fragile construction of white, American patriarchy.

The transformation narratives in which the ethnic female is often situated are a reflection of a need to strictly control the ideological meanings she carries – meanings which could signify the undoing of a number of taken-for-granted notions of identity which are maintained by the exclusion or denigration of the Other. The representational prominence of ethnic femininity threatens to expose the fact that there is no innate, unique and ahistorical whiteness, Americanness or masculinity. Thus, the figure must be neutralized through a narrativization process which emphasizes incorporation into the white ideal, Americanization, and domestication. For these reasons, then, the means by which ethnic femininity is encompassed and managed by dominant commercial cinema practices will be illustrative of the history of twentieth century power relations in America.

Reading stardom

Stardom is one of the most devalued forms of social knowledge, yet it is a form of knowledge that we all possess, often with a high degree of expertise. Discourses on celebrities are capable of carrying a range of significant forms of information in regard to what we think we know about the world. What we say about stars is often a displaced form of discourse about our culture at large, and the belief systems that structure it.

In this book I read star personae as cultural texts in which our understandings of gender, ethnicity and national identity are embedded. A substantial component of cultural studies research has been devoted to the critical exploration of stardom, yet the work of Richard Dyer in theorizing stardom remains paramount. In discussing the complexity of stars' relationships to ideology, Dyer has noted that 'stars may reinforce aspects of ideology simply by repeating, reproducing or reconciling them.'[22] As he points out, many star personae are illustrative of an attempt to reconcile apparently disparate facets of social experience. Judith Mayne has suggested 'that the appeal of stardom is that of constant reinvention, the dissolution of contraries, the embrace of wildly opposing terms.'[23] Taking a cue from these suggestions, we might, for instance, theorize that ethnic female star personae would work to alleviate tensions between the myth of American culture as all-incorporating and the reality of a fragmented, divided society.

At the same time, however, stars can function as sanctioned sites for ideological irruptions – that is, they can serve as comfortable cultural 'fictions' for social realities. By distancing ourselves from the star through an understanding of that individual's extraordinariness, we can pleasurably partake of the meanings they are associated with, without having to directly confront questions of social relevance. In this respect, the continual foregrounding of the energies (productive or disruptive) of the ethnic woman in the film narratives in which she appears may be enjoyed for its own sake, without necessarily inspiring questions about the nature of ethnic identity or the relation between dominant and peripheral social groups.

A number of authors have undertaken to examine the fluctuations of star personae and their evolutions and adaptations in relation to social history.[24] I will also devote considerable attention to the specific historical variables that impinge on the celebrity of the actresses whose careers I discuss. Of course, the degree of alteration in a star persona is subject to the longevity of the star's career. In addition, some stars linger significantly in the popular imagination long after the height of their success, a phenomenon I discuss in the conclusions to several chapters.

Not only do stars function to present the organizing concept of a film, but they also serve as a crucial link between representation and reality, and in many instances, are indicative of the complex relationship between representation and social history. As Jane Gaines has observed, 'The star is crucial to the study of meaning and the cinema, since it is one element within the system of the motion picture which always has prominence in the social realm.'[25] In 'Stardom as an Occupation,' Barry King links stars to the taken-for-granted elements of social experience:

> In principle, the role of stardom must be seen, if I can coin a phrase, as that of providing a 'collective register.' This term is intended to indicate two aspects of a recurrent process. Firstly, that the stars are taken

to indicate something about the state of collective experience, conscious or unconscious. Secondly, that what the stars represent is otherwise suppressed by the prioritized realities of the dominant culture.[26]

My method of linking stars to social context in some ways resembles that of Gaylyn Studlar, who in her discussion of Jazz age male stardom, notes:

> Intertexts are not meant to suggest a single determination of meaning, but instead are used to suggest how cultural frameworks often figure importantly in the creation of a star who is presold in the sense of being constructed to appeal to an audience's established interest in controversies, dilemmas, or spectacles that are already in cultural circulation.[27]

For Dyer, stars are 'embodiments of social categories' and, as such, they tend to be experienced as representative types. In light of the many overlapping determinations of star meaning, it is clear that where there are constituent 'ethnic' parts to a star persona, it seems likely that these would forcefully define and implant the meanings of ethnicity.

Important work on ethnic star 'imports' has been carried out by Adrienne McLean and Shari Roberts. In 'The Construction of Rita Hayworth,' McLean analyzes the discourses of ethnicity and transformation in Rita Hayworth's star persona.[28] She questions the notion that process is always de-emphasized in favor of product in star images, noting that the process of Rita Hayworth's transformation – from Margarita Cansino to Rita Hayworth, from all-purpose ethnic to American love goddess – was a strong, consistent discursive element of her publicity and promotion. Moreover, the preservation of Hayworth's 'former self' was likely to have, in fact, broadened the range of roles she was able to play and deepened her cross-gender appeal to audiences. McLean asserts that 'Hayworth's ethnicity provides the means by which she is able to integrate wholesomeness with eroticism in her film texts' often allowing her 'to escape the drastic punishments normally inflicted on sexually potent women in classical Hollywood narratives.'[29] Through a connection to her ethnic origins and an emphasis on the extent and nature of her transformation into the kind of mainstream femininity required to attain star status, Hayworth's persona serves to reconcile and reduce some of the contradictions of female sexuality as it is depicted in Hollywood, incorporating such 'disparate' elements as sexuality and respectability.

In ' "The Lady in the Tutti-Frutti Hat": Carmen Miranda, a Spectacle of Ethnicity,' Roberts reads Miranda's star text as a vehicle for recuperating fears of ethnic difference and solidifying a shared sense of identity with Latin America during wartime.[30] Because Miranda's image successfully exaggerated and parodied signifiers of femininity and ethnicity she became a kind of spectacle of containment. By overplaying the nature of the threat she represented (in two senses – as non-American, and as performing, public woman) she undercut that very threat. Thus, her sexuality (highlighted through revealing costumes), her desire for consumer goods ('I say monee, monee, monee' she was quoted) and her connections to non-Hollywood representational traditions (Spanish song, a Latin style of dress) became so strongly associated with excess that they were rendered comically harmless.

McLean's work is particularly useful for its emphasis on the ideological pleasures that accrue to the spectator in engaging with the transformative work of the Hollywood industrial apparatus applied to an 'outsider.' In this formulation, Hollywood appears as a microcosmic America, skillfully assimilating and improving the female immigrant through the refinement of basic materials and application of industrializing techniques. Roberts' discussion of Carmen Miranda offers insights into the ways in which ethnic star personae can work to familiarize and reduce the threatening ethnic Other. I will discuss these two methods of recuperation at length in the context of the pleasures of consuming ethnic star images that mobilize a sense of shared American community.

A number of interesting possibilities suggest themselves in relation to female spectators and the potential ability of the ethnic female star to catalyze spectatorial fantasies of resistance and agency. In many of the narrative forms in which she appears, the figure of the ethnic woman is located (even if in apparently minor ways) outside of dominant American cultural values. What this may have meant for female filmgoers was the opportunity to engage and identify with a figure uniquely privileged to defy the social order of white, patriarchal capitalism. The ongoing association between ethnic femininity and disruption, unruliness, excess, and innovation makes it more likely that female spectators could enjoy such representations from a safe distance – that is, without ever having to interrogate the dominant culture into which ethnic femininity did not quite fit. The extent to which representations of ethnic femininity facilitated the fantasy of evasion from cultural strictures that disempowered American women cannot be gauged, but it remains a resonant possibility. Near the end of the book, I return to the question of such 'ethnic fantasy' in the context of a contemporary star, Marisa Tomei, whose persona forcefully engages this issue.

My discussions of star personae are necessarily limited in scope, and it is inevitable that my analysis will leave some aspects of these stars' often lengthy public tenure untouched. Yet in order to consider the co-deployment of gender and ethnicity discourses in these star personae, it will be important to look as comprehensively as possible at the packaging, promotion and performances of these actresses. Where information is not available, (films are lost, publicity materials and fan magazines no longer in existence, etc.) the claims that are made will be based on necessarily limited evidence. This analysis will encompass the many extratextual determinants of the construction of the female ethnic star persona, and therefore, will include evidence culled from fan magazines, popular magazines and newspaper articles, publicity materials, and other such sources. I am also forced to make selective choices about which of these stars' films to discuss and in some cases have reduced discussion of film roles in favor of what might seem to be less consequential modes of discourse such as fan magazine stories, publicity photos and gossip. I hope it will be clear from my analysis that despite their low cultural status and presumed transparent signification, such textual material can be both complex and richly illuminating. These materials are significant on the one hand for their ability to mediate 'the space between films and their paying publics,'[31] and there is significant evidence that particularly in early phases of Hollywood history, fan magazine discourse provided a key interpretive foundation for spectators. Richard Koszarski observes that:

> Fan magazines in this period served a highly educative function, rather than simply providing readers with data on the latest releases or the private lives of movie stars. While critical standards were generally diffuse, these magazines did suggest various aesthetic bases for differentiating 'good' from 'bad' and supplied their readers with enough technical, social, and economic background to help inform their decisions. The interviews and features were often quite detailed and contain material of considerable value to scholars and historians.[32]

Fan magazines are also crucial in implanting the meanings of stardom, and a star persona has its own kind of continuity that precedes and transcends any individual film role. As Richard DeCordova points out:

> Since the identity of the actor was elaborated not only in films but also in fan magazines and the general press, it remained in process long after the individual film's production of meaning had ended. Star discourse thus worked to extend the contract between the spectator/consumer and the cinema at large. More accurately, it might be said that this discourse extended the boundaries of the cinema as institution so that it could more fully occupy people's lives.[33]

Thus, in examining the popular culture discourses generated around the ethnic female star persona, I hope to track a process of construction that occurs in but is not exclusive to film texts themselves. To do this, other important extra-cinematic sites of analysis such as film reviews, publicity photos, and captions will also warrant close consideration. Such a project is in keeping with Charles Wolfe's observations about the historiographical usefulness of such materials. Wolfe argues that star photographs, in particular, convey much useful information:

> Around the production, distribution and exhibition of films a host of photographic images proliferate: production stills, celebrity photos, photographic poster art, illustrations for pressbooks, programmes, interviews and reviews. They whet our appetite for moving images yet unseen and prolong our pleasure after the act of seeing. They can be

held, examined at leisure, collected and catalogued. With time they
serve as an archive of images to be drawn from for coffee-table antho-
logies, journals of history and criticism and monographs of various
kinds. They are an important part of the institution of cinema even
if we do not at first think of them as related to the film-as-text in a
meaningful way. Reproduced and recycled, captured and captioned by
authors and editors, these images bear an historical trace, a trace worth
pursuing.[34]

Publicity photos tend to emphasize the more spectacular elements of a star
persona (as the cover of this book well illustrates), and yet they also tend to
reduce the star's meaning to certain foundational essences that lodge quickly
and easily in public consciousness. They can interact with other sites of persona
construction in complex ways, occasionally serving to maintain the foundational
facets of a star's meaning even when those particular dimensions are not being
activated by a single film role. In Chapter 3, for instance, I discuss the way in
which Pola Negri's publicity photos continued to promote her as the exotic
foreign other throughout a period when Paramount was casting the actress in
film roles intended to domesticate her foreignness. At such moments as the end
of her American career, the public condemnation over her elaborate grief at the
funeral of Rudolph Valentino, and even in her afterlife as a star in Europe where
she was alleged to have had an affair with Adolf Hitler, such photographic constructions of Negri as a cultural threat served to make meaningful her presumed
innate transgressiveness. In this way, publicity photographs and portraiture served
to maintain a low-level, operative discourse of Negri's excessiveness and duplicity
which distinctly emerged only at certain particular moments, where American
ideals were directly or obliquely threatened (i.e. Negri's proprietary claims toward
a beloved (Italian) American film star, her return to Germany in the buildup to
World War II, etc.).

Organized as a series of linked star studies, this project focuses attention
on stars who illuminate different forms of ethnic types in Hollywood, balancing 'imported' ethnic actresses including Pola Negri, Sonja Henie and Hedy
Lamarr, with 'homegrown' ethnic stars such as Colleen Moore, Marisa Tomei,
and Cher. I have gravitated toward stars who were (or still are) economically,
industrially and culturally significant, but for whom there is a vacuum of critical
commentary. The actresses discussed in this study were also chosen because
they are consistently narrativized (in both film texts and extra-cinematic discourses) in ways that emphasize the thematics of transformation. Certainly, to
some extent, all star personae do this, simply as a function of the way in which
stardom constitutes a balance between typicality and exceptionalness (i.e., our
identification with stars is predicated on our perception that they are both like
and unlike ourselves). The transformational shifts that stars embody are often
highly complex, and yet they tend to personify transformations that are ideologically crucial. For instance, the celebrity of any star signals the possibility of

uniqueness being produced by a social system that essentially desires conformity. In this book I specifically highlight the film role and public persona transformations undergone by Euro-American female film stars in a process of popularization much like assimilation. I will put in play (both to conceptualize and problematize) the notion of Hollywood (particularly in the early decades of the twentieth century) as a type of 'assimilation machine,' very much driven by immigrant ethnicities as raw materials 'produced' through such processes as publicity and promotion to serve the larger goal of ideological incorporation. Hollywood's representational model of assimilation relates to the way in which stardom in general involves rather deft negotiations of similarity and difference. Americanizing ethnic femininity does not so much entail a renunciation of ethnic attributes, as it does an attempt to codify and delineate those attributes that are meaningful within an American ideological system.[35] As the figure of the ethnic female is made to work for the interests of American patriarchal capitalism, she tellingly illuminates the representational means by which cultural power is maintained and consolidated.

White ethnicity in the Hollywood system

Many film historians have represented Hollywood as significantly shaped by European ethnicity, but they restrict formative influence and crucial contributions to male auteurs – Jewish immigrants from Central and Eastern Europe who became early studio heads, and imported male directors such as F.W. Murnau, Ernst Lubitsch, Michael Curtiz, and Alfred Hitchcock.[36] Such limited assessments of the genius of the immigrant director or mogul make up a disproportionate share of the limited literature on European ethnicity and Hollywood film. They are also sometimes factually incomplete – Ernst Lubitsch, after all, was able to make the transition from European filmmaking to Hollywood production largely as a function of the star power of Pola Negri.[37] In this analysis, I seek to balance the scales somewhat by turning to ethnic femininity and its place in Hollywood representational output. Film history has tended to celebrate male labor as genius while rendering women's labor invisible, natural or simply a reflective facet of the male authoring process. I am working from an alternative, non-male-centered conception of authorship that encompasses female stardom as an important (though sometimes qualified) mode of agency.

From a representational perspective, significant critical literature on white ethnicities and film is scant. This seems due to a variety of factors, ranging from the relative newness of film studies as a discipline, to a desire to establish the importance of film in its own right, leading sometimes to a neglect of social, historical and cultural factors. Sumiko Higashi, for instance, maintains that the reason why ethnicity has not been sufficiently attended to in film studies is that:

> Film history, as it has evolved thus far, has limited usefulness for
> critics studying ethnicity because focus on mode of production or film

language leaves little room for a consideration of the broader political, socioeconomic, and cultural context.[38]

A thorough cultural history of American film needs to take into account the extent to which our culture is organized in ethnic terms and Hollywood's role in disseminating cultural fictions marked by notions of normativity founded on ethnicity. As Catherine Hall has observed in the context of a discussion of Britishness, 'Ethnicities do not only belong to those on the margins – every culture has its own forms of ethnic identity.'[39] By focusing on those more mainstream European ethnic identities whose 'difference' is sometimes downplayed or denied and at other times emphasized, celebrated or caricatured, we can begin to explore what our representations of assimilating groups say about our sense of national identity. In this respect, my project is somewhat similar to Ella Shohat's work in which she argues that ethnicity 'haunts' even the most homogeneous film texts. In 'Ethnicities-in-Relation: Toward a Multicultural Reading of American Cinema,' Shohat discusses the problem of identifying the ethnic dimensions of American culture where ethnicity is 'culturally ubiquitous and textually submerged.'[40] She goes on to note:

> The disciplinary assumption that some films are 'ethnic' whereas others are not is ultimately based on the view that certain groups are ethnic whereas others are not. The marginalization of 'ethnicity' reflects the imaginary of the dominant group which envisions itself as the 'universal' or the 'essential' American nation, and thus somehow 'beyond' or 'above' ethnicity. The very word *ethnic*, then, reflects a peripheralizing strategy premised on an implicit contrast of 'norm' and 'other,' much as the term *minority* often carries with it an implication of minor, lesser, or subaltern.[41]

I need to point out, of course, that the kinds of European ethnicities explored here tend toward the more valued end of the spectrum of ethnicity in American culture. As I have suggested, my analysis is centered around these in part because of the way in which, in our cultural experience, such ethnicities have been naturalized to the extent that they are seldom put under scrutiny. They are also of particular interest because in the existing literature on cinematic ethnicity we have generally first explored the most de-valued (especially non-European, non-white) ethnicities, assuming that those who were self-evidently 'white' were on more stable and privileged ground.

Yet whiteness is far from a monolithic category in American culture, and one of the goals of this book is to consider the historical and contemporary dimensions of the hierarchization of ethnicity and its attendant relationship to gender, to cultural production and to power. In beginning to write a relational history of gender and ethnicity in American film, I hope to more fully grasp issues of ideology which become necessarily reductive when isolated to a single context (such as gender or ethnicity alone). As Gina Marchetti writes:

By seeing ethnicity as ideological, the power dynamics behind representations of ethnic groups become clearer. Moreover, ethnicity's cultural and historical aspect surfaces, and the contradiction becomes less obscure between the lived experience of any given individual and the way the dominant culture represents that individual's race, class, ethnicity, age, or gender.[42]

The ethnic woman has often symbolized excess and exaggeration. (Of the six actresses discussed in this book, three gained fame for their hyperbolic exoticism and transgressive sexuality). The fact that the figure of the ethnic woman in Hollywood film has so often been overdrawn (as 'the vamp,' 'the seductress,' as 'the homewrecker,' as the 'woman we love to hate') should not preclude the interest of the critic. Rather, we should ask why this image has been so persistent within Hollywood typology and further why it is rendered with such vituperation.[43] In this project I suggest that the common denominator amongst representations of ethnic femininity (whether positive or negative) is cultural fear about her potential exercise of power.

Perhaps one of the reasons for the general avoidance of the figure of the ethnic woman among feminist film scholars has to do with a certain feeling of discomfort generated by this unusually active and empowered female figure who, instead of opposing patriarchy, often attempts to make it work for her own ends. In addition, one of the most persistent representational stereotypes of the ethnic woman tags her as competitive with/envious of other women, with whatever triumphs she achieves generally won at other women's expense. For these reasons, the transgressive, ethnic woman is an image that in the past has in many ways been difficult to 'rescue' for feminism. Nevertheless, just as the field of queer theory has undertaken analysis of the embarassingly stereotypical images of gays and lesbians in the mass media, feminist scholars have realized that we too need to come to terms critically even with those images which most repel and disturb us. This seems an opportune moment in the evolution of feminist analysis of Hollywood cinema to begin to attend more closely to images of ethnic femininity. I hope also to demonstrate that even when she is at one level a clear caricature, the ethnic woman frequently offers a polysemous image which can, at times, present itself as pleasurably different from other Hollywood formulations of femininity.

While facing clear constraints in being able to encompass all the numerous examples which I might take up, I hope to offer a suggestive typology of white ethnic femininity in Hollywood film. Such a typology assumes the importance of investigating the complex ways in which knowledge of the past helps to construct gender in the present. The historical scope of this analysis will also make it possible to gauge the longevity of media representations that do not simply reflect social realities, but work to construct and perpetuate a social milieu that systematically disempowers women and particular ethnic groups. While early film narratives tend to manifest rather direct links to social anxieties about threatening new immigrant groups, Hollywood speaks ethnicity as a more complex and circuitous discourse in more recent phases of its history. The ethnic character of silent cinema was expressed most evidently in attempts to representationally enact anxieties connected to 'New Immigration' and to chart shifts in the white ideal. After the silent era, at a period of time when the contours of the assimilation crisis shift radically, European ethnicity comes to serve as an innocuous representational means to figure difference, a kind of sliding signifier that at certain historical moments offers a way to articulate more fundamentally divisive social discrepancies. Studio era protocols for ethnic representation became relatively solidified, with ethnicity receding somewhat and the ethnic woman most consistently figured as a permanent outsider or a trophy of American achievements abroad. In post-classical Hollywood ethnicity is a discourse spoken with increasing sophistication in the interests of cultivating ethnic nostalgia or as a means of evading more contentious social differences at a time when we openly identify our society as a 'multiculture.'[44] By fictionally enlarging the parameters of ethnic difference, contemporary films establish a safe plane on which to enact crises of difference far less volatile than crises of race or class, in the end working to conceal them. As I discuss in the last two chapters, a variety of modes of 'ethnic fantasy' have been deployed in recent Hollywood films and film culture, posing ethnicity as a representational response to the perceived sterility of contemporary American whiteness. If early films often featured the acquisition of whiteness at the expense of ethnicity, contemporary Hollywood has just as often inverted that formula in films whose protagonists trade a negatively-valued or bankrupt white identity for ethnic vibrancy.

Ethnicity, whiteness and performance

Laura Browder draws our attention to the unsettling effects of seeing ethnicity as performance,[45] yet American twentieth-century culture was particularly dependent on just such a performative mode. Electing or rejecting ethnic identity has been a key dynamic of contemporary American life. As Richard Alba observes:

> Whites are largely free to identify themselves as they will and to make these identities as important as they like. This is especially true of the emerging majority of white Americans who come from mixed ethnic backgrounds, who can present and think of themselves in terms of a hybrid identity, or emphasize one ethnic component while recognizing the other (or others), or simplify their background by dropping all but one of its components, or deny altogether the relevance of their ethnic background.[46]

A common assumption about ethnicity in Hollywood is that ethnic stars have been pressed to leave their ethnicities behind, yet there are a striking number of cases where stars amplified ethnic identities or invented them altogether. The history of Hollywood performance is littered with examples of stars who constructed entirely fictionalized ethnic biographies.[47] That this phenomenon of ethnic impersonation was by no means confined to Hollywood is amply demonstrated by Browder in a series of analyses of individuals who gainfully undertook ethnic impersonation from the mid nineteenth to the mid twentieth century. In this book, however, I concentrate upon a set of film stars who have lived a version of their 'original' ethnicity so romanticized/distorted as to be almost fully separate from that original experience. The meanings of their ethnicity were restricted and codified; in the silent and classical eras stars often worked to guarantee versions of ethnicity that rationalized its renunciation by assimilated Americans. In contemporary Hollywood, in keeping with a turn away from the direct promotion of whiteness, stars more frequently demonstrate how to reclaim an ethnic identity through performance and consumption.

Two studies adjacent to mine in the area of femininity and performance have illuminated a number of concerns which I will elaborate on in the course of this book. Linda Mizejewski's study of the Ziegfeld Girl elegantly examines the production of the idealized, white American girl in the Ziegfeld Follies of the first three decades of the twentieth century.[48] The Ziegfeld Girl materialized the symbolic reconciliation of all the disparate ingredients of American culture and the inevitable promotion of certain ethnic and national pedigrees deemed most valuable. Containing potential category crises of gender, class and race through her guaranteed and indisputable whiteness, the Ziegfeld Girl contributed to the indigenizing of whiteness by establishing an American definition of the white, female body.

In a more contemporary setting, Sarah Banet-Weiser explores beauty pageants as 'sites for cultural work that produces national female subjects in postindustrialist United States.'[49] If icons of nationalized femininity such as Miss America do indeed 'assuage fears about ambivalent definitions of who and what a nation should be,'[50] they do so by directly nominating a national ideal. In the case of the film stars I examine, ethnic celebrity can turn in either direction, to exemplify the beneficial effects of Americanization, or to express residual concern about national homogeneity when it appears ethnic traits are retained. In either case, 'bodies of [ethnic] difference – become validations of the availability of the norm for everyone.'[51] The value of Mizejewski and Banet-Weiser's analyses for my purposes is to underscore the importance of female characters in the stories we are constantly telling ourselves to suture citizenship and promote a sense of national unanimity.

Ethnic femininity has been most frequently associated with unauthorized sexuality, permitting audience members the pleasures of using the foreign body to interrogate sexuality from a safe distance. Even when she is not intensely sexualized (Colleen Moore, for instance, is associated with safe, 'non-adult' sexuality), the ethnic feminine body is nevertheless posited as an important site of social control. Its potential exuberance and excesses are figured against the controlled American social body. From the figure of the vamp whose body threatens to evade sartorial containment, to the 'New Woman' or flapper, whose frenetic dancing signals resistance to the conventions of bodily regulation, to such scandals as Hedy Lamarr's nude scenes in *Ecstasy* (1933), the film that brought her to the attention of Hollywood, ethnicity and femininity taken together almost inevitably lead to a circulating discourse of fears about the ungovernable body. In large part, the ethnic female body serves as a repository for fears of difference that play out across several registers, activating anxieties pertaining to femininity, to 'foreign' ethnicities, even to the uncontrollable, lower-class body.

In this book I consider the co-deployment of gender and ethnicity discourses in the packaging, promotion and performances of a number of female stars who have attained success in the American film industry, ranging from 'good girls' such as Colleen Moore, Sonja Henie and Marisa Tomei, to 'bad woman' figures including Pola Negri, and Cher. In all of these cases, the ethnicity of the performer has to be 'worked through' in a kind of rewriting process that enables a potential obstacle to be recoded as a selling point. For the ethnic girls, this leads to the construction of fundamentally demystified star personae, while the personae of the ethnic women tend to emphasize their essential mystifica-tion. Whether presented in incorporative or excorporative discursive terms, examination of the narratives constituted in these actresses' careers reveals im-portant interconnections between stardom, assimilation and the social meanings of whiteness.

Throughout this book, I employ the dichotomy of girl/woman as a func-tional conceit, in part to draw attention to a broader pattern of differentiation in Hollywood between the safe sexuality of the girl and the often troublesome sexuality of the woman, but also to indicate how female ethnicity has been particularly subject to representation on these polarized terms. The girl/woman pairs of the silent (Colleen Moore and Pola Negri), classical (Sonja Henie and Hedy Lamarr) and post-classical eras (Marisa Tomei and Cher) help to illu-minate patterns and trends which draw our attention to features of ethnicity, gender, consumerism and class at work in American culture. Indeed, the celeb-rities in each of these star pairs might be said to turn around a particular, topical question, generally positing opposed answers. For the silent era stars that ques-tion would be: Who can be assimilated into unqualified US citizenship? For the classical era stars the question that takes shape is: Who can embody the nation? The contemporary stars offer modes of response to the question: How can we reconstitute identity in an age of problematized American whiteness?

Contrasting the girlish persona of Colleen Moore with the mature style of Pola Negri, the cuteness of Sonja Henie in comparison to the continental glamour of Hedy Lamarr, the newcomer status of Marisa Tomei with the longevity of Cher in these paired terms serves both organizational and ideo-logical goals. Ethnic female film stars mobilize different forms of response to social anxieties concerning the state of US culture, whether in the 1920s, the

1940s or the 1990s. I argue that whether an ethnic star presents as a girl or as a woman makes a considerable difference in the constructed and received meanings of her ethnicity and sexuality. Further, the ethnic girl is far more likely to be celebrated as an exemplary American; even if her ethnicity is prominently displayed, the very fact of her girlishness promises that it may yet be traded away.

While each of the case studies in the book reveals that star personae (particularly those that are developed over decades) tend to be both dynamic and multifunctional, certain generalities in regard to the function of the ethnic girl and the ethnic woman are sustained across the eighty-year period I am concerned with. Where the ethnic girl typically disclaims any of the potentially negative attributes associated with her ethnicity, the ethnic woman flaunts such attributes. The girl is especially well-suited to act as a cipher for dominant interests, a particularly energized image of personal freedom that is utterly deceptive. As Ann K. Clark has written, 'The context of no context is where The Girl invites us to live. It is the source of the freedom she represents. And I think it is also the legacy of the destruction of history as part of our lives.'[52] Understanding the figure of the girl as the byproduct of the destruction of history, enables us to perceive the girlish ethnicities so lightly worn by stars such as Colleen Moore and Marisa Tomei, for whom ethnicity is style, a tenuous link to a malleable past. Certainly, the energized, nationalized figure of the girl in American culture precedes the advent of cinema, as Martha Banta observes in discussing the late nineteenth century: ' "America" was female, young, pretty, Protestant, and northern European. She was the heiress of America's history as edited by the American Whigs. Her features were "regular" and Caucasian. Her bloodline was pure and vigorous.'[53] The ethnic girl, whether she personifies Irish, Norwegian or Italian ethnicity, whether she is named Heidi or Colleen or Anna, is always innocent. In this project I seek to examine the ideological effects of these presentations of ethnic innocence, arguing for instance in Chapter 4 that the girlish ease of Sonja Henie matched her persona in helping to rehearse the unproblematic character of uncontroversially white ethnic groups in the United States.

This situational use of ethnicity contrasts with the ethnic identities of stars such as Pola Negri and Hedy Lamarr, whose maturity is often figured in the terms of an inescapable historical inheritance. Although ethnic women can be occasionally and temporarily rendered girlish (this occurs, for instance, in the stardom of Hedy Lamarr) and girls may graduate to womanhood (Colleen Moore moves toward this at the end of her career) generally speaking these designations remain fixed.

In this project, then, I examine the careers of a number of Hollywood actresses as paradigms for the cultural construction of gender and ethnicity. My goal is not to recast the history of American film representation, but to inflect it in specific ways, by accessing a crucial, and yet frequently overlooked area of evidence in popular culture. In the course of examining the incarnations of the ethnic woman in Hollywood films and considering the interrelatedness of these various manifestations, I hope to make clear that studies of the representational history of film have been insufficiently attentive to the role of ethnic femininity. I see this study as one which begins to remedy this lack in feminist film scholarship. My focus will be not so much on questioning received ideas, but rather on beginning to examine and to theorize a representational pattern. I am particularly interested in the ways in which the figure of the ethnic woman has functioned to 'disturb' the conventions of Hollywood representation. As I will demonstrate, the foreign woman often poses an ideological problem for the Hollywood narrative which has difficulty emplotting her into its generic formulae. Both the early and late decades of the twentieth century resonated with debates about the incorporation of difference in American culture. I contend that notions of normativity are largely based on a hierarchical sense of white ethnicity, and a highly ambivalent relationship to European ethnicities in particular. Examination of the meanings attached to ethnic femininity can help to complicate the apparently 'undifferentiated' American white social body.

Stardom and exemplarity

Having enumerated the various constituent elements of this project, I now want to attend to a more synthetic description of their inter-relatedness. It will already be evident on the basis of the foregoing discussion that this project is designed to explore white ethnic stardom through the application of multiple synchronous lenses of analysis. From the more primary goal of contributing to the current level of knowledge about the films and careers of ethnic female stars, to connecting stardom as a social practice to the maintenance of cultural boundaries, to the formulation of Hollywood as an assimilation machine, this project considers the representation of ethnic femininity as a means of investigating a number of broad lines of analysis. Nevertheless, while attempting to offer a critical contribution on numerous fronts, some of the project's goals are more continuous and centralized than others. It may also seem at times that in attempting to remain sensitive to the complexities and nuances of each of these actress' ethnic personae, that there is tremendous variety and multiplicity in the questions being posed in each chapter. In weighing the project as a whole, however, one finds that these different strands of analysis are carefully interwoven with one another in such a way that several large, ongoing areas of interest emerge. These areas are as follows:

1   The usefulness, frequency and adaptability of ethnicity as a discourse capable of investing Hollywood narratives with greater ideological power;
2   Ethnicity's participation in a thematics of national and sexual incorporation;
3   Ethnicity's capacity to expose and/or disrupt taken-for-granted notions of American whiteness, solidarity and heritage.

In this book I attach critical importance to understanding the construction of female star personae and their relationships to the ideological operations of patriarchal culture over time. Investigation into the careers and constructed meanings of actresses whose personae are ethnically inflected can begin to elucidate what it has meant to filmgoing audiences to be gendered 'female' in conjunction with a clearer sense of what it has meant to be 'Irish,' 'Polish,' or 'Italian,' for example. By making plain the ways in which these actresses' films make use of ideologically freighted imagery, I hope to point toward the ways in which Hollywood cinema functions to naturalize hierarchies of power. By reading star personae as complex discursive systems that actively work to construct standards of indigenousness, attractiveness and acceptability, I hope to connect the phenomenon of stardom to the maintenance of American social boundaries.

The historical scope of this analysis will make it possible to gauge the longevity of media representations that do not simply reflect social realities, but help to construct and perpetuate a social milieu that systematically disempowers women and particular ethnic groups. In addition, this study represents an attempt to amplify the ethnic feminine voice, arguing that this voice can and should be heard amongst a cacophony of more privileged speakers in Hollywood discourse who have dominated historical accounts.

The book is organized into the following sections: Chapter 2 looks at co-medienne Colleen Moore, a box office phenomenon of the mid-1920s, whose emblematic girlishness was linked to a secure, positively-valued white ethnic identity. In electing to amplify her Irish heritage, Moore crafted an acceptably ethnic version of the 'All-American Girl' whose Irishness explained her fundamental innocence. Chapter 3 is focused upon another silent-era star, but one whose ethnicity generated suspicion rather than acceptance. In reading the stardom of 'Polish import' Pola Negri I argue that Negri's vamp persona mimicked cultural stereotypes of the New Immigrant such that her 'failure' in Hollywood seemed to confirm the unassimilable status of marginally white groups from Eastern and Southern Europe. Chapter 4 turns to Sonja Henie, the Norwegian figure skating star who segued into MGM musicals in the late 1930s and early 1940s. In direct contrast to the career trajectory of Pola Negri, Sonja Henie's ethnic stardom was founded on a positively nationalized version of whiteness. Indeed, her athletic acumen and foreign nationality served as mutually de-complicating explanatory features within her persona. Henie's success well illustrates a tendency to proffer national, racial and ethnic explanations for success in American life. Chapter 5, a study of the celebrity of Hedy Lamarr, considers the attempt to balance the European exoticism/eroticism of the Austrian-born star with an Americanization process that implicitly rationalized US interventionism overseas. Lamarr's status as an ethnic trophy came to the fore in a series of film roles in which she was rescued by benevolent American males, an extension of the narrative of her 'discovery' by MGM's Louis B. Mayer. Chapter 6 illustrates how Marisa Tomei, the 1992 Academy Award winner for Best Supporting Actress represents an important turn in late twentieth-century

American culture toward nostalgic reconstructions of the ethnic ties left behind by earlier generations of assimilating immigrants. I read Tomei's mid-1990s stardom as a balance between long-standing fears of ethnic female agency and an increasing turn toward positing ethnic vibrancy as an antidote to the sterility of contemporary culture. Chapter 7 reads the career trajectory of Cher, who has consistently taken on and sloughed off a variety of exoticized identities in a process of ethnic chameleonism that reflects new postmodern options for ethnic indeterminacy. As the only star in this study without significant structuring connections (factual or fictional) to a white European homeland, Cher represents an exceptional case, and in this chapter I discuss how some of the rules of ethnic female representation are unmade by her celebrity.

My choice, then, to consider these six actresses' careers as examples, or as selected points if you will, along a historical continuum in Hollywood history, has been a highly self-conscious one, and predicated on an awareness of the care which must be taken in deriving broad conclusions from specific and limited case studies and examples.[54] In considering the variant textuality of ethnic femininity, I try to negotiate the delicate balance between the whole and the part, drawing broader and more definitive conclusions where they seem warranted, but understanding at the same time that each of these case studies sustains an internal integrity valuable in and of itself.

The twentieth century ended, as it began, with crucial transformations in the population of the United States. Immigrants from Southern and Eastern Europe were key contributors to the composite 15 percent of foreign-born Americans in the 1900s and 1910s; in the 1990s another immigration boom (composed primarily of those from Latin America and Asia) once again raised the percentage of foreign-born (up according to census reports, to 10 percent).[55] As in the early years of cinema, the waning years of the twentieth century were rife with debates over the definitional borders of American whiteness. Far from conferring legitimacy on such debates, *Off-White Hollywood* seeks to probe the social foundations for them by analyzing the role of stardom as it enacts and is acted upon by prevailing conceptions of nation, race, ethnicity, gender and class. In part, this project reconstructs via the history of stardom, those ideological developments that led up to the late twentieth-century emergence of the New Nativism in the US. With its discursive emphases on patriotism and monolingualism, and its commitment to a certain version of family values, the New Nativism also seeks to bolster identity bonds between the US and Europe, as Americans are invited to construct and perform a heritage relationship to white homelands. In the 1990s nativism strikingly emerged in new hysterical discourses of white, American middle-class defensiveness and immigrant criminality. Such discourses are predicated in large part on perceptions of white citizenship and entitlement, in tandem with fears about the calcification of a permanently disenfranchised, largely invisible American underclass.

Alongside these developments and not altogether contradictory to them has been the emergence of a politics of white ethnic performativity, one which showcases ethnic identity as a new kind of national, class and consumer credential. Marilyn Halter's research on the contemporary marketing of ethnicity shows that 'although the impetus to reclaim roots often stems from disdain for commercial interests, paradoxically, consumers look to the marketplace to revive and reidentify with ethnic values.'[56] As part of this marketplace, stars operate totemically in the processes of ethnic retention, invention and resuscitation now broadly taking place in US society.

Arguing that ethnic female stardom can uniquely showcase the characteristics, fluctuations and oppositions of American social life, this multidisciplinary project is designed to draw from the fields of film studies, women's studies, American Studies and critical ethnic studies to consider the ways in which icons of popular culture distill contested social issues and express/subtextualize issues of history. While the meanings and pleasures of the ethnic woman clearly vary in accordance with social, historical and industrial variables, this study will offer evidence that during periods of ideological transformation, popular culture tropes play a key role in shaping and sustaining cultural debates about gender roles and valued ethnicities. In what follows, I demonstrate the ways in which tropes of ethnic femininity have generated some of the most potent and enduring images to be deployed in this process.

2

THE WEARING OF THE GREEN

Irishness as a promotional discourse in the career of Colleen Moore

In an article that appeared in 1921, Theodore Dreiser locates the primary and fundamental appeal of the Hollywood film in the constructed body of the American girl. He writes that:

> The thing which is giving the motion picture its enormous popularity is the physical splendour of American girlhood . . . where else in the United States would one turn for a similar picture of fresh American girlhood, as smooth and hale and rosy as the flowers of the plains and mountains from which she springs – possibly as pagan? The clarity and lustre of skin and eyes, the perfection of form and manner! The world is literally agape and athirst over the beauty of the American girl. It is she who is making, whether she knows it or not, the American motion picture the success that it is.[1]

A keen observer of the Hollywood scene, Dreiser makes plain a tendency in dominant film representations that provides the starting point for this analysis – and that is Hollywood's use of femininity as the prime signifier. As the emergent American film industry promulgated cultural fictions that functioned to produce the American woman, it also produced competing versions of femininity tied to ethnicity. Nevertheless, in the late 1910s and 1920s, both the categories of femininity and indigenousness were highly contested as women and immigrants made threatening forays into public space that led to a definitional crisis in the 'American girlhood' posited by Dreiser. Onto the body of the 1920s 'American girl' (or at least her cinematic incarnation) were converging both nationalist and gender discourses that have had a special relevance to the shaping of Irish feminine identity in the US. During this period of time, as I hope to show, Hollywood colonized Irish femininity for representational purposes that supported certain cultural goals. Not the least of these goals was the attempt to check the emerging power of the 'New Woman' – the figure who embodied (though somewhat problematically) female freedom from repressive Victorian ideals. At a historical moment when traditional American femininity was 'under siege' to some extent due to the ascendancy of the New Woman as a dominant female stereotype, the figure of the Irish Colleen, a constituent element in the actress Colleen Moore's persona, served as a comforting return to natural and unproblematic femininity.[2]

It could easily be argued that no other period of Hollywood history has been as strongly marked by discourses of Irishness (whether positive or negative) as the 1920s, and I am not sure that I can fully account for this.[3] What is clear is that the moderate re-writing of the female immigrant's sexual status that takes place in the 1920s did not extend to Southern and Eastern European female sexuality, which was being demonized and made strange during this same period of time via the figure of the vamp, the exotically threatening Other, who in some ways is the counterpoint to the good-hearted, virginal, transparent Irish Colleen. Without proposing a kind of bad girl/good girl dichotomy with the vamp on the one side and the Irish Colleen on the other, which would fail to encompass many representational complexities, it would seem that these two female stereotypes were positioned on opposing sides of an economic divide, with the vamp announcing herself as finished product of her own labor in a way that foreclosed the shaping influence of patriarchy and the Irish girl as a raw re-source to be acted upon by patriarchal and capitalistic influences. In such a fashion, gender and modernization discourses begin to be thoroughly imbricated with one another in a way that will be central to the concerns of my argument.

The promotion of Colleen Moore as Irish was far more than coincidental.[4] In the 1920s, some of the cruder cinematic stereotypes of Irishness were on the wane, and when they did recur, as for instance, in the 1927 film *The Callahans and the Murphys*, Irish-American societies such as the Ancient Order of Hibernians were able to mobilize extensive and effective protest. It is clear that in the 1920s 'Irish-American' was becoming a more valued ethnic hyphen, in large part as a function of longevity. As Joseph Curran has noted:

> Indeed, 'Paddy' and 'Bridget' were on the verge of assimilation in the twenties. Most Irish Americans were now second or third generation, Irish immigration having crested well before the turn of the century. By 1920 more and more Irish were moving up into middle-class jobs and middle-class neighborhoods; the Irish had even risen above the national average in college attendance.[5]

Analysis of Colleen Moore's star persona thus needs to be informed by some sense of the historical shifts taking place with respect to the status of Irish-Americans. In this context, it becomes increasingly clear that Irishness was an appropriate correlative discourse to the transformations of star-making in early Hollywood. The figure of the Irish woman implicitly modeled assimilation into American patriarchal values by standing for the history of the Irish immigrant's successful assimilation into American capitalistic values at a time when the Irish in America were beginning to attain the status of a 'model minority.' This tacit activation of the history of Irish immigrants transforming themselves through

Figure 1 Colleen Moore's publicity billed her as 'The Irish Flapper'. Courtesy Joseph Yranski

assimilation is another instance of the way in which we may read gender and economics off and through one another.

This exact linkage is suggested by William Lord Wright in a 1914 piece in which he discusses the crucial role played by film in upholding the melting pot myth (though he would not quite characterize it as such). For him, motion pictures are integrally tied to the consolidation of a national consciousness. He observes that:

> The Motion Picture has created reverence for the banners of other nations and has also taught respect and love for the starry banner of Young America. There is a great lesson written on the old flag; and Young America needs and is given, thru [sic] the Motion Pictures, the refreshment of the memories that lie within its precious folds.[6]

If motion pictures were quite directly viewed in the 1910s as opportunities to indoctrinate immigrants (and it is, I believe, immigrant culture that Wright refers to as 'Young America') and to foster appreciation for 'correct' American values, there were others who championed the movies for their potential to cultivate hybrid American identities. Carl H. Grabo, for instance, deplored sweeping attempts to homogenize the United States, and urged 'a greater sympathy with and appreciation of the foreigners now among us.'[7] According to Grabo, discussing the American political and social climate of 1919:

> There is under way a widespread movement to Americanize the immigrant more efficiently than in the past. For in how few quarters is there any clear notion of what Americanization means . . . hybrid civilizations have always, as history shows, been the most rich. In the United States we have now, undeveloped and unappreciated, the materials for a new and richer civilization than the world has yet seen.[8]

Colleen Moore's career and promotion in terms of her Irish ethnicity took place at a moment when discourses on immigrant ethnicities were clearly contested. Such debates no doubt colored the reception of Moore's films and probably strongly affected public consumption of Moore's persona. At the same time, as a function of the new influx of lesser valued Eastern and Southern European ethnic immigrants, Irish ethnicity was less de-valued than it had been. Thus, in conjunction with Irishness, such features of Moore's persona as safe sexuality, playful energy, and ultimate recuperability all served to assuage cultural fears associated with immigrant identity.

A sense of the social historical context around Moore's films helps us to better track the celebrity of the most prominent Irish-American actress of the 1920s. Joseph Curran has identified Moore as 'probably the most popular Irish actress during the 1920s, a time when performers such as Dolores Costello, May McAvoy, and Sally O'Neil were also associated with Irish roles.'[9] Moore (whose real name was Kathleen Morrison) signed her first studio contract at age fourteen and followed a steady but unspectacular course in the late 1910s and early 1920s. Then in 1924, she made two decisions that galvanized her career – she appeared as the flapper incarnate in a film called *Flaming Youth* and (perhaps more importantly) she bobbed her hair. The haircut and the role led to Moore being tagged as 'The Modern Girl' in Hollywood and through the remainder of her career in the 1920s and early 1930s she was cast chiefly in roles that directly or obliquely explored the contradictions of the shifting feminine ideal. From 1924 to 1927 Moore appeared in films with such titles as *The Perfect Flapper* (1924), *We Moderns* (1925), *Her Wild Oat* (1927), and *Naughty But Nice* (1927). Many of these films cast her in the role of a woman being transformed, usually from public to private, or from autonomy to domestication, but the film which most clearly foregrounded the transformative process was *Ella Cinders* (1926), to which I will return later in the chapter.

Moore's celebrity was constituted across and through such sites as fan magazine articles, interviews, film reviews, news accounts, publicity photographs, and the actress's autobiography, all of which I draw from in the course of this discussion. Because very few of her films are extant, I also offer close readings of several films based on the following criteria: 1) the film still exists; 2) it was commercially successful; and 3) it seems to be significantly illustrative of the dimensions of Moore's persona. In many respects, however, this analysis is founded on those materials which are peripheral to Moore's film roles but central to her star persona. As Richard Dyer notes:

> The star phenomenon consists of everything that is publicly available about stars. A film star's image is not just his or her films, but the promotion of those films and of the star through pin-ups, public appearances, studio hand-outs and so on, as well as interviews, biographies and coverage in the press of the star's doings and 'private' life. Further, a star's image is also what people say or write about him or her, as critics or commentators, the way the image is used in other contexts such as advertisements, novels, pop songs, and finally the way the star can become part of the coinage of everyday speech.[10]

The promotion process built around Moore consistently foregrounds her Irish identity. Typical of the publicity photos and layouts, blurbs, articles and other press pieces on Moore is a photo of her from a 1926 movie magazine. The caption to the photo reads:

> Sure, this Irish Colleen is married to another Irisher, John McCormick, and between the two of them, they're putting on some grand picture shows. Our Adela says flapper Miss Moore is the potential great among younger actresses. Colleen wears this pond lily costume in 'Irene.'[11]

The caption is significant not only for its efforts to position Moore as the embodiment of Irish femininity, but also for the way in which it incorporates a

discourse of 'stage Irishness' and co-opts the linguistic signs of Irishness (use of words such as 'sure' and 'grand') through a process of discursive assimilation. The notion that Irishness was reducible to a certain set of linguistic markers permeates the publicity and review discourses on Moore, as well as the intertitles of some of her silent films.

To explore what 'Irishness' might have connoted to filmgoers in the 1920s, we might consider some of the implications of the ways in which Moore was promoted. In this case being Irish corresponded with such values as natural-ness, freshness, and diminutiveness and the resulting ideological valence was one which had a particular currency in 1920s Hollywood. Moore's Irishness estab-lished a connection to purified, virginal sexuality at a historical moment when American female sexuality was suddenly (and to some Americans, shockingly),

OFFICERS

PRESIDENT—Miss. Dorothy M. Thompson,
13 Fifth St., Aspinwall, Pa.

VICE-PRES.—Miss. Dorothy E. Brown,
5839 Nicholson St., Pittsburgh, Pa.

TREASURER—Miss. Mary E. Dodd,
22 Fifth St., Aspinwall, Pa.
SECRETARY—Mrs. Margaret Langhein,
115 Western Ave., Aspinwall, Pa.

❖ ❖ ❖ ❖

DUES 50¢ PER YEAR

WHICH GO TO FURTHER THE
INTERESTS OF THE CLUB

ACCOUNTS KEPT—NO SALARIES

❖ ❖ ❖ ❖

COLLEEN MOORE PICTURES

Turn up the corners of the mouth permanently, and make flowers grow in the
waste spaces of the heart

WELCOME BUDDY!

THE PURPOSES OF THIS CLUB ARE

1. To create additional interest and enthusiasm for COLLEEN MOORE pictures all of
which are elevating and entertaining in their
wholesome fun.

❖ ❖ ❖ ❖

2. To watch for, and notify members, of
contests being held in magazines and papers
so that they can vote for COLLEEN MOORE,
and try to put her first.

❖ ❖ ❖ ❖

3. To write to the Fan magazines prais-
ing her pictures and her work. People who
read these magazines are enthusiasts, and
appreciative.

❖ ❖ ❖ ❖

4. To write to COLLEEN MOORE herself
covering points of appreciation of her work,
as often as possible.

5. See all her pictures and try and get
your friends to go with you. Dress up the
occasion with a picnic before or after so they
will always associate COLLEEN'S pictures with
good times.

❖ ❖ ❖ ❖

6. When you leave the theatre tell the
proprietor how you liked the show and ask
him when he will show her again. This helps.

❖ ❖ ❖ ❖

7. Keep a scrap-book of COLLEEN MOORE
clippings, photos, etc., and ask your friends
to please help collect for you. That helps.

❖ ❖ ❖ ❖

8. And send to the officers any suggestion
or information of benefit to the Club. They
will be most welcome.

Figure 2 (this page and opposite) Stationery from the Colleen Moore Fan Club, 1927.
Courtesy Joseph Yranski

unbounded. Thus, not only was the Irish Colleen an effective counter-image to the prevailing liberalization of sexual norms in the 1920s, but she also furnished part of the raw materials for an updated version of the Victorian 'True Woman' disguised as the New Woman.

Early in the century some conservative commentators had feared that the advent of the New Woman spelled the release of the social, economic and political energies of the immigrant. In 1910 novelist Margaret Deland contended that 'We have suffered many things at the hands of Patrick; the New Woman would add Bridget also.'[12] Yet in the ensuing years of silent cinema, Irish femininity as depicted onscreen and through stardom was marked by a thoroughgoing conservatism – the Irish girl in particular appeared as engaging performative, yet chaste and unthreateningly white.

'Your little sister:' the construction of Colleen Moore as waif

In many ways, Colleen Moore's career takes on the terms of a colonialist narrative in which she functions as a resource framed within a narrative of exchange and development, first 'discovered' by D.W. Griffith, and subsequently 'managed' by John McCormick. If Moore is originally posited in typical ways as a 'discovery' (though if anyone discovered anything, it was Moore herself, who resolved to become an actress in childhood), she progresses through certain stages of development during the course of her Hollywood career.[13] Moore's film roles and publicity can be organized into sedimentary layers within an overarching assimilation narrative. The three distinct stages of Moore's persona are as follows:

1   THE WAIF (in which Moore's relationships to family are stressed – in her private life she is referred to as sheltered by her Irish mother and grandmother, in her films she plays the orphan who must endure trials and tribulations to secure the protection of an adoptive family). This stage is typified in films such as *Little Orphant Annie* (1918).
2   THE WILD GIRL (here Moore is the free-spirited 'flapper' best known for her bobbed hair and limited social experimentation). These sorts of parts made Moore famous in films like *Flaming Youth* and *The Perfect Flapper*.
3   THE WIFE (Moore, now married to John McCormick, is featured in film narratives which conclude with coupling and the promise of marriage, frequently to a man who is socially and economically superior, as in *Irene, Ella Cinders*, and *It Must Be Love*).

I will discuss in detail four of Moore's films as representative of these stages in the Moore meta-narrative: *Little Orphant Annie, Come On Over* (1922), *Irene* (1926) and *Ella Cinders*. The first three of these give us a good indication of the various qualities associated with the phases of Moore's career, while *Ella Cinders* will be discussed as the quintessential Moore film, for it retains the elements of all three stages and tracks them back within a single narrative.

The first stage of Moore's persona is marked by a kind of childlike innocence and ignorance signified in a variety of ways from naive comments and behavior to physical stature. Moore is continually referred to in terms of her diminutiveness – as if to insist upon her inability to present a threat. This is especially evident in her publicity photos, an important repository of information about Moore, and therefore a significant site for analysis in this study. For instance, in a publicity still from *Synthetic Sin* (1929) the caption reads, 'Don (Antonio Moreno) is completely captivated by the bubbling personality of attractive little Betty (Colleen Moore).' The photo features the actors framed in a mock tug-of-war in front of a fireplace, with Moreno in a seersucker suit and Moore in a frilly white dress. Moreno is seated in a wooden, straight-backed chair, making distinct eye contact with Moore, who crouches between his legs, both hands in his in a playful pose that suggests she is trying to cajole him into standing. Moore is crouched down so low that, despite the fact that he is seated, Moreno's figure is distinctly taller in the frame. Another publicity still from the film *Orchids and Ermine* (1927) is even more striking in presenting Moore as a child. Here she is pictured with a very young Mickey Rooney, who plays a cigar-smoking midget in the film. Moore stands behind a wooden bar with Rooney sitting on it. In this (rather overdetermined) image, Moore again stands so that she is positioned as the smaller figure in the frame. Rooney is leaning back to chuck Moore under the chin.

In addition to the emphasis on her physical diminutiveness, early fan magazine articles also highlight Moore's energy, exuberance, and apparent blithe ignorance of her own fame. For instance, Frederick James Smith enthuses that 'Colleen Moore is positively the most unsophisticated movie favorite we ever met.'[14] He relates that:

> We first met Miss Moore by chance at the Hotel Algonquin. She had just arrived for her first New York visit, and she was still gasping at her initial subway experience. She told about it with wide-eyed wonder and called the subway 'the underworld.'
>
> 'Can such things be?' we questioned ourselves mentally?[15]

Smith then goes on to contrast Moore's guilelessness and straightforward enthusiasm for New York with his own jaded perspective, recounting how in a brief visit, the actress toured the Statue of Liberty and the Woolworth Building, two places he had never gone.

Gordon Gassaway details an interview with Moore preceded by his 'sense of wonderment as to what the much-in-demand "leading lady" was to be like.'[16] From this point forward, the structuring irony of the piece is the way in which Moore falls comically short of the standards of Hollywood glamour. Gassaway goes on to relate his reaction upon meeting Moore at her home: 'There was an abrupt stopping of piano playing within, a whirl of light footsteps and the door was thrown open by – your little sister! . . . I looked at her – she's an elflike little thing – and wondered if I hadn't come to call on the wrong girl.'[17] As the interview went on, according to the author's account, Moore herself implies this when in response to a question from Gassaway about her 'wonderful and romantic past,' she replied 'Oh, dear, there's only eighteen years of "past" and it's not a bit "vampy" or subtle or anything.'[18]

In the early stages of her career, Moore's persona was essentially founded on the idea of the naive child. Such positioning is revealed through her film roles and early publicity, and is even supported anecdotally. One Hollywood rumor centered upon Moore's performance in her second film, *An Old-Fashioned Young Man* (1917), a small-town comedy-drama in which she played an urban vamp who tries to lure the hero away from his country sweetheart. Just fifteen, Moore reportedly stumbled around so badly in high heels that she had to have a double for long shots. This was clearly the first phase of Moore's career, in which the uncertainty of her successful 'adoption' by Hollywood decision-makers and filmgoing audiences matched the typical adoption narrative film in which she appeared.

One such film was *Little Orphant Annie*, loosely based on the James Whitcomb Riley poem, and featuring Moore playing a Pickford-style gamin. Reviews of the film highlight the dominant themes of the first stage of Moore's Hollywood persona – the Waif. In one, Moore's performance is written of in the same complimentary terms that would recur throughout most of her career:

> Colleen Moore is Annie and she plays with such artistry that one's sympathies immediately go out to her in her misfortune. She has all the wistfulness of a homeless waif, which she is, until she goes to live with the squire and his wife and their nine children. It is amid these surroundings that the 'dream child' finds the little happiness she has ever known.[19]

Little Orphant Annie features Moore as the eponymous heroine who as the film opens is regaling other orphans with stories of the supernatural. In her visions, which are strikingly brought to life through the appearance of a cast of odd-looking dwarves she calls the 'Gobble-uns,' a whole nether world is opened up. In time, it becomes clear that Annie's ability to activate a nether realm inhabited by these 'little people' serves as a projection of her awareness of social forces beyond her control. When she warns the orphans not to be surprised that 'Gobble-uns' could be about, her evil uncle arrives to take her from the orphanage. At the end of a day when she has been mistreated by both her uncle and aunt, Annie looks down from her attic, and imagines a fantasy metamorphosis in which they transform into a goblin and a witch.

While one couple is demonized, Annie and her 'protector,' a local farmer named Dave Johnson, make up an idealized couple, whose contrasting imaginary transformation is into a knight and a lady. On a trip to town, Annie meets Squire Goode and his wife, who, shocked at the behavior of Annie's relatives, who berate and strike her in public, agree to take her into their home. This event is heralded in intertitles as 'The Beautiful Tomorrow' and we soon learn that 'the waif was very happy in her new home.' In the meantime, Dave says a poignant goodbye to Annie as he leaves to assist in the war effort. At the end of the film, Annie learns that Dave has been killed in the war. She collapses, crying 'The Gobble uns have got my Dave!' Ultimately, however, she recovers, bolstered by the support of her new family, and, an intertitle assures us, grows up and lives happily ever after. Clearly *Little Orphant Annie* presents a fantasy of class advancement, but it is one that is particularly predicated on a family of origin whose lower-class status is irrevocable, and where the 'aristocracy' (embodied by Squire Goode and his family, and Annie's fantasy of Dave Johnson as a knight) are more established, American types. The film is typical of Moore's early roles for its emphasis on morality, good behavior, and resignation – one model of immigrant success.

This phase of Moore's representation as the pitiful orphan is also reminiscent of historian Donna Gabaccia's discussion of American perceptions of immigrant family life. According to Gabaccia, one way in which American social service organizations rationalized the confiscation of immigrant children was by mythologizing the immigrant family as exclusively and primitively organized according to 'outmoded' patriarchal cultural traditions. Understanding immigrant families to be made up of women and children ruled by violent men justified social service intervention, and in some cases, the classification of immigrant children as orphans even when their immediate relatives or other family members were still living. As Gabaccia points out:

> Americans past and present have focused on the material poverty and moral backwardness of peoples from the other side. Through the lens of Social Darwinism, they saw foreigners at worst as racially inferior ('unassimilable') and at best as benighted children waiting to be raised through contacts with white Westerners. Because they have viewed men as breadwinners, Americans imagined the women of the other side more with pity than with fear or scorn.[20]

In this context, the nativist overtones of *Little Orphant Annie* become evident. In depicting the rescue of a female child from her primitive and abusive relatives, who is then appropriately sheltered by a WASP family, the film traded both on Moore's ethnic identity and her construction as a vulnerable child. In this respect, the narrative epitomizes the broader construction of Moore's ethnically-inflected waif persona. From this basis, Moore's career would follow a trajectory of assimilation in which Hollywood, much like the Goode family of *Little Orphant Annie*, would subject Moore to a process of incorporation representative of its benevolent patrimonial stance.

'The greenest aura:' Colleen Moore as assimilating immigrant

After appearing in dramatic films such as *Little Orphant Annie* and Tom Mix westerns in the late 1910s, Moore was playing more Irish roles in the 1920s. By

1920 Moore had come to the conclusion that her aptitude was for light comedy, and she signed a contract with Al Christie, whose slapstick shorts were rivaling Mack Sennett's comedies. After *Dinty* in 1920 (in which Moore played a young Irish mother), she again appeared as an Irish woman in *Come On Over*. As Moore began to play more Irish roles in films, her publicity was increasingly infused with traditional Celtic stereotypes and her fictionalized ethnic biography was amplified. In 1922 Elizabeth Peltret characterized Moore's rise to fame as her evolution into 'Colleen Moore, the personification of all the lovely colleens of the sentimental Irish poets.'[21] Other representations were not quite so heavy handed, although they came close. Fan magazine articles on Moore in this period are replete with descriptions of her as a simple, unpretentious Irish girl whose dream of stardom came true as the result of hard work and determination.

This in itself is interesting because of what such a construction both omits and amplifies from Moore's biography. For instance, such accounts neglect to mention Moore's valuable family connections which included her Uncle Walter Howey, editor of the *Chicago Examiner*, who was able to capitalize on a favor owed to him by D.W. Griffith to arrange Hollywood introductions for his niece. In addition, these accounts also selectively focus on and exaggerate one aspect of Moore's ethnicity; although she was of Irish descent, her ancestry was also German and British, but this is never mentioned.[22] Instead, Moore was publicized as consummately Irish. For her part, Colleen Moore attributed the inflation of her Irishness to a very conscious decision made by Howey. Kathleen Morrison being too long a name for theatre marquees, her uncle, she reports, set about to create a new professional name for her:

> Uncle Walter had taken the problem to his archrival and sometime friend Teddy Beck, editor of the *Chicago Tribune*. Over a beer in a friendly neighborhood tavern they decided the time had come for introducing an Irish actress to the movies. There was a lot of good publicity in it.[23]

From the outset of her career, Moore was linked to the guidance of her 'Irish' family. Jack Spears describes Moore as arriving in Hollywood 'under the protective watch of her grandmother, Mary Kelly, an Irish matriarch who regarded movies with a suspicious eye.'[24] Other accounts, however, paint a different portrait of Mrs. Kelly and imply that she served as a savvy business manager. For instance, Patricia Moore writes: 'The pretty little girl was helped by a number of persons in Hollywood, including her chaperon grandmother who advised Colleen to double her price each time she signed a new movie.'[25]

Many accounts sought to authenticate Moore's Irishness through heritage discourses and through her placement in a coterie of Irish performers and directors in Hollywood. In 'The Irish in the Movies,' George Mitchell commented good-humoredly:

And here we come to the moving picture industry and find the screen on Broadway, in one week, literally overrun with Irish actors. The Meighans, the Murrays and the Moores, Thomas, Mae and Colleen waving the Irish flag and big genial Tom Geraghty, smiling behind the backs of Zukor and Lasky, running Famous Players in good-humored Celtic large-handedness.[26]

Such positively valenced accounts of the Irish in Hollywood extended also to the celebration of Irish heritage. One article that focused on the community of Irish-American actors and directors in Hollywood even describes Moore hanging around the studio lot with directors Mickey Neilan and Pat O'Malley strumming a guitar and singing 'Kathleen Mavourneen,' then asking of O'Malley, 'Pat, do you think we'll ever any of us get back to Ireland?'[27] Gordon Gassaway also links Moore to both her Irish relatives and Irish friends:

Colleen comes by her brogue naturally. Her grandmother, one of the dearest little Mrs. Kellys in the world, came over on whatever was the Irish equivalent for the Mayflower, and so when D.W. Griffith, who has the distinction of discovering Colleen for the movies, changed her name from Kathleen to Colleen, he did not choose amiss. In keeping with her descent, she has created a green aura about her which rivals that of Mickey Neilan. As a matter of fact, I think Mickey put her up to it. At present she owns a little Irish terrier called Mike, with a green collar and green leash. Her personal notepaper is monogrammed in green and the shamrock is her coat of arms. For a time there was much rivalry between Mr. Neilan who directed her with John Barrymore in *The Lotus Eaters*, and Colleen, to see who could have the greenest aura.[28]

Moore's links to well-known Irish figures in Hollywood, including Neilan and publicity agent John McCormick, were sometimes described in upbeat terms, but they were just as often colored negatively. McCormick presented Moore with a diamond engagement ring cut in the shape of a shamrock, and the two married during the shooting of *Flaming Youth*; after this, McCormick would become the producer of Moore's films until their divorce in September 1930. There are significant traces of abuse in press accounts of Moore's marriage to John McCormick, whose renowned temper apparently caused problems for Moore both personally and professionally. In one article Moore is reported to be returning to First National after a dispute triggered by McCormick:

Colleen, you will remember, walked off the First National lot last year after following her husband's resignation as production manager. John McCormick is Irish, and, therefore, hot-headed. Even when the war was at its height, Richard Rowland and the rest of the F.N. executives admitted a sneaking liking for young McCormick and believed that he would get over his spell.[29]

Discourses of Irishness are prevalent in many accounts of the Moore/McCormick marriage. Just as McCormick is figured in the foregoing article in ways that strikingly conform to stereotypes of Irish masculinity (that is, rash, mercurial, and yet ultimately so charming that he wins over even studio executives), Moore emerges as long-suffering Irish wife. In an article detailing the couple's 1930 divorce proceedings, Moore is even described as giving testimony 'with a slight Irish accent,' which seems highly implausible given that she was born and raised in the United States. Thus, although by this late stage of her career, Irishness was by no means the dominant discourse of Moore's persona, it is strikingly activated here in the context of emotional upheaval and marital discord. In this respect, Irishness is not an indiscriminate but a selective discourse in Moore's persona, and it is clear that her image was infused with associations of Irishness at certain key moments that appear to conform to stereotypes of positive and negative 'Irish' emotionality.

After being figured as a wayward child in the first phase of her career (both in her film roles and in extra-filmic publicity and promotion efforts), Moore was increasingly promoted as 'the modern girl' at the same time that her Irishness was highlighted. At this juncture, she was perceived to be evolving from an ingenue with a flair for light comedy into a more resonant figure in keeping with the times. Moore bobbed her hair, inspiring a national trend for American women, and began to be more strongly associated with the perky style of the flapper, appearing in films such as *Flaming Youth* and *The Perfect Flapper*. During this phase of Moore's career, as Angela Taylor has observed, 'Her Dutch bob was copied in every village and hamlet and so was her pert, emancipated air.'[30] This was the Moore of whom F. Scott Fitzgerald would write, 'I was the spark that lit up flaming youth. Colleen Moore was the torch.'[31]

Assessments of Moore's career make clear that she was a figure linked more to the co-optation of free female behavior than to an actual expansion of women's roles or any overt critique of patriarchy. One article suggests that Moore's association with autonomy was reducible to good fashion sense, citing the actress giving the following advice to American women in 1925:

> Don't worry girls. No edict of fashion arbiters will ever swathe you in long and cumbersome skirts . . . Long skirts, corsets and flowing tresses have gone . . . The American girl will see to this. She is independent, a thinker [who] will not follow slavishly the ordinances of those, who in the past, have decreed this or that for her to wear.[32]

In the sense that the freedom Moore embodied was more sartorial than ideological, this middle phase of her career represented a natural evolution from the Waif, into a phase of moderate experimentation before settling into domesticity as the Wife. Lois W. Banner characterizes the flapper as just such a figure, noting that she 'glamorized the working world for women while trivializing it,' for she was 'anxious for a good time, but intent on securing a husband, and that goal was the ultimate message.'[33] Banner reads the Flapper as a symbol of the dawning of consumer culture in America:

> An adolescent quality permeated the 1920s as Americans were first exposed in quantity to consumer goods like radios and automobiles destined to change radically the nature of their lives. Advertising celebrated the leisured, consumption-oriented life. The flapper, with her frenetic dancing, represented the vitality of these developments, with their promise of a new life.[34]

If Moore personified free behavior in the middle phase of her career, she nonetheless remained anchored to standards of normativity. As Jack Spears has observed, 'She had no difficulty whatever in projecting, practically simultaneously, gay abandon and a righteous awareness of the eternal verities.'[35] In this phase of her career, the energy and vivacity of Moore's Irishness were a way of positing women's social advancement as childlike play and interim pre-marriage freedom.

Moore's connection to discourses of modernization was not incidental, but in fact reflected a logical discursive progression if we read her persona as an evolving assimilation narrative in which Moore is first presented as an immigrant child, but one whose exposure to American culture broadens and enlivens her, enabling her to be contextualized as an American product. During this phase of her career and presentation as 'the modern girl,' the notion of Moore as product was continually underscored in her publicity portfolio.

One of the ways in which Moore's position as the autonomous, modern girl was neutralized was through a discourse of masculine production. From the beginning of her career Moore's success was represented as having been filtered through a layer of male sponsorship (her editor uncle, D.W. Griffith, her husband John McCormick). In a publicity photo for *Her Wild Oat* for instance, Moore is obliquely presented as her husband's accomplishment with the caption to her photo reading, 'John McCormick presents Colleen Moore in HER WILD OAT.' Similarly, a review of *Irene* describes that film as 'First National's release of John McCormick's presentation of Colleen Moore.'[36] As has been discussed, Moore's relationship to the industrial apparatus of Hollywood was considerably mediated through her domineering husband (a fact that would seem to work against her 'modern' status). Nevertheless, her links to modernization and industrialization during this phase of her career were strong. One publicity photograph of the period makes this manifest as Moore is featured alongside a Ford automobile with the caption, 'Colleen Moore was one of the first Hollywoodians to acquire one of the new Fords.' The line between two separate commodities is blurred as Moore poses beside the car, holding up a reflective panel used to conceal the engine. The panel reflects her face, underscoring certainly her asso-

Figure 3 Colleen Moore as Moyna Killilea in the 1923 immigrant drama *Come On Over*. Courtesy Joseph Yranski

ciation with modernization discourses, but also suggesting in rather blunt terms that, like the Ford automobile, Moore is the byproduct of a routinized, industrialized (masculine) system of production.

In 1926 when Moore appeared in *Irene*, it was one of the greatest hits of her career. Yet that film is anticipated to some degree by *Come On Over* in 1923. Like *Irene*, *Come On Over* narrativizes the assimilation of a poor Irish girl into American urban life. However, the two films present considerable differences in the extent of the heroine's economic advancement and the degree of incorporation into mainstream American culture she attains. It will be helpful to consider these two films as a pair, with *Come On Over* working as a first stage assimilation narrative, and *Irene* as a second stage drama of broader Irish incorporation into American cultural and social life.

In the first film, Moore's character is represented as virtually pre-civilized, inhabiting an Ireland which is constructed to accord with the terms of Irish-American nostalgia for the old country. She plays Moyna Killilea, a devoted Irish girl, whose boyfriend Shane O'Mealia (Ralph Graves) emigrates from Lisdoon-varna[37] in Co. Clare to New York. When we first see Moyna, she is sitting in a glen; as she waits for Shane she roams the cliffs and hills of Lisdoonvarna in sequences (much like those of *The Quiet Man* [1952]) designed to endow Irish femininity with elemental, natural simplicity. Shane leaves Moyna (significantly, an orphan) in the care of the elderly Mrs. Bridget Morahan (Florence Drew) and heads to New York. Although well-intentioned, Shane is not able to raise the money to send for Moyna, who is finally able to leave Ireland for America with the help of Michael Morahan (J. Farrell MacDonald), another Irishman who has had more success in the US than Shane. Michael's visit to his mother's cottage is a natural narrative progression in a film which depicts no one in Ireland who is not passing their time thinking of relatives in America. When he stoops to enter his mother's home, Michael comments that 'Either this door has grown shorter or I've grown taller these twenty-five years.'[38] He takes pity on Moyna and tells her 'Moyna, you've been an angel to me mother. Come on over with us.' Moyna is so elated she begins to dance a jig, and the Morahans soon join her. When Moyna arrives, she is embraced by Michael's wife Delia (Kate Price) who tells her, 'Oh, Shane's well and grand. But it's yourself that's had the use of the May dew on your cheeks.' As a gift, Moyna brings Delia a literal piece of the old sod, a clump of Irish soil with shamrocks in it.

While Moyna is cast as the embodiment of 'the old country,' other Irish characters in the film must contend more directly with the pressures of change and modernization. Unbeknownst to Moyna, Shane has become friends with Judy Dugan (Kathleen O'Connor), whose drunkard father is the butt of many jokes early in the film for his inability to keep any kind of employment. The film presents a moderate contrast between Moyna's purity and primitivism and Judy's more modern style. In one scene for instance, Judy cajoles Shane into dancing with her, despite his protest that '[I] can't learn these modderen [sic] dances.' As the two begin to dance, Moyna materializes in his imagination just over Judy's shoulder. Although the scene well illustrates Moyna's status in the narrative as a shining icon of traditionalism, the contrast between the two female types is somewhat ineffective, in light of the film's conceptions of Irishness. For Judy to serve as an effective foil to Moyna, she would need to be more completely Americanized, something which her Irishness prevents. Yet the film's complete inability to imagine Irish characters associating with non-Irish beyond an enclave mandates this ethnic identity. Although Judy is too nebulous a figure for the viewer to make much of her one way or the other, it is clear the film intends for Moyna to represent the crossing over of Irish femininity with its virtue and morality intact.

In a crucial sequence Moyna, under the mistaken belief that Shane is planning to marry Judy, runs out into the street without hat or coat. The ensuing drama of the lost girl in the big city entirely conforms to Moore's waif persona as I have discussed it thus far, but it is also significant as the one episode in the film where Moyna must confront American public space. The film presents Moyna's flight into urban chaos as a crisis which can be effectively managed by the combined efforts of the Irish immigrant community. A high-angle shot emphasizes her vulnerability on the street as a stranger immediately attempts to take her arm and walk with her. Meanwhile, Shane arrives and upon hearing that Moyna has fled, he exclaims, 'That poor darling lost in the strange city! I'll scour the world for her.' Delia, however, offers a more expedient solution by telephoning her police officer brother and providing a description of Moyna, 'She's red-headed, bare-headed, grey dress, Irish shoes on her feet, and a wild look in her grey eye.' Moyna immediately instinctively seeks out a more rural setting, and is spotted in the park by a police officer and brought in.

In an effort to find a job for Shane, Michael Morahan calls his friend Carmody, and as Moyna is returned to the house, Carmody is being introduced to the Widow Morahan as 'the little Danny Carmody that owns all the railroads in the United States.' Bridget recalls that the last time she saw Carmody in Ireland '[you] were fightin' a pig for a crust of bread. I disremember who won.' Carmody announces that his sister has married and that her name is now Mrs. Van Dusen. 'Mrs. Van Dusen!' says Delia. 'That's a he – l of a name for an honest Irish girl!' Before leaving, Carmody invites them all to dinner.

Shane then arrives and chases Moyna around the dining room table before she runs into a bedroom, threatening to jump out the window. Michael advises Shane to 'Try a bit of force. It's that that the women admire.' Delia and Michael then have a spat in which he threatens to hit her, but then they quickly laugh and make up. With things at an uncertain point between Shane and Moyna, the group arrives at the Carmody mansion for dinner. Overawed by her surroundings, Moyna demonstrates her unfamiliarity with the concept of dressing for dinner. When offered the loan of a gown, she says, 'Gown? Is it going to bed I am so soon?' In her new borrowed clothes, Moyna later sees her reflection and visualizes a transformation back to her former self, costumed in more functional, rural attire. It is clear that despite her sartorial transformation, she remains innately the same rural Irish girl. Shortly thereafter, events quickly resolve as it is revealed that Judy had merely enlisted Shane's help in getting her father to take the pledge before a priest. Moyna realizes her mistake, Shane begs her forgiveness, and she responds, 'I'll forgive you for everything but forgetting the old Irish dances.' A piper is brought in, and opulent rugs are put away in favor of a door so that the group can engage in traditional dances. At the film's conclusion, the Carmodys, the Morahans, the Dugans, Shane and Moyna, and even the priest dance an energetic jig in a scene that establishes that even in an American mansion, the Irish resist complete socialization into American ways, relying on community and family networks to overcome social differences and reverting to rural rituals.

In *Irene* Moore for the first time plays an Irish character who assimilates through marriage, and the film places heavy emphasis on positively valued transformative skills. Moore's character is a shanty-Irish model for an exclusive New York designer whose business interests are linked to a young millionaire she marries at the film's conclusion. To some reviewers, the inclusion of Irish ethnicity humanized the stock plot. One described the film as follows: 'The awkward little tenement girl becomes the graceful model winning the handsome prince-of-trade in a blaze of costumed glory. *Irene* is a modern fairy tale – but it comes in a most human Irish edition.'[39]

Even with the inclusion of Irishness as a relative novelty, this was familiar stuff for Moore's fans. *Irene*'s most innovative quality seems to have been its inclusion of a fashion show sequence shot in two-color Technicolor. Publicity stills from *Irene* feature Moore in an extra-diegetic fashion show of her own, in a variety of elaborate costumes, many in shades of green designed to imply her character's Irish identity. Like *Come On Over, Irene* trades on stereotypes of Irish pugnacity, emotionality and alcoholism in its narrative about a working-class Irish girl who marries into WASP aristocracy. It emphasizes a later phase of assimilation, depicting a female protagonist who is a less recent arrival, possibly even a second generation Irish-American, who must make her own way in the world. Irene O'Dare (Moore), as we first meet her, delivers the laundry her mother (Kate Price) takes in as a result of Pa O'Dare's (Charlie Murray) inability to work due to alcoholism.[40] She also has a job displaying beds in a department store display window where her excessive horseplay finally destroys the merchandise and she gets fired. When Irene tells her mother of this, Ma O'Dare impetuously throws her out, and Irene is forced to seek help from her friend Cordelia Smith, whose 'large income gave her a large choice of apartments – and the young gold-digger had taken her pick.' In contrast to the experienced Cordelia, Irene is represented as comically virtuous. When Cordelia receives a note from her date that uses the salutation 'Flaming Baby,' Irene naively assumes her friend is having dinner with her father. At a dinner party that evening, a young man of Cordelia's acquaintance makes aggressive advances toward Irene, who runs out into the streets.[41] Meanwhile, Ma O'Dare calls for Irene out the window, wondering if she believed her to be serious.

Weeks pass, and the O'Dares are on the verge of eviction for lack of rent, when they get a letter from Irene relating that she fell asleep in the back of a truck and wound up in New York. (As in *Come On Over* Irish ethnicity seems to connote lack of education, as the letter is full of misspellings). Irene invites her parents to join her, saying the laundry business will be good in New York. One day shortly thereafter, Irene arrives bearing laundry at Marshallmere, the home of Donald Marshall, the scion of a family of wealthy industrialists. Directed to the back entrance, she sneaks in the front door, and amuses herself while she waits by playing dress-up with the furnishings, putting a lampshade on her head, and wearing a silk throw as a dress. This moment of childlike play is typical of many of Moore's later films (as I discuss further with respect to *Ella Cinders*), and it is significant that it takes place here, following Irene's audacious refusal to accept the strictures of class positioning. These exhibitions of childlike play, impersonation and masquerade often lead to social advancement through marriage for the heroine while defusing the political charge associated with the immigrant's promotion. True to form, it is during this moment of play that Irene meets Donald Marshall, who will later tell a friend, 'There's a little girl I'm interested in.' Marshall mistakes her for one of his mother's guests, and she ambiguously replies only, 'I was asked to wait here.' When she knocks down some curtains in an attempt to flee, they share a significant brief embrace. As she is invited to sit, Irene pricks her finger with a needle to be sure she isn't dreaming. She tells Donald that '[I'm] always praying for a chance to meet nice people – so I can be somebody and take care of Ma and Pa and the kids.' Clearly attempting to prolong their acquaintance, he replies, 'Miss Irene, I think that opportunity you prayed for is coming your way,' and invites her to model for 'Madame Lucy,' a milliner client of a friend whose business is floundering. She objects, 'It doesn't sound quite – quite – er – respectable,' but he reassures her, and Irene is sent home in style. Thus, *Irene*, like so many of Moore's other films, foregrounds ethnic female bravado. Here she enters the mansion as a delivery girl, and departs a guest, sent off with flowers and candy and a car at her disposal.

Returning home, Irene finds her parents have arrived. Pa O'Dare goes out to the stoop to smoke a cigar, and gawks at the names on store signs all around him. Seeing signs for Meisenfeld the Tailor, Kokalinski & Rabinivitz, Druggists, and Brunoshefski Rubenstein Co., he is clearly bewildered. In an exchange that is crucial in establishing the film's incorporative stance toward the Irish, O'Dare asks a man beside him, 'I lived here about twinty [sic] years ago. What's become of all the Irish?' and the man replies, 'What's become of the Indians?' The response implies the increasingly secure place of the Irish in a hierarchy of ethnicities and assimilating immigrant groups, at least in comparison to other ethnicities (the new immigrants who make the Irish look virtually like native Americans).[42]

When he sees her, Madame Lucy (a man using a female professional name) refuses to use Irene as a model. Donald, however, tells him rather bluntly, 'I've seen you take a stick and make it beautiful. Give her a chance.' Scandalized by the dress she is given to wear, Irene puts a hand to her cheek to hide her blush. As she stands on the elevated modeling platform, Donald accidentally activates a control and Moore begins to rotate around, for a few moments being transformed into the performing doll the film and many press accounts make of her. In this strange moment of the Irish girl's transformation, it is as if the forces of mechanization suddenly run rampant and in a gesture of self-reflexive excessive production, the 'machine' (creation of the beauty ideal) threatens to destroy its part (Moore). The scene plays out as a highly self-reflexive instance of the transformative apparatus suddenly and starkly revealing itself.

Meanwhile, Ma O'Dare deduces from a conversation with the mother of another girl that 'There's somethin' wrong, somewhere!' When an invitation to the Fashion Fete is discovered in a book, the three mothers set out to discover what is going on. At the fashion show, Irene is an instant success as a model; her beauty, grace, and poise charm the audience. Yet the fact that her success comes so suddenly and abruptly at the end of the film is significant, for it underscores Donald's successful production of Irene as a desirable commodity to his social and class stratum. Because the film places heavy emphasis on Irene's transformation after recognition has been conferred on her by a rich WASP, the fashion show is as much a celebration of Donald's perception and construction of Irene as it is a recognition of her attributes (of course, the film as a whole credits Irene with very few of these apart from the stock Irish traits of charm, endurance and luck). It is also important to observe the contrast that is presented between Donald Marshall and the Frenchman, Madame Lucy, with only the former authorized as agent of Irene's transformation and legitimization. It is clear that Donald's elite class status and uncompromised masculinity qualify him to perceive Irene's value as a resource, while the foppish Frenchman is disqualified on both ethnic and gender grounds.

As the fashion show concludes, (predictably enough) the brawling Irish family members arrive, led by Ma O'Dare. Their physical placement in the orchestra pit between the performing Irish girls and the WASP audience highlights how little these older immigrants understand the transformations of their own offspring. As each girl in turn opens a fur coat to reveal a rather skimpy outfit underneath, a scandalized Ma O'Dare calls a halt to the proceedings, warning Irene, 'Stop! Don't ye dare open that coat!' As the Fashion Fete disintegrates into chaos, Mrs Marshall reproaches her son, 'You did this! Foisting these common creatures on me as society girls –' She then directs her anger to Irene, '– and you certainly tricked me nicely. I suppose you were angling for my son.' Irene protests, 'I don't want your son – and you can't insult my mother and me. We're not common – we're just poor – and that's no crime!' Turning to Donald, she tells him, 'You made me dream of being a lady – but I'm awake now – and I never want to see you again!' As Mrs Marshall summons her butler, 'Paxton, show these – VULGARIANS – off the premises!' Ma O'Dare is given one last opportunity to comically demonstrate her ignorance and rejoins, 'Bulgarians to you, Mrs Marshall. I'm Irish, I'll have ye understand!'

At the O'Dare apartment, shortly thereafter, Donald is able to placate Ma O'Dare who praises 'his gift of blarney.' Donald goes out to the fire escape where Irene is waiting and tells her, 'I've fixed things with Mother – and it's all o.k. with the O'Dares' and the couple embrace to close the film. Yet Donald's last lines resonate strangely – in referring to Irene's family in such distancing terms (as 'the O'Dares,' rather than 'your family' or 'your parents'), it is as if she is already not one of them any longer. Thus, particularly in its conclusion, *Irene* manifests an ambiguous view of Irishness. The film presents a paradox in that Irene is prized as a desirable romance partner for the purity and virtue signified by her Irishness (and policed by Ma O'Dare) yet she is also obliged to overcome her ethnicity to ascend to the upper classes. In order to take up a more elevated class role, she must leave her Irishness behind. Thus, if Irishness connotes transformative potential, such an association seems to carry with it a fundamental dismissal of the desirability of retaining Irish characteristics. As the film would have it, Irishness is assimilable in large part due to the fact that it can become something else, conceptualized here as a public state given up upon entering the 'privacy' of marriage. For the Eastern European vamps, such as Pola Negri, whose stardom I discuss in the next chapter, the public state is irrevocable, while for the Irish Colleen it is convertible upon marriage, an interiorized version of social incorporation.

'The Cinderella girl:' the heritage encounter and the domestication of Irish ethnicity

Lois W. Banner writes that:

> Early in the nineteenth century, a Cinderella mythology became for women the counterpart of the self-made man mythology for men. Just as it was commonly believed that for men hard work and persever-ance would bring success, beauty was supposed to attract wealthy and powerful men into marriage. Young men in business dreamed of rising to the top through entrepreneurial skill. Young working women dreamed of marrying the boss's son.[43]

In the third phase of her career, as we shall see, Moore's connections to Irishness and assimilation were significantly mediated through the ongoing trope of the Cinderella story. This served to render her success intelligible within prevailing American norms.

By 1924, Moore was a major star whose name and image were being used to open new films even in medium-sized and small American cities.[44] In 1924, a poll of exhibitors in *Film Daily* ranked Moore as the eighth biggest box office attraction (tied with Mary Pickford and Reginald Denny).[45] There are indica-tions that Moore's Hollywood clout by this time was considerable – not only did First National build a luxurious bungalow for her use during filming, but Moore also exercised considerable freedom over her choice of projects and scripts. In 1926 and 1927 film exhibitors consecutively voted Colleen Moore the country's top female attraction.[46]

In addition to her domestic success, Moore also sold well abroad, an impor-tant factor in the 1920s when American films were establishing dominance in foreign markets. One of the most striking events in Moore's career occurred in 1925, when she went to Dublin on a promotional visit. Significant publicity attended the trip even before Moore left the United States. Many articles repres-ented the trip as a return to their homeland for Moore and John McCormick.[47] However, despite such proprietary claims, the relationship between Moore and Ireland was constructed as fundamentally touristic, a fact which is partly given away in the incessant invocation of the Blarney Stone as the marker of a heritage encounter between Moore and Irish culture. One article reported that:

> Colleen Moore is happy! Her last words as she boarded the train in LA some weeks ago en route to Europe were to the effect that she would not return until she had pressed her lips against the blarney stones. A

cablegram from Ireland signed by the First National star advises she has made good her promise and that the rock which has been the recipient of countless thousands of kisses has added her name to its never ending list.[48]

Coverage of Moore's visit in Irish newspapers also echoed the theme of a heritage encounter for Moore and McCormick. In a Special Interview previewing the actress's visit, one article quotes Moore expressing her life-long desire to visit her homeland:

> Ever since I was a tiny child I have always wanted to come to Ireland, the home of my parents. I felt that I knew it as well as if I had lived there all my life, for as far back as I can remember my mother was never tired of telling me about her homeland.
>
> I shall see this land which hitherto has been more like a fairy story. I shall be able to meet and talk to people that knew my parents before they ever crossed the Atlantic. I shall feel that I have come home.[49]

Two days later the same newspaper reported Moore's arrival as a joyous homecoming: ' "Sure it's God's country, it is," said Colleen Moore, the famous Irish-American film star after landing at Dun Laoghaire Pier with the first glimpses of the Irish coast in her mind.'[50] While the majority of the visit seems to have been spent privately, Moore did appear in person at the Irish debuts of two of her films, *So Big* (1924) and *Sally* (1925) (contrary to Moore's claims later in life that it was *Flaming Youth* being premiered). The premieres (in addition to being advertised in the *Irish Times*) were hyped through gimmicks that also de-politicized white ethnicity. The La Scala Theatre hired eight men to patrol the streets in blackface, carrying cards reading 'No wonder I look black. I can't see Colleen Moore in *Sally* at the La Scala this week.' Another strategy (referred to as 'a clever way of announcing the event in an Irish setting')[51] used announcers wearing chest-to-waist placards that made them resemble the political protesters of the early 1920s. While the *Boston Post* and other American newspapers reported that Moore's appearances caused chaos ('police reserves were unable to check the mobs determined to shake Colleen's hand'[52]) there are no comparable reports in the Irish newspapers to corroborate these accounts. This disparity intriguingly suggests that Americans wanted to believe in the international appeal of American film stars, even to the extent of exaggerating their reception abroad.

The significance of Moore's trip with respect to Hollywood's use of ethnicity in its burgeoning attempts to cultivate an international market should not be under-estimated. As accounts in the Irish press make clear, Moore's visit represents a striking instance of Hollywood successfully selling Irishness to the Irish. At the same time, however, there may have been significant incentives for the Irish press to publicize Moore's visit at a cultural moment when Ireland appears to have been learning to commodify the heritage impulse, particularly to attract

Figure 4 Colleen Moore goes from miniaturization to marriage in *Ella Cinders*

Irish-Americans.[53] A piece entitled 'Advertising Ireland' indicates a high degree of awareness and mobilization behind an incipient Irish tourist industry. The article alludes to such initiatives as a postal stamp reading 'Tour Ireland' and a 'See Ireland First' tag to be affixed to all mailed letters, the production of tourist posters, an 'Official Guide to Dublin' and the Tourist Association's booklet 'Ireland in 1925.'[54] Thus, it would appear that the construction of Colleen Moore's visit 'home' to Ireland had the effect of serving two simultaneous ends – authenticating the Irishness that was seen to be explanatory of Moore's comic style and desexualized persona while also positioning Moore as the embodiment of the heritage-seeking American tourist who could contribute to the Irish economy.

A year later, Moore would appear in *Ella Cinders*, the film that most successfully wove together the various threads of her star text. Moore plays the eponymous heroine in a remarkable assimilation narrative. An aspiring actress, Ella wins a local contest, and with it the opportunity to travel to Hollywood. When she arrives, she learns that in fact the contest was a fraud. But the film continually showcases Ella's abilities to adapt to circumstance, as she perseveres, eventually stumbling unaware into a film shoot, where her genuine reactions of terror to a staged fire make clear that her own natural, instinctual behavior is better than the performance of the film's leading actress. In the end, Ella gets a chance at a film career, not so much through her own design but because she possesses those qualities which we have consistently seen associated with the Irish female immigrant – perseverance and lack of artifice.

While there is no direct evidence that filmgoers or reviewers saw *Ella Cinders* in any way as a self-reflexive account of Moore's own rise to fame, the film readily serves as a culmination narrative for Moore's star persona.[55] The reviewers of the film seem to have judged its sincerity a bit boring, yet it is clear that in the context of Colleen Moore's star persona, the possibilities for satirizing or critiquing the Cinderella myth were severely limited. One wrote:

> Paste, soot and soap are generously employed as comedy material in 'Ella Cinders,' Colleen Moore's latest photoplay, which now is sojourning at the Mark Strand. From one or two points in this fractious film, it is obvious that it might have been an entertaining satire on the fairy tale 'Cinderella.' Those responsible for it, however, apparently decided that while satire is all very well on Broadway, it misses fire on Main Street.

> Here, dear little Ella seems to have her share of fun through breaking up the parties of her severe step-mother and her plain sisters. One bright afternoon she stands on a bridge-table and then goes through to the top to the amazement of the guests. Persistence is her chief virtue . . . Miss Moore is energetic and vivacious.[56]

It is important that the film narrative represents Ella/Moore as a ready performer, willing to demonstrate her own transformative skills at any moment. In two striking instances in the film, Moore's performing body is reduced in size at the same time that it is shown to be maneuverable and adjustable. Moore's heroine first miniaturizes herself to entertain a male admirer by substituting her face for the face of a baby in a soap billboard promoting the product's ability to cleanse/transform children with the slogan, 'After one rub you'll never know your baby.' In another instance, she impersonates a dancing puppet for the entertainment of a group of children, placing shoes on her hands and standing behind a table so that she becomes a performing doll.

Interestingly, Moore became very well known in the late 1920s for doll collecting and dollhouse furnishing – hobbies which she had maintained since childhood and apparently did much to popularize for American women.[57] This type of connection fostered an understanding of the actress herself as a kind of doll, both childlike and undeveloped, and as I have been suggesting, this presentation was facilitated by being combined with certain stereotypes of Irish femininity. Thus, in a sense it is almost poignantly ironic that Moore should have written a piece for *Ladies Home Journal* in 1927 entitled 'My Career and My Doll's House' that links those very topics in an odd-seeming juxtaposition unless one considers that Moore herself was a kind of doll in the house of the Hollywood studio system.

In a startlingly self-reflexive conclusion, *Ella Cinders* plays out the domestication of Moore's public performance. In this scene, the film undervalues Ella's work by depicting her performing domestic rituals in public – on a film shoot, she is scrubbing a railway platform while a director calls instructions to her through a megaphone. In the middle of the shoot (and as the cameras continue to roll) the hero arrives to whisk Ella away, mistaking her public performance for private service. (Arriving on a train which pulls in between Ella and her director, he literally interrupts the public action). Even after his misunderstanding has been corrected, he still warns 'Tell them to find another star to do their scrubbing.' Thus, just as in *Irene*, public performance is traded in for private legitimacy. In a highly self-conscious coda, the film's falling action then has us flash forward to the happily married Ella and her husband proudly observing the antics of their small son. By this point, Ella is no longer the public performer; she has now become an onlooker along with 'us.' It is significant that this scene is stylistically at odds with everything that has come before it – this is the only time we have seen Moore in fashionable, contemporary clothing throughout the film, and as the couple wave at the child offscreen, they appear to be waving at us. For these reasons, and because the scene's placement encourages us to read it as a kind of 'curtain call' that acknowledges the work of the performers, this vignette plays out as a moment in which Moore suddenly steps out of character, no longer Ella Cinders, but herself, the actress whose persona in this phase was strongly linked to the Cinderella trope.

In figuring a heroine who achieves her goals through perseverance and naturalness rather than design or artifice, and whose career success is cheerfully discarded in favor of domesticity, *Ella Cinders* encapsulates the entire ideological trajectory of Moore's persona. For both Ella Cinders and Colleen Moore, the requirement that display be accompanied by miniaturization/reduction relates to a broader ideological vision of the containment of ethnic femininity. The woman who knows her place understands her necessarily limited participation in adult economies, just as the dependent nation recognizes its delimited role in political and industrial economies. In this regard, Moore's early positioning as waif, her publicity photos' ongoing emphasis on her diminutiveness, her association with the miniaturized world of dollhouses and her appearance in films like *Ella Cinders* which directly thematize the connections between display and miniaturization all come together to endow Irishness and femininity with a sense of vulnerability and helplessness which implicitly worked to legitimate the hegemony of American patriarchy.

Fan magazine coverage of Moore in this period runs in tandem representationally with films like *Ella Cinders*, extending the domestication narrative through emphasis on the actress' comfortable home life where she finds richer rewards than can be attained through professional accomplishments. A number of magazine articles also allude to Moore's old-fashioned, traditional nature in ways that would seem to belie her tag as the 'modern girl.' According to one interviewer, despite all of her efforts at 'modernization,' Moore was clearly nothing but a traditionalist who inspired an equally traditional male response:

> She seems quite out of her century. Somehow all sorts of old-fashioned phrases and gallantry begin to stir within you. And the modern male, so long a serf to the equal-rights-lady-on-the-pedestal, finds himself distending his bosom and talking throatily, with a feeling, I fancy, akin to that of the rooster just before he crows.[58]

In addition to identifying Colleen Moore as 'the essential feminine' (perhaps essentialized feminine would have been the better phrase), the author goes on to characterize her in terms that suggest the futility of experimentation and imitation. The caption beneath her picture in the article reads, 'She wants to look like Gloria Swanson, but she confesses it's no use – she's just a simple Hollywood girl.'[59] These sorts of apparently paradoxical constructions are extremely important for the way in which they reveal the recuperative function of Moore's 1920s persona. On the one hand, as 'the modern girl' Moore was packaged as a typical flapper, yet other features of her image significantly undercut the 'New Woman' persona and steered it in a direction that suggested that women's attempts to modernize themselves were inevitably futile and a bit silly. In this sense, these two dimensions of Moore's star image were fundamentally inter-related – for she came to represent a transformative process that only began with the construction of the New Woman, and then significantly reversed course. Stated another way, Moore personified the transformation *back* just as much as she personified the transformation to. The promotion of Moore as Irish enabled the transformational energies associated with Irishness to be

hijacked to stand for a reversion to dependent, passive femininity. This positioning of Moore as disqualified from taking part in the modernization process is
crucially connected to her ethnic status as an Irish woman with the message
being that women (or colonized, traditional cultures) need men's (or dominant,
modern cultures) help to transform themselves. In this respect, Irishness as a
category was more recuperable within the Hollywood ideological system than
were, for instance, Polish or Italian ethnic identities which offered no 'safe'
stereotypes comparable to the figure of the Irish Colleen.

Moore's career is emblematic of a certain ideological matching process between
femininity, culturally sanctioned white ethnicities and social advancement. Over
and over again throughout her career, she personified the model immigrant
who is safely assimilated into dominant American culture. Narrativized as the
girl who finds family shelter, the rambunctious pre-marriage flapper, or the
'good girl' who marries up, the shared ideological problematic is the smooth
incorporation of Irish femininity into American life. In the later stages of her
career, this is accomplished through the particular activation of the Cinderella
trope, with its implications of social advancement through complacent acceptance and dues-paying. Moore herself acknowledged the centrality of the Cinderella
narrative late in her life, when, in discussing her career, she told Joe Collura:

> I turned out to be essentially a comedienne, therefore, it was my
> dramatic pictures I liked the most. Comedy or drama, we just made
> one story after another – and it was always Cinderella![60]

Even after her Hollywood career had ended, Moore was celebrated for her
ongoing transformation into domesticity. The actress's graceful acceptance of
the limits of professional transformation and accommodation to shifting circumstances are praised, for instance, by Jon Anderson in his review of Moore's
autobiography. He writes that:

> Colleen has managed to make the transitions in her life and to move into
> new roles with grace and charm. And this, perhaps, is her greatest accom-
> plishment: the ability to solve problems, and get on with something new.[61]

It is extremely important here that Moore is lauded for her adaptation from public
to private, and that her willingness to recede from public view is suggestive of an
assimilation trajectory which entails a kind of amnesia about the pre-domesticity
phase.[62] Very much in keeping with the conclusion of films like *Irene*, (which
figures ethnicity as disposable at the point of social incorporation symbolized by
assimilation/marriage) the 'ending' to Moore's career is predicated on a happy
transformation from public performance to private, domestic life. Constructions
of this sort correspond to the ideological trajectory of Moore's persona by
obliquely activating a sense of the endurance and adaptability of the immigrant,
and valuing Moore for displaying moderate ambition and essentially, for knowing her place. In sharp contrast to the kind of ethnic femininity embodied by

the Eastern European vamps who were often associated with an intense covetousness for enduring fame, Moore was linked to a class status which functioned to confer a sense of decorum about the limits of public performance.

Even Moore's obituary in *The New York Times* in 1988 associated her with the rejuvenating energies of desirable immigrant ethnicity, quoting the actress as saying of her career, 'Here was a chance for a girl who had straight hair, who was not buxom and not a great beauty,' she told an interviewer half a century later. 'A new type was born – the American girl.'[63] Such accounts tend to reinforce a sense that American femininity is crafted out of disparate immigrant materials, having no distinct, original formulation of its own (a notion strikingly at odds with Theodore Dreiser's representation of American femininity at the start of the chapter as an ahistorical incarnation of the land itself). They are also expressive of the degree to which Moore was constructed as the assimilable outsider who ultimately becomes an emblem for the porousness of the system and a sign of the incorporative ideal (however far this ideal may have been from actual social conditions).

In *Silent Star* Moore discusses her transition from public to private life as a process of Americanization, and she is effusively enthusiastic about her 'discovery of America' on tour with the Colleen Moore Doll House. She writes that:

> Almost everywhere I went the mayor presented me with a small gold key to the city. I have hundreds of them mounted in a shadow box. To me they are wonderful souvenirs – the keys to the doors that opened America for me.[64]

Thus, just as Irishness recedes upon marriage for Moore's characters such as Irene O'Dare in *Irene*, retirement from public to private life is linked with Americanization in the larger narrative of Moore's life. As in *Ella Cinders* miniaturization and display are linked to domestication, forging a sense of assimilation predicated on reduction and privatization.

I do not want to overstate the ways in which gender and modernization discourses seem to merge in the representations of Colleen Moore, to create a kind of feminized, colonized Irish identity. Yet it seems to me that there are a number of troubling undertones to these images that link both femininity and Irishness to a helplessness suitable for and subject to the corrective interventions of more privileged gender and national identities. It should be evident on the basis of this analysis that during virtually her entire career Colleen Moore was constructed in publicity and promotion materials in terms that are essentially thinly-veiled descriptions of a pre-sexual child. The success of Moore's infantalized positioning is made clear by Moore's own later comment that 'my public wouldn't accept me grown up.'[65] In this respect she may have been similar to other actresses of the period (notably Mary Pickford)[66] but she significantly differs from other actresses in being promoted as Irish, and I would suggest that this ethnic identity helped to consolidate her connection to childlike simplicity and functioned, in effect, to set limits on her public tenure. Moore's Irishness required assimilation and neutralization leading to a natural decline of her public-ness in favor of a domestication associated with narrative closure and invisibility. To characterize Moore as a perpetual child was to deny her full development in a way that is akin to the process of colonization. In a sense, this is the flip side of figuring Ireland as a woman in a representational process that denies Irish political and social agency – here women are figured as Irish in what I read as an unconscious capitalization on the notion of Ireland as the passive feminine. The sort of promotional strategy at work in both these cases engaged in and traded on a particularly debilitating cultural meaning of Irishness.

To describe Colleen Moore as Irish was to implicitly relegate her to a state of initial underdevelopment, so that she was then seen to require the enculterating influence of male auteurs such as D.W. Griffith and Marshall Neilan, the guiding influence of her husband John McCormick, and the broader power of early Hollywood machinery to develop her in a star-making process modeled on an idealized conception of American assimilation. Moore's attainment of success and consolidation of cultural power was at every stage contextualized (and neutralized) through a discourse of male management. As we have seen, Moore was subject to a process of hegemonic narrativization whereby she was implicitly cast as the ideal Irish immigrant. Taken together, her energy, her wholesome and virginal sexuality, her disconnection from ambition and apparent willingness to abide by broader cultural powers all rendered Moore ideal immigrant fodder for an ideological machine seeking to establish its relevance to an increasingly heterogeneous audience and to produce fictions that would be meaningful to that audience at home and abroad.

Cinematically and extracinematically figured as a foundling beneficently adopted (by film families, by male mentors, by Hollywood itself), deployed as a controlled symbol of modernization or recuperated through domesticity, every stage in the evolution of Moore's persona provides striking evidence of the successful formation of an ethnic hyphen predicated on the increasingly sanctioned social incorporation of Irishness. By selectively activating associations of Irishness, Hollywood publicity efforts on behalf of Colleen Moore smoothly managed to promote her as an ethnic type in the least threatening way possible, such that her star persona could function as a smooth cog in a representational machine fundamentally oriented toward the consolidation of patriarchal capitalism, in effect permitting Hollywood to demonstrate its own inclusivity to itself and to its audiences. Colleen Moore's Irishness served as a sign of Hollywood's growing power to control the meanings of a broad range of cultural resources – her ethnicity was functional only in the sense that it activated stereotypes which linked Irishness to strictly regulated patterns of transformation and assimilation. Hollywood's management of Colleen Moore as an 'Irish' resource suggests that the circulation of a quasi-colonialist message can relate more to selling strategies than to conscious political ideologies. This, of course, does not insure that such messages are devoid of political or ideological impact.

3

IMMIGRANT STARDOM IN IMPERIAL AMERICA

Pola Negri and the problem of typology

Arriving in America from Berlin in 1922, with a $3,000-per-week Paramount contract, and long famed for her-coal-black hair, camellia-white complexion, and fiery temperament, she was Hollywood's first imported international star. . .

'Pola Negri,' *Who's Who In Hollywood* (1992)

Historically positioned as she was between the passive, pure ideal woman of the late 1800s and the 'New Woman' of the 1920s, the vamp of Hollywood silent film has ties to both stereotypes. In this chapter I briefly consider these relationships and then examine the career of Pola Negri – one of the actresses most associated with vamping – for the evidence it may provide about the images and understandings of transgressive ethnic femininity in early twentieth century American culture.

Negri's American career was not congruent with what might be called the 'golden era' of the vamp, (1915–1919), launched when Theda Bara appeared in *A Fool There Was* (1915). Although Negri was making films at that time (and principally ones in which she starred as an exotic, threatening woman), these films were made in Poland and Germany, and Negri did not come to be known to the American moviegoing public until the early 1920s. I want to critically consider the standard account that Pola Negri simply resuscitated Bara's persona in order to argue both that it was ideologically necessary to attempt to type Negri as vamp, and that her particular incarnation extended and complicated the type. Furthermore, given the failure of Negri's American career, I also want to look into the reasons why the actress was not successfully subsumed into operative Hollywood typologies of femininity and to argue that Negri's unincorporable status was largely a function of her resistant ethnicity. My assumption is that the production of Hollywood film stars (particularly in the case of 'imported' stars such as Negri) has much to do with celebrating the idea of American global power.

In an account of Pola Negri's career, Jeanine Basinger has written that, 'She had a real talent for front-page publicity, and she represented, as well, that inevitable lure for Americans – the European sensibility.'[1] In this chapter I will argue that such a claim needs to be significantly complicated and developed and that the dynamics of Negri's celebrity were seldom as straightforward as this. To better track these issues I investigate the discursive tension between Negri's extra-filmic construction as vamp (particularly in the pages of 1920s fan magazines) and the continual recuperation of that figure in her American film roles. Arguing that at a time when attempts were being made to pitch American individualism as a global manifesto, film stars played an especially important role in fantasies of American cultural and economic dominance, I consider Negri's vamp as a form of ethnic sexuality which impeded rather than facilitated that ideological agenda. Given the classificatory dilemma catalyzed by Negri's arrival in Hollywood, the anxious discourses on the credibility of and motives for her Americanization, and her final categorization as rigidly and intransigently European, the trajectory of Negri's American stardom offers a telling instance of resistant female ethnicity.

Almost all of the accounts of Negri's early life contradict one another, and it was in fact this very idea of a shadowy, mysterious past that formed the cornerstone of her initial publicity in the US. In her autobiography *Memoirs of a Star* Negri says that she was born Apolonia Chalupec in 1899, and raised primarily in Warsaw. She took as her professional name the last name of Ada Negri, an Italian poet she admired, and continued to use the diminutive form of Apolonia as a first name. After her training in the ballet was curtailed by a diagnosis of tuberculosis, Negri spent time in a sanitarium, and when she returned to Warsaw, began acting on the stage. She was widely praised for her performance as an exotic dancer in the play *Sumurun* and shortly thereafter began making films. Negri's American stardom was initiated as a function of the fact that in the silent era foreign films could obtain national distribution in the United States by simply translating their subtitles into English. She became well known in the US playing Carmen, Madame DuBarry, and other roles as a woman exploiting her sexual liaisons with men for economic and political gain. Her German films, particularly those directed by Ernst Lubitsch, won her international fame, and Negri left Berlin for Hollywood in 1922 under contract to Paramount.

Between 1923 and 1928, Negri made twenty-one films, none of which equalled her early successes in Europe. Negri's exotic image, while played up in her publicity, was generally tamped down in her American films. Known for her roles as a femme fatale, she made films in Hollywood which often ended happily. The moral rehabilitation imposed upon her was matched by an aesthetic re-orientation. Remembered for the vividness of her physical presence in earlier films (the actress would apply kohl underneath her eyes, whiten her face and paint her lips dark red), Negri was given the soft-focus, atmospheric treatment in Hollywood.

In addition to these stylistic modifications in her image, Negri was cast in films which tended to de-emphasize the ethnic and class dimensions found in many of her earlier films. Because she represented a problem of type, she was cast early on in vamp parts which were then undercut by the demands of 'goodness morality' in 1920s Hollywood. Nevertheless, throughout her Hollywood career, press accounts of Pola Negri consistently cast her as the vamp – unassimilatable in terms of both her sexuality and her ethnicity. Yet, like other ethnic stars of the period like Nita Naldi or Natasha Rambova, Negri did not embody a single clear and distinctive ethnicity – rather, she stood for a broader pan-ethnic threat. With her Italian surname, Polish ethnicity, and connection to the German film industry, Negri remained ethnically vague in the public imagination. Indeed, in *The Twenties in Vogue*, (a collection of selected writings from the magazine in that period) the actress is recalled as 'the German Pola Negri, with her smouldering eyes and blackened eyelids.'[2] Such confusion did not, however, in any way detract from Negri's association with alterity and exotic excess. When we consider her career in more depth, it becomes evident that Pola Negri is in many ways an ideal example of Hollywood's ambivalent relationship with continental glamor. Known for such practises as walking a tiger on a leash down Hollywood Boulevard, Negri, according to Michael Bruno, 'never quite caught on with the plain folks who were going to the movies at the rate of a hundred million a week.'[3] While other imported female film stars such as Greta Garbo, Marlene Dietrich, and Ingrid Bergman would enjoy successful Hollywood careers by apparently balancing the stakes of exoticism and domesticity, with Negri this 'balancing act' somehow never worked. Instead, she seemed to continually confound journalists, the Hollywood community, and film audiences during her American tenure. Since virtually every account of Negri's career takes note of her strong acting skills, and her remaining films testify to the power of her on-screen presence, it seems that the reasons for her lack of success are more industrial and ideological than aesthetic.

Immigrant stardom in imperial America

Michael H. Hunt has argued that in turn-of-the-century American culture a number of factors combined to produce an inspiring 'vision of national greatness' that remained uppermost in the minds of politicians, business leaders and social reformers alike. As the end of Reconstruction eliminated barriers to national unity, the extension of European imperial interests in the Pacific, East Asia and the Americas began to incite competitive rivalry in the United States. Furthermore, as Hunt observes:

> Industrialization, urbanization, and the arrival of millions of immigrants created internal (or at least elite anxieties) that were ultimately vented in overseas adventures. These trends, as reflected in the troubling fragmentation of the nation into antagonistic blocs of capital and labor and diverse ethnic and regional cultures, may have made the unifying effect of an assertively nationalist foreign policy particularly attractive.[4]

In a similar vein, Andrew Erdman has written of the development of American mass media in the context of early twentieth century political and economic rhetoric, noting that in this period Americans were trading in the traditional frontier of the American west for a 'frontier of world markets' (oftentimes through specularization of the exotic or foreign). Erdman locates vaudeville and early cinema as nodes within a rich matrix of urban attractions which permitted Americans, in essence, to 'find' the rest of the world and their place in it.[5] Historian Emily Rosenberg also sees the early twentieth century as a moment of crucial ideological transition as the terms of American expansion shifted away from the cultivation of the western frontier toward a broader, global frontier to be staked out by American capitalist interests. Like Hunt and Erdman, she identifies this period as one in which the US was actively transforming itself from a regional entity into a nation with distinctly global ambitions, and represents this shift as the result of a confluence of social and economic factors, noting that, 'Thus, the entire rationale for overseas expansion was shaped in a domestic crucible. Economic need, Anglo-Saxon mission, and the progressive impulse joined together nicely to justify a more active role for government in promoting foreign expansion.'[6]

In the specific case of the American film industry, economic and social conditions were highly conducive to a colonization of European markets in the 1920s. As Rosenberg has observed, European film studios had largely collapsed under the economic strain of World War I, and audiences grew dissatisfied with the inferior production values of non-American movies. Furthermore, in her view American films were predisposed to appeal to a wide range of audiences:

> Created not out of the traditions of elite art but designed to entertain a diverse, multi-ethnic patronage at home, early American films were perfectly suited to a world market. The movies' appealing, highly sanitized version of American life was, in effect, an extended commercial for American products.[7]

It is important to bear in mind that an increasing consciousness of American empire was emerging in relation to an irrevocably altered, postwar view of Europe. In the 1920s American leaders such as Herbert Hoover were attempting to promote American individualism as a global manifesto, believing that 'A new international system, built by American hands and money, and based on American principles, now had to be erected on the bloody ruins of the old European order.'[8] If Americans sought the rebuilding of Europe on American terms, this would not entail, however, simple eradication of European economic and political power, for European recovery was economically crucial for US prosperity. The resulting complexity in American/European relations in the 1920s meant that American interests were integrally tied to the management of European recovery, and to some degree, American business and political interests benefited from the position that European nations might serve as imperial partners, as long as US superiority was fundamentally unchallenged. As a result, American cultural, linguistic, ethnic and social ties to Europe were stressed as a means of justifying American involvement in European affairs, and as a route to establishing a critical block in opposition to the demonized Soviet Union.

In this context of shifting global relations, the ideological imperatives behind the consolidation of American mass media are strikingly illuminated. To some degree, the promise of empire had always been implicit in the nineteenth-century notion of Manifest Destiny. At a time when that imperial promise was being supplanted by a commercial rhetoric of American global destiny, American films offered an attractive, profitable mode of entertainment that had the added advantage of enhancing cultural consolidation among the far-flung components of empire. Or, as Ann Douglas puts it:

> America needed the media for the same reason it favored all technological developments. England and France might over the course of their history acquire empires that mandated communication among their parts, but America – with its geographic sprawl, divided and interrupted by mountain ranges and rivers that obstructed the free flow of goods and people from one part of the country into another – started with this mandate; indeed the national identity, as advertised in its name, the *United States* of America, depended on fulfilling it.[9]

Like Erdman and Douglas, I am seeking to investigate what John MacKenzie has called 'popular imperialism' – in other words, the relationship between the materials of mass culture (which could include such things as advertisements, parades and pageants, songs, slogans, and the mass media) and the popularization of imperial ideology. Such forms are indispensable in fulfilling MacKenzie's notion of empire, any definition of which, as he notes, 'must also embrace the control and exploitation of existing Empire and the communication of the justifications for that to the populace of the imperial state.'[10] Robert Rydell has found such justifications to have been on display in the intensely nationalistic American international expositions (or World's Fairs) of the late nineteenth and early twentieth centuries. One function of these fairs having been to make the social world comprehensible, the international exposition functioned (as, it seems likely, the cinema did as well) to propound ideological consensus in a pleasurable form, participating in a process whereby 'the possibility of constructing alternative visions of progress became increasingly hemmed in and attenuated.'[11] If, as Erdman points out, it is important to contextualize early mass media in a similar fashion with respect to their relationship to an emerging imperial frame, it seems that one of the first questions to be asked about early film is: Did cinema (like vaudeville or the World's Fairs) communicate ideological justifications for this imperial shift, and if so, by what representational means did it do so? We may quite interestingly speculate that not only might cinema have permitted Americans to situate themselves within sweeping global expansion, it may also have promoted the fantasy that the entire world was available for the taking. In this way, at the level of culture, film may have assisted in removing obstacles to American imperialism.

Cultures of United States Imperialism, an anthology edited by Amy Kaplan and Donald Pease, takes as its subject 'the multiple histories of continental and overseas expansion, conquest, conflict, and resistance which have shaped the cultures of the United States and the cultures of those it has dominated within and beyond its geopolitical boundaries.'[12] The editors seek to rectify three distinct omissions in the study of American culture: 'the absence of culture from the history of US imperialism; the absence of empire from the study of American culture; and the absence of the United States from the postcolonial study of imperialism.'[13] The anthology offers a useful reformulation of imperialism, pointing out that any definition of empire should attend both to its international features (foreign relations, political, social, and economic oppression, etc.) and to its domestic dimensions as well. As the editors note, it is essential 'to examine imperialism as an internal process of cultural appropriation and as an external struggle over international power.'[14]

It should be clear that the development of a national and international culture of American film stardom has the capacity to engage both levels of this definition. However, my particular focus is on the ways in which stardom has functioned in tandem with the cultivation of empire at home, for ethnic female stars like Pola Negri had the capacity to serve as significant characters in a national narrative supportive of imperialist aims. Imported stars were particularly important in this regard, for if the United States could take a 'raw talent,' package her and turn her into a saleable commodity, then Hollywood was, in effect, enacting American ability to control the international commercial marketplace (not to mention the representational/ideological arena when these films were marketed abroad).[15] Through the packaging and selling of such international stars, US culture industries were establishing something about American global reach and power.

An actress and her location in a film narrative can serve as a register for overt and implicit discourses of imperial consolidation. This is very much the case in Negri's 1927 film *Hotel Imperial*, the fourteenth film of her American career, and one which both the actress and the studio seemed to regard as potentially restorative to her earlier fame. Set in Austria during World War I, the film features Negri in the role of Anna Sedlak, a chambermaid in the Hotel Imperial, who shelters an Austrian Lieutenant during the occupation of Galicia by the Russian Imperial Army. The film's first intertitle makes plain Negri's role as the custodian of a displaced empire, reading 'Thrones and empires might be tottering – but there were still floors to be swept in the Hotel Imperial.' In the role of a servant, Negri is somewhat unusually situated in this film narrative – she is neither the upper-class aristocrat nor the lower-class arriviste of many of her earlier films. *Hotel Imperial* takes on the rather difficult task of camouflaging Anna's class rise within a narrative of imperial restoration. Toward this end, the film attempts to re-channel the energy in Negri's persona that is associated with class rise into the preservation of legitimate empire. Thus, in the film's conclusion, the coupling of Anna (a servant) and the Austrian aristocrat Lieutenant Almasy is subsumed into a spectacle of national consolidation, as the couple are reunited during a ceremony in which Almasy and others are being decorated for their wartime contributions. Here, Negri is a figure of passive piety and patriotism – as Almasy is commended, she kneels and prays. Though she notices him first, she makes no move to approach him, and it is only when he notices her and relays the story of her help to the Austrian General Sultanov that Anna is officially recognized, as Sultanov tells her, 'My dear young lady I am honored to thank you in the name of our country.' The film closes with its most emphatic equation of romance and war as a close up of a kiss between Anna and Almasy fades to images of marching troops.

Hotel Imperial is a useful film text for its ability to shed light on the typological tension that undergirds Negri's image, and its relation to the question which I will suggest underscored the actress' entire American career: how could her persona be made meaningful in an American context? This film suggests one possible (though failed) route for the conversion of Negri from a European exotic to an American type. Since the narrative trajectory of *Hotel Imperial* is shaped to reflect the discrediting of a complacent, aristocratic empire and re-assertion of a legitimate empire in its place, the film capitalizes on the aristocratic discourse of Negri's persona[16] and her unique status as a shifting symbol of imperial ambition. In indirect fashion, the film plays out an idealized conception of Negri's Americanization, as she is first an obscure European girl, converted to the status of an aristocrat. (The Russian General Judschkiewitsch dresses Anna in lavish costumes and tells her, 'It is not I who command here – it is you!' When she rejects him, and is restored to her servant status, another worker taunts her, 'So you are not the Queen around here any more.') By the film's conclusion Negri as Anna has renounced one empire for another, rejected an elevation to privileged, aristocratic status, and accepted a more subdued and passive role in a coupling relationship charged with connotations of national solidarity and empire.

Having begun with an instance of Negri's production in conformity with American imperialist ideology near the end of her career, I now want to proceed achronologically to consider how the formation of her role as an ethnic vamp more frequently troubled such representational endeavors.

Vampire sexuality and cultural predation

In a broad sense, the vamp is a particularly potent marker of the transition from women's sexuality as in need of regulation for its own sake to a deep cultural investment in that process of control and regulation to bolster patriarchal norms. Differently deployed at different moments, the vamp's vitiated sexuality consistently stands as an indictment of combination across class and ethnic lines. This use of the figure of the vamp as the locus for a number of different discursivities is consistent with the cinematic vamp as incarnated by actresses such as Theda Bara, Nita Naldi, Lya de Putti, and Pola Negri in the 1910s and 1920s. Promoted and publicized as *culturally and sexually* predatory, all of these actresses either emanated from Southern and Eastern European countries or were given fictional biographies to suggest that they had. For instance, Theodosia Goodman from Cincinnati was transformed by Fox studio publicity into the mysterious Theda Bara, daughter of an Arabian princess and an Italian sculptor, raised 'in the shadow of the Sphinx.' At a moment of apparent prosperity but underlying fear about the efficacy of American economic policies and ability to maintain cultural isolation, the vamp was a charged figure indeed. She personified a whole category of newly arrived immigrants who (in the eyes of some Americans) called up these economic and social anxieties. Ann Douglas writes:

> Immigrants were now coming mainly from eastern and southern Europe rather than, as had long been the case, from northern Europe. The Germans, Scandinavians, and Irish of the older immigrant groups were being replaced by countless Poles, Italians and Jews; 2.5 million Jews arrived from Russia and eastern Europe between 1880 and 1930, and most of them settled in New York. Some of the newer immigrants were visibly different from America's older white population, and they were no longer dispersing themselves across the nation but collecting ominously in vast city enclaves fast becoming 'ghettos.'[17]

If new immigrants symbolized the threat of national erasure, and the possibility that American cultural consensus might be irretrievably lost, female immigrants were particularly subject to attempts at ideological management. The hypersexual cinematic vamp of the 1910s and 1920s was in essence, a thinly disguised incarnation of the threat of female immigrant sexuality. This figure was multiply deployed to quell both fear of uncontrollable female desire and the spread of immigrant values into the dominant culture. Just as the sexually insatiable woman might somehow enervate seminal substance, the ambitious immigrant might drain the country's resources dry.

Positioned as the improperly (or more threatening yet, unsuccessfully) socialized woman, the vamp reflected an intense cultural need to regulate woman's sexuality. She was an ideal figure to manage such cultural anxiety for she represented a site of intersection for the two most important reproductive resources at a time of national expansion – birth and immigration. Thus, Hollywood representations built on Victorian formulations of the death-dealing woman for a specific purpose – to lend support to the definition of appropriate femininity as life giving. In the case of Pola Negri, whose publicity represented her as having come out of a culture marked by death, Americanization was supposed to invigorate and revitalize her. In a *Photoplay* article previewing a series of features outlining Negri's autobiography in installments, the actress recalls her childhood in suggestively apocalyptic terms:

'Poverty and suffering in my childhood and tragedy always,' she writes in the opening chapter. 'Before I knew happiness I saw death. Death, imprisonment, the Black Plague and Cossacks killing, killing. Torture and oppression, war and revolution, starving children and frantic mothers and friends shot down by my side . . . The Four Horsemen always riding over my country.' On the screen she achieved renown as the pagan, soulless Carmen. Since coming to this country she has been termed ruthless and temperamental.[18]

Such accounts reinforced emergent American anxieties about the new character of immigration. For the first time, it seemed possible that European emigres might have the most powerful incentive to achieve (always considered an American characteristic). In the eyes of some Americans, it seemed that immigrant women, given the freedoms afforded by their entrance into a new culture, might indeed prove to be ungovernable, even ambitious. Such fears well complemented other contemporary anxieties about the 'foreign' character of ethnic female sexuality.

In their history of sexuality in America, John D'Emilio and Estelle Freedman have documented the numerous economic and social factors that militated against the easy continuity of the nineteenth century Cult of True Womanhood into the twentieth century. Not only were the fissures in the smoothly repressive sexual decorum of the 1800s very much in evidence by the turn-of-the-century, but by the 1920s, 'erotic life was assuming a new, distinctive importance in the consciousness of some Americans.'[19] D'Emilio and Freedman write that:

> By the early twentieth century, the sexual values of the middle class were on the edge of a decisive transformation. Old and new coexisted in an uneasy balance. That tension would make the first two decades of the century a time of conflict, as defenders of the past and proponents of change contended for hegemony in sexual matters.[20]

These authors are not alone in characterizing the early twentieth century as strongly marked by shifting social and sexual norms, and they are typical in excluding the representational history of the period from their analysis. Yet popular culture tropes played a key part in shaping and sustaining cultural debates about gender roles. Just as cinema 'provides an ideal vantage point from which to observe the making of the new woman,'[21] it also betrays a level of anxiety about her incipience. Close study of Pola Negri's career exposes the distinct limits faced by some ethnic women in terms of their access to the freedoms of 'New Womanhood.'

Of course, the extent of such freedoms has been appropriately called into question. Lisa Rudman, for example, has observed that 'Rather than a radical break from Victorian perceptions of womanhood, "modern womanhood" can be seen as a response to urbanizing and industrializing society and an adaptation of Victorian ideology so that it could exist in a new context.'[22] Thus, it would seem that the vamp represented a kind of 'outburst of sexual anxiety which still appealed to a sexual, moral and ideological absoluteness while responding to confusion over a newer expansion of and inquiry into sexual roles.'[23]

If the female vampire is, on the one hand, a figure with the capacity to disturb gendered relations of power, she is also a figure well-equipped to articulate certain social tensions in early twentieth century American life, for she is pre-narrativized in ways that resonate strongly with the condition of the female 'New Immigrant.' *Dracula* and other vampire myths represent the vampire first and foremost as a liminal figure, caught between an old world and a new one, at first a welcomed visitor but ultimately a new arrival who comes to be seen as a menace. Vampires are superficially incorporable, yet after a period of time their profound alterity and destructive influence necessitate their extermination. The vampire's destructive power, moreover, is a function of his connection to a malignant homeland; though he may travel the world, he is fundamentally linked to his recondite origins, a connection which he regenerates and fosters by sleeping in a coffin filled with his native soil. Most threateningly, rather than adjusting to their new cultural context, vampires are always engaged in a seditious campaign to convert others to become like them. As we have seen, these were exactly the qualities some Americans feared new immigrants to be in possession of; to nativists, these new arrivals had the capacity to insidiously infect the American body.

The vampire is almost always represented as in possession of a strange energy that seems to speak both to a sexual and cultural threat. Furthermore, the vampire's appearance seems to be interestingly correlated to the consolidation of power. As Nina Auerbach notes, 'Vampires go where power is: when, in the nineteenth century, England dominated the West, British vampires ruled the popular imagination, but with the birth of film, they migrated to America in time for the American century.'[24] If we can trace the proliferation of vampire representations to moments of national consolidation, one could plausibly argue that the vampire's status as a symbol of deadly energy and a threatening return of the past makes this figure a unique symbol of empire, taking shape as an expression of the fear of an insider with a different, destructive agenda who cannot be subsumed into national interests. The vamp is clearly the outsider who is able to get inside the (national) body. In this context, the multivalent implications of the vampire's de-energizing influence become evident. It is clear that the female vampire functions simultaneously as a sexual, economic and ethnic contaminant.

The cultivation of Negri as type

By all accounts, hopes were very high for Pola Negri's potential cultivation as an American film star at the time of her arrival in the United States. However, the negotiations for her arrival tend to be represented as unproblematized, when, in fact, they were conducted with a great deal of delicacy and sensitivity to the possible negative repercussions of importing a European star for the nascent American film industry. Examination of Paramount files reveals that both Adolph Zukor and Ben Blumenthal (Paramount's agent in Berlin) saw a need to gingerly handle Negri's contractual arrangements. While highly enthusiastic about the artistic merits of Negri and Ernst Lubitsch (whom it is clear the studio perceived as a set),[25] Paramount cautiously proceeded to arrange for the arrival of these foreign stars, remaining attentive to a possible nativist backlash. A Western Union cable from Zukor to Ralph Kohn at Paramount, Berlin on July 18, 1922, advised strongly against bringing Negri and Lubitsch to America at the same time:

> Would be very bad from all angles bring over more than one at a time. Should leave reasonable period between to avoid propagandist criticism and be sure make no promises.[26]

Thus, fears that even a small number of stars brought over from Germany in the period immediately following World War I might be perceived as an exodus provoking jingoist criticism were a crucial structuring element of the promotional efforts undertaken by Paramount on Negri's behalf. Upon Negri's arrival, her own enthusiasm and appreciation of her American sponsors is evident in a letter from Negri to Zukor dated October 10, 1922, reading in part:

> California agrees with me wonderfully and since arriving in this beautiful country I have felt splendidly. After getting settled at last in my new home in a new land, I anticipate I will start in my new picture next Tuesday.[27]

Despite such positive exchanges and the apparent goodwill between Negri and the studio, an immediate typological problem was becoming evident as Paramount and the American moviegoing public grappled with the question: Who is Pola Negri?[28]

When Negri emerged as a star-in-the-making in the early 1920s, she represented a problem of type for those who wrote about Hollywood culture and Hollywood stars. Fan magazine articles of the period tend to reflect this classificatory dilemma, frequently addressing (directly or obliquely) the problem of her unknowability.

In one fan magazine, Negri's imminent arrival was described in these terms:

> Pola Negri has the paradoxical distinction of being one of the most famous and yet at the same time one of the least known of motion picture stars. Announcement made recently that she is coming to this country in September under contract to star in a big Paramount picture has aroused curiosity as to details of her life and career. About all

that is known about her over here, except that she is an actress of remarkable ability and during the last two or three years has given some of the vivid characterizations of the screen is that she is Polish and now makes her home in Berlin.[29]

In another Joan Jordan wrote:

> Ever since Pola Negri turned her eyes upon us beneath the famous powdered wig of Madame DuBarry, we have been hearing about her. First, in the dim recesses of Continental Europe, impressionistic glimpses of the alluring, the foreign, the thrillingly different and wonderful Pola Negri.
>
> Then – she was coming to Hollywood to make pictures. She sailed. New York greeted her briefly – a smiling, mysterious, monosyllabic Pola. Chicago drew hardly a breath of exotic perfume as she swept her skirts through. Pasadena saw her pick a real orange from an orange tree. The American public read this and that – intriguing flashes that merely whet the appetite.[30]

Herbert Howe described the difficulty of even seeing Negri for a scheduled interview and devoted half of an article entitled 'The Real Pola Negri' to a chronicle of his attempts to actually see and speak with the star. Similarly, Rose Shlusinger framed an article on Negri as a kind of detective narrative, with the actress endlessly one step ahead of the journalist as she attempts to locate her for an interview appointment through Paris, Berlin and Dresden.[31]

Invariably, however, Negri did become well-known to the American public, apprehensible now as a vamp – the social type that most closely fits the filmic and extra-filmic information known about her. Typical of the kinds of characterizations that were made of her in the fan magazines during this period is this description: 'La Negri – A tiger woman with a strange slow smile and a world-old lure in her heavy-lidded eyes. Mysterious, fascinating, an enigma.'[32] Throughout her Hollywood career in the 1920s writers would frequently employ deliberate misspellings and grammatical errors to convey a sense of Negri's imperfect and heavily-accented English. Quotations such as 'I suffer much. It is terribl' and 'Miss Negri do not feel like today to work' abound in the fan magazine articles that attribute remarks to the actress.

In a fan magazine piece which claimed to be 'the first authoritative personality sketch of Pola Negri, the Polish Star,'[33] the reasons for the actress's rise to fame were straightforwardly given:

> First of all she was new; secondly she appeared in a 'vamp' part – a type of part which having been rendered ridiculous by Theda Bara and subsequently abandoned, stood in real need of resuscitation; and, most important of all, she was not camera-wise.[34]

In this article, as in others, Pola Negri is discussed in terms that obliquely suggest her status as 'new blood' (so to speak), or as a new resource to be exploited within the Hollywood system. As one writer speculated at the time of her arrival in Hollywood:

> I wonder if other directors will understand Pola as Lubitsch does or whether they will expect fire to always be cool and a tiger cat as tame as one of the curly ingenue lambs. Will Pola escape the standardization process? Or will she have to submit to being a perfect lady, always kind to directors and always diplomatic with pestiferous interviewers who ask her all sorts of absurd questions like whether or not she is to marry Chaplin?[35]

It is tempting to read these kinds of questions about how this new resource (Negri) would fit into the social system (Hollywood) as pointing toward a broader cultural level in such a way that we might interchange the terms Immigrant for Negri and America for Hollywood. Certainly the discourses of the fan magazines would support such a reading. For example, one early magazine piece on Negri before her arrival in the US concluded:

> So Pola steps from the Old World into the New. From the old life into the new. Let us hope that her dream of America will be realized as adequately as America's dream of her. As for me, I say, see Pola and die![36]

Negri herself was attributed with comments that reflected a variant of 'the streets are paved with gold' conception of the American Dream:

> Always America has been my dream from the time I was a child in Poland. You do not know how Polish children look toward America. It is like heaven to which people go for eternal happiness. Always people return rich or send money back.[37]

But far from being able to definitively prove this kind of connection, (and I am not sure that I would want to), I do want to suggest that Negri's interrelationship with immigrant identity played a substantial part in generating the huge amount of popular interest that preceded and accompanied her arrival in the US. I also want to raise the possibility that Pola Negri's huge publicity buildup served in some sense as an analogue to the idea of the welcome mat offered to the new immigrant, and that this limited her possibilities in Hollywood by requiring her 'Americanization.' Negri's intense professions of her own immigrant desires suggest the beginnings of an anxious discourse on the rationale for and success of her Americanization. Negri's later resistance to being Americanized – to being typed – perhaps constituted a brand of ideological transgressiveness that resonated beyond the parameters of actress/studio.

In any event, it is important to emphasize that Negri's American career (by this I mean the films she made for Paramount in the 1920s)[38] followed the period of the popularization of the vamp. Because she was seen as reviving this type, Negri's vamp is thus to be distinguished from prior incarnations, and in ways that will prove to be extremely important. Negri's positioning as vamp is perhaps most apparent in the publicity photos circulated of her by Paramount. In these photos, the black/white 'mask' of the characters of her German films tends to be very much in evidence. Her full-figure poses are regal and remote, or suggestively threatening. Her gaze is sometimes unsmilingly direct – more often she is shown glancing sidelong at the camera. Often she leans back in a way that facilitates the vamp's trademark heavy-lidded look. In all of her photos a certain knowing quality emerges that, to some degree, overshadows other representational elements. In the accompanying illustrations (two representative publicity photos produced by Paramount in the mid-1920s) Negri's hands are the most forceful representational component (apart perhaps from the actress' striking face and eyes). Typical of her publicity poses in most respects, these two images, I contend, subtextually engage the question of agency which was so problematic in Negri's re-making as an American film star. In the first image, she hides her hands below her elbows, giving her an almost straight-jacketed look, while in the second her hands are prominently displayed as a frame for her face, testifying, in effect, to a lack of guile. Thus, through different means, both photos render in visual terms a complex (and hardly complete) disavowal of Negri's agency.

As has been discussed, the vamp was a multivalent image, embodying not only unsupressed female desire, but (especially in the case of Pola Negri) the potential ascendency of a new immigrant class from southern and eastern Europe. It will be suggested that Negri was particularly well situated to activate this latter set of meanings. Helen Plunkett has called the Vamp a 'cipher' and perhaps she was especially so as activated by Negri.[39] As the figure who troubled the rigid regulation of sexuality, Negri was positioned as aberrantly destructive. Fan magazine articles about her in the 1920s constantly allude to her in this fashion: 'Beneath the silken charm of Pola Negri there is the tigress-claw, with threat of instinctive cruelty,'[40] writes one author in an article entitled 'The Loves of Pola Negri.' In a *Photoplay* piece in which well-known actresses were asked to provide their definition of love, Negri is attributed with the comment, 'Love is ruthless. In pursuit of its desires it will destroy that it may achieve. That it may lavish upon one of its largesse, it will crush a thousand who stand in its way.'[41]

As the figure who troubled the hegemony of white northern and western European ethnicity, Negri was certainly more potent than vamps such as Theda Bara and Gloria Swanson. Rather than being fabricated as ethnic 'Other' in the fashion of Theda Bara, whose name was known to be an anagram for 'Arab Death,' Negri's construction in such terms had a far greater claim to 'authenticity.' As an actual ethnic import with a foreign accent and a well-publicized

Figure 5a Publicity portraiture for Negri attached key importance to the placement of her hands as a sign of her agency

European past, Negri was well positioned to restore a seriousness to vamp characterizations that had become increasingly lampooned by stars such as Bara herself. This 'authentic' dimension of her persona, however, became increasingly problematic throughout the duration of her American career, as I will later discuss. In its most benign form, the suggestion that Negri was intransigently

Figure 5b

Old World was even underscored in a 1926 article about her home, 'A Bit of Europe in Hollywood,' a piece which details the house's formal style, and 'Old World charm,' and is peppered with observations such as 'it is more of a Continental salon than an American living room.'[42] At the time of her arrival in the US (under contract to Paramount) in the fall of 1922, Negri would have been best known to American audiences for her roles in the films *Gypsy Blood* and *Passion*.[43] In the former film (a re-telling of the *Carmen* story originally written as a novel by Prosper Merimee),[44] Negri plays La Carmencita, a gypsy girl who enthralls soldier Jose Navarro. This version of *Carmen* is one which continually plays up the gypsy's role as sexual threat. When the pair first meet it is as Jose Navarro sits reading a letter from his sweetheart Dolores. He is accosted by La Carmencita, who mockingly tosses him a rose. The two meet again when the gypsy girl is jailed for fighting with a co-worker who has snatched away an admirer's note. When she escapes, Navarro is then himself jailed for losing her. La Carmencita attempts to help him flee by smuggling in a file hidden in a loaf of bread, but Navarro resists this temptation, inspired by a vision of his virtuous sweetheart. Eventually, though, stripped of his rank and commission, he joins the gypsies. Tormented by the conflict between his passion for La Carmencita and his sense of degradation, he tries to leave her, but cannot. The gypsy becomes disgusted by his weakness, and begins an affair with another soldier. Later she meets and falls in love with Escamillo, a matador. The film culminates in a confrontation between Jose Navarro and La Carmencita in an alley where he murders her, then commits suicide.

In many ways typical of the vamp narratives that seemed to best showcase Negri's talents, *Gypsy Blood* is also noteworthy for its subtext of destructive regional collaboration. When La Carmencita first meets Jose Navarro, she comments on their shared background, 'By your speech, you are from the provinces, like myself.' When he visits her in jail she addresses him repeatedly as 'my countryman' and 'comrade of my heart.' When he is imprisoned, and she attempts to free him, the loaf of bread she carries takes on the status of a symbol of shared regional attributes. La Carmencita tells the guard she has brought a loaf of Alcala bread, and a remarkable footnote reports that Alcala is 'a hamlet close to Seville, famous for its excellent bread.' In the context of the film then, close connections based on regional affiliation tend to produce treachery.

Thus, those roles that made Pola Negri a star in the United States even before she had ever set foot on American soil, tended to emphasize her guile and her primitivism, and to strongly link these attributes and her broad destructive influence to a vaguely 'ethnic' and regional identity. In this respect, her pre-1922 persona represented a balance between the cosmopolitan and the regional, two terms employed by Timothy Brennan in his book on myths of nationalism. In *Salman Rushdie and the Third World* Brennan argues that within post-colonial subjectivity the cosmopolitan is designed to replace the regional. In an earlier and quite different cultural context, Negri cultivated an extra-diegetic association with the cosmopolitan, becoming a symbol of European glamour and sophistication, while enacting film roles that thematized the malignance of regionalism.[45] In an earlier section I have indicated the relevance of imported stars to Hollywood as both a business and a producer of cultural representations and discourses. I am further suggesting that as the US film industry (particularly Paramount) colonized Europe in the 1920s, emblematic

Europeans such as Pola Negri were expected to be cosmopolitan and not regional. This was partly because the US was actively engaged in repressing regional difference in favor of national solidarity – to Americanize a star who connoted the fractious regionalism of Europe as opposed to the coordinated national harmony of the US would be impossible.

However, the tension between cosmopolitanism and regionialism in Negri's persona was only one of a number of functional paradoxes she embodied. Such paradoxical constructions tend to apply at a number of levels in Negri's persona. On some occasions, they were celebrated as part of the actress's allure. Writing in her syndicated column in 1923, Gladys Hall observed:

> You know, so long as a woman remains a paradox, she is perfect. After all, she hasn't been proven imperfect. She hasn't been proven anything at all, and as gallantry still persists in a world and age that would defy it, and as it particularly persists concerning a charming woman, the woman who is the paradox is safe. Pola Negri seems to be that paradox.[46]

Framing Negri as a paradox also served as a means of acknowledging and disavowing her erotic attraction. If a commentator like Hall tended to read Negri's enigmatic persona as a positive attribute, others associated her appeal with sordidness, creating an image of Negri where her superficial cosmopolitan attractiveness was undercut by an omnipresent regional sordidness. In some accounts, interestingly enough, it is suggested, that Negri had not been fully 'cleaned up' and that her cosmopolitan glamor always had a slight tinge of 'regional dirt.' Richard Griffith, for instance, writes, 'She was, someone said at that time "sexually irresistible" – and you had the feeling that the back of her neck was dirty.'[47]

The vamp as canny laborer and uncertain commodity: Pola Negri in the context of industrial production

In this section, I will show how the vamp's transgressive ownership of her own labor was especially problematic at a time when Imperial America wanted to codify the range of female types and channel female ethnic labor for its own use. As Pola Negri was incorporated into an American social frame of reference, discourses of work became more prevalent in her persona. This is, on the one hand, not surprising, for as Richard Dyer has noted, stardom and labor are integrally tied to one another. Not only are 'stars examples of the way that people live their relation to production in capitalist society,'[48] stars are also inevitably 'involved in making themselves into commodities; they are both labour and the thing that labour produces.'[49] It is certainly true that the work that goes into image making and image maintenance has been the subject of ambivalent discourse throughout Hollywood history. Yet Negri's gender and ethnicity contributed to a further contradiction in that her links to immigrant ethnicities entailed a positive value be attached to her working status, while her gender mandated that her work be invisible. The strong preoccupation with the performance of Negri's work seems to indirectly reflect the question that underscored her celebrity: How could Negri be *made* to work for American interests?

These concerns, I suggest, were really only a logical extension of anxieties about the depth and legitimacy of her Americanization. Her border-crossing persona implicitly raised issues in regard to the international exchange of labor that some of her film roles quite interestingly enact. On the other hand, playing a courtesan, prostitute or 'kept woman,' Negri also shaped a response to discomfort with women working outside the home and with a sexual activity that escapes the controlling power of the home and family. The ethnic woman's relationship to public space was particularly fraught and it seems that the connection between ethnic femininity and the 'working woman' presupposed that the kind of labor she performed was inevitably sexual.

In this section, I want to contextualize a reading of the Negri film *Passion* (1919) by considering two proximate phenomena: the rapid growth in the number of women entering the workforce, and the proliferation of vamp roles in the silent films of the 1910s and 1920s. Here I will argue for the vamp's significance as a complex image mobilized in part as a response to younger women's advent into the workforce in large numbers for the first time. As an incarnation of the predatory woman stereotype, the vamp has had successors as well as predecessors, and popular culture discourses generated around the predatory female persona continue to be numerous. Nevertheless, the meanings and pleasures of the transgressive woman clearly vary in accordance with social, historical and industrial variables. One crucial variable which has tended to remain unexamined by historians and critics is the vamp's relation to the shifting landscape of the American workforce.

Perhaps the most striking labor trend in the period under consideration here is the entrenchment of the woman worker, whose numbers increase in the late decades of the nineteenth century and continue to rise throughout the early decades of the twentieth century. In this period, the transition of women (especially young, urban women) from family worker to wage worker was increasingly normalized. For this reason, labor historian Leslie Tentler locates the period 1900 to 1930 as formative in establishing the labor climate for women well into the century. She argues that these years 'can be seen as a first and critical chapter in the history of modern female industrial employment. In this period important precedents regarding women's work were established or confirmed.'[50]

The vamp is not merely a figure who demonizes working women; rather, in an evolving consumption economy, she is too aware of her own commodity status. In personifying a mingled sexual/economic threat (we may think of the implication of the female vampire's bloodsucking as both kissing or some other kind of erotic embrace and an assertion of economic 'bloodlust'), the vamp is consistently linked to the ramifications of women's work. As will be demonstrated, Negri's vamp announces herself as manufactured in a way that foregrounds her own laboring efforts and her appearance/sexuality is shown to be a hazardous commodity in a way that codes women's labor itself as duplicitous.

In *Passion* Negri plays Jeanne, a milliner's apprentice at the outset of the film, who rises to power as Madame DuBarry, mistress of Louis XV. Although Jeanne is overtly represented as a working woman for only a brief section of the narrative, her disconnection from home and hearth and ascension to a position of power marks her with the same anxieties attached to contemporary working women. The problem at the heart of the film is the problem of the woman who works to further her own interests outside of appropriate domestic channels.

Made for UFA and directed by Ernst Lubitsch, *Passion* was, though not American-made, an enormous American success in both commercial and critical terms. The film was originally produced as *Madame DuBarry* but was re-titled for its American release in part to disguise the circumstances of its production in Germany. When First National premiered the film in 1920, it played five times a day at the sumptuous Capitol Theatre in New York, and attendance during the first week was estimated to be about 106,000. Trade journals reported gross box office receipts of $10,000 per day, and excitement over the film ran so high that on December 19, 1920, a reported 40,000 people tried to gain admittance to the theatre and extra policemen were dispatched to 'maintain order and clear traffic.'[51] As a result of the enthusiasm generated around *Passion* (and to a lesser extent other collaborations between Negri and Ernst Lubitsch, such as *Gypsy Blood*) Negri was heavily recruited by the major American studios before ultimately signing with Famous Players-Lasky (Paramount).[52] Part of the film's success, in my view, has to do with the way in which it presents the sexually transgressive woman and the working woman as very close categories.

Briefly, the plot of *Passion* has to do with Jeanne's expanding sphere of influence in the French court, as she is first the companion of the proletarian Armand, then Spaniard Don Diego, Count DuBarry, and the French king. In the course of the film, Don Diego is killed by Armand in a duel, Louis XV dies of smallpox, and Armand is shot by his friend Paillet, after attempting to defend Jeanne. As the king's consort, Jeanne shows herself to be capricious and self-indulgent, and she begins to encroach on the territory of Choiseul, the King's Minister of State, who then launches a popular campaign against her. At the conclusion, she is guillotined at the hands of a bloodthirsty mob, although in its American release, the film ends just before Jeanne is beheaded.

Historian Robert Smuts has written of the geographical circumstances that conditioned women's labor at the turn-of-the-century, noting the far greater likelihood of non-domestic work for urban women.[53] Part of the vamp's connection to women's work is established through her links to city life. Jeanne Vaubernier (later DuBarry) is described in *Passion* as 'freshly strayed from country lanes.' From the beginning of the film, two of Jeanne's other traits are very much in evidence. She is shown to be highly aware of the value of commodities and she understands how to transform work into pleasure. In fact, the film continually conflates work and sexuality for Jeanne. Sent out on an errand, she subordinates her work to her pleasure by stopping to visit her lover Armand on 'work time.' On her return, the hat she carries is accidentally crushed by the Spanish envoy Don Diego's horse, and she weeps because she knows its value and anticipates her employer's anger. The encounter, however, has provoked Don Diego's interest, and he follows her to the milliner's shop and promises her that 'Mademoiselle could be better employed.' To conceal a liaison with Don Diego, Jeanne later tells Armand she has to work, inventing the excuse that she is visiting the residence of the Spanish envoy in order to pin his wife's gown, and he is so completely deceived that he walks her to the door.

Once under Don Diego's 'protection,' Jeanne finds herself still constrained by the demands of work, for Don Diego now expects her to work for him. She is barely installed as his mistress when he rouses her out of bed yelling 'Wake up you lazy baggage and earn your keep!' He forces her to the dressing table to work on her appearance, telling her that she must go on his behalf to attempt to collect a debt from the King of France. At the palace, the King is predictably smitten by Jeanne, and sends his Minister, Choiseul, to find out where she lives. When Choiseul discovers her at Don Diego's house, an exchange is quickly made although not before the Spaniard acknowledges Jeanne's commodity value, protesting, 'My broken heart – I must be paid!'

From here Jeanne ascends to the pre-eminent position of power in France, but through it all she undergoes a kind of development process not unlike the routines of industrial production. In fact, the entire film consists of a kind of assembly line process of commodity production with Jeanne as the developing commodity and each of her lovers in turn playing a part in refining/honing her worth. The warning that is offered by the film centers on the fact that feminine duplicity ensures that Jeanne will become an excessive commodity that threatens to disturb the control of the production process. And indeed, she does this, ultimately achieving control over the agents of production who do not perceive her own self-commodification. By the time she is the consort of the King of France, Jeanne's control is such that Louis buffs her nails for her while matters of state are left waiting, behavior that the film strongly condemns.

According to the film, non-domestic female labor is seen as inevitably self-serving and the vamp's self-absorption is heavily contrasted with the unity of the family. *Passion* provides a ruptured family victimized by the actions of the predatory woman, although the significance of this family is not made clear until the revolution led by Armand near the end of the film. At this point, we are re-introduced to a minor character from the early part of the film, Armand's friend and an early acquaintance of Jeanne's, Paillet the tailor. When Jeanne has Paillet thrown in prison, the film emphasizes his family's deprivation, articulated through the neediness of a child – Paillet's small daughter – who inspires Armand's revolutionary spirit with the words 'Monsieur Armand, I am so hungry.' Thus, the vamp's characteristic tendency to put her own interests before the interests of the family jeopardizes the role of the male breadwinner, and if this were not already clear enough, we cut quickly to Armand crying out 'Friends, we must save Paillet!' and leading the masses with Paillet's daughter on his shoulders. Thus, in this creative reworking of historical fact, the French Revolution is fought solely on behalf of the dispossessed male breadwinner. In this account, even Louis XVI and Marie Antoinette are represented as innocent victims of the consequences wrought by the vamp's evil – an intertitle proclaims them 'waiting helplessly' as the revolutionaries descend.

It is important to consider in some depth the complex codes of the vamp body, since *Passion* represents women's labor as wholly readable on and through the body. The film ties the woman whose production is solely in her own interest to bodily display, and presents the vamp's making up, combing her hair, or inspecting her appearance in a mirror as actions that constitute labor in the service of the feminine form as commodity. The film emphasizes a number of instances when the vamp pauses to enhance her appearance and these are coded as labor activity, moments of self-manufacture. Just as in the quintessential vamp film *A Fool There Was*, Theda Bara's Vampire looks out from a porthole, watches the Schuyler family saying goodbye, and takes out her compact to check her appearance, so Jeanne Vaubernier announces her designs by performing 'work' on her appearance. Our first glimpse of her is at work, and when her employer sends her out on an errand, she stops to powder her nose in a mirror and is looked at reprovingly. In this respect, female labor is criminalized, and it is implied that non-domestic women's work is both surface-oriented and deceptive. Women's labor outside the home is also always and inevitably sexual in *Passion*. Jeanne's work as a milliner serves only as a pretext for her efforts to snare a male protector. Thus, the film codes female labor as both sexual and duplicitous, serving as a front for the only feminine concerns that the film takes to be legitimate – the search for male sponsorship. Of course, the vamp's connection to makeup is not insignificant, as it ties her to discourses of transformation and implied class rise. In the early decades of the century, makeup was integrally tied to a cultural sense that the boundaries of class were collapsing and the vamp iconography of pale skin and heavily made-up lips and eyes might well have connoted transformative desire to audiences of the time.[54] Beyond the vamp's dark hair and eyes which work to imply the threat of transgressive ethnicity connecting her to devalued, 'suspicious' ethnic groups, it is important to observe further that the vamp is inevitably a woman whose origins are unknown or obscure. Jeanne Vaubernier is not shown to have any family connections, and in a film which charts the dangers of a woman's rise from the working class to the nobility, it is clear that the vamp's ability to win the male provider away from his more appropriate partner is very much a threat to destabilize the boundaries of class and the hierarchy of valued ethnicities.

The vamp's tendency to posture and her inclination to wear distinctive, vivid makeup combine to render her an excessively produced body. In some sense, she threatens to be out of bounds at any moment, and her body seems always to be in danger of showing. Her laboring efforts help her to carry off a kind of masquerade – a false femininity, whose veneer is continually slipping. The vamp's meaning is also strongly articulated by means of costume. Heavily sexualized, her clothing tends to be dark in color or to feature aggressive prints and stripes which serve to mark her sartorial threat. The vamp draws attention to her labors through her costume, and so represents a sharp break with the patriarchal requirement that women's labor be invisible. Since we are culturally committed to effacing the female laboring body, part of the threat of the vamp is that she presents herself as the evolving site of her own laboring efforts. This potentially empowers the female body and authorizes it as a site of identity formation. This is strikingly apparent in a scene in *Passion* in which Jeanne, the milliner's apprentice, decides her fate by reading the codes of her own bodily display. As she counts off the bows on her bodice to decide between Armand and Don Diego, Jeanne interprets her own work efforts, subordinating her emotional decision-making to her own working body, and defining her identity according to her own achievement rather than to an externally defined patriarchal standard. In short, she threatens to produce herself. Moments such as this one strongly suggest that one of the vamp's most distinctive threats centers on self-production.

The vamp's problematization of women's work was coincident with the rise of female labor outside the home. As both producer and product, the vamp threatens to close the gap between labor and its results. She responds to cultural anxiety that if women take part in industrial production, they may learn to produce themselves in opposition to patriarchy. By presenting herself as a commodity in process, whose appearance is deceptive and whose use value in patriarchy is highly questionable, the vamp is crucially involved in the gendering of industrialized mass culture, for she demonstrates the dangers of both contemporary commodification and women's participation in the production of useful commodities. She also serves to perpetuate a superannuated discourse of women's invisibility and concealment, for the vamp's crime is that she is too much seen, she makes her labor visible. Thus, in addition to her status as a figure of ethnic threat, the vamp is also of interest for the way in which she uniquely articulates a set of concerns about women's access to work and to its rewards.

Negri consistently plays the role of a woman who exploits her sexual liaisons with men for economic and political gain. She inspires death and destruction not by design, but seemingly inevitably. Onto the vamp cipher were merged two discourses – one having to do with sexuality and the other with ethnicity – both delineating the dimensions of the 'problem' of woman in the 1920s. In a broad sense, Pola Negri's persona, as constituted in extra-filmic terms, connoted unenculturated femininity. As the unassimilatable woman, both in ethnic and sexual terms, she stood for a type that was in fact far more transgressive than the thoroughly American, upper-middle class flapper of the period who for all her supposed flouting of social conventions, was nearly always safely married off in the end.

Negri's unsuccessful typological conversion

In Pola Negri's case, as I have argued, the American film narratives in which she appeared were not always co-extensive with the persona being constructed. Rather, for the most part, they exist in contradictory relation to one another. Michael Bruno contends that:

> Hollywood did not know what to do with her, after the first flurry of excitment had abated. She was pulling in the carriage trade, but was establishing no real audience rapport, nor was she building a consistent cinematic image.[55]

While Negri's film roles failed to coalesce into a single recognizable persona, they also ran counter to the fundamental direction of her publicity. In fact, while Negri was being constructed through fan magazine articles and publicity photos as vamp, that persona was being undercut by a series of film roles which contained vamp energy. The resulting typological tension created a kind of ongoing recuperation of the vamp via the career of Pola Negri in the 1920s.

Negri's 1923 film *The Spanish Dancer* is especially illustrative of the differences between her German screen portrayals of the late 1910s and her American films of the 1920s. In a number of interesting ways, this film 'corrects' many of the more transgressive elements of *Gypsy Blood* and *Passion*. In it Negri plays Maritana, a gypsy dancer who falls in love with Don Cesar de Bazan, a nobleman who is to be put to death for dueling. Although still the woman whose beauty and sexuality can motivate class ascension, Negri is here a savior rather than a femme fatale. When she saves the life of the Queen's child, Maritana pleads for clemency for Bazan. The King, however, plots to marry Bazan to Maritana before executing him, thus giving her a legitimate place at court so that he can make her his mistress. The lovers are married, but Bazan escapes death when a friend substitutes bread pellets for the bullets of the firing squad's guns. The King follows Maritana to a hunting lodge where he plans to seduce her, but is interrupted by Bazan, who begins to engage him in a duel. They are interrupted by the arrival of the Queen, who is assured by Maritana that the King had only come to bless their marriage. Order is then restored at the end of the film as Bazan and Maritana are reunited with one another.

Not only does this narrative deprive the gypsy woman of the agency of her own social rise, it more generally robs her of the level of self-awareness and self-interest that made her earlier roles so interesting. In *The Spanish Dancer* Maritana must be shown to be pure-hearted despite her social and ethnic background. Here, rather than destroying her lover, she rehabilitates him, for as an intertitle claims, before their meeting. 'All Spain knew Don Cesar as a reckless, carefree noble to whom gold was made for gaming, and life but a stage for rash adventure.'

Even while films such as *The Spanish Dancer* were narrativizing the recuperation of the vamp, the publicity surrounding Pola Negri ran sharply counter to any type of containment. Indeed, Negri was consistently associated with a discourse of erotic and cultural aggression that seemed to challenge American morality and American empire. One especially important source for the kinds of extra-filmic information about Negri which literalized the myth of the vamp was the publicity about her romantic relationships in Europe and America. Reports linking the actress to such beloved icons of the American cinema as Charlie Chaplin (British) and Rudolph Valentino (Italian) seemed to inspire much disquiet in the American press. Herbert Howe's 'The Loves of Pola Negri,' for instance, begins:

> When I facetiously asked Pola Negri in Berlin if she intended to marry Charlie Chaplin, she tossed back her head and laughed heartlessly. I felt a pang for Charlie, because even a comedian would not care to get a laugh like that.[56]

The building of a public idea of Negri as 'deadly woman' was reinforced by stories of her deadliness in real life. She was widely attributed with the quote 'In Poland we kill,' supposedly uttered during the shooting of one of her films and directed at someone who did not share her artistic point of view. Interviewers suggested that Negri was quite capable of making good on such a threat since her allure was inevitably fatal. There were suggestions that she used men to gain social power:

> With stardom and high salary came her marriage to the Polish Count Domska. It is significant that this marriage, according to German report, was very much like that of Madame Du Barry in 'Passion.' You will recall that the little milliner married in order to gain a title that would permit her to move in aristocratic circles.[57]

There were also dramatic accounts of her fatal influence over the men unlucky enough to have fallen under her spell. Many such accounts described Negri's professional success as having come at a high personal price, as if her growing strength was enabled by her debilitating effects on her lovers. In one fan magazine, Negri describes her 'first love,' a painter whom she met just as she was beginning to attract notice for her performances on the stage:

> He was in delicate health. I knew that. It did not matter . . . I loved him. He became worse . . . It was the dreadful quick consumption. I saw the life going from him. I thought I could save him somehow. I had overcome so much by my will, I thought I could even conquer death. Then one night he died. He died in my arms.[58]

Accounts of Negri's romantic history testified again and again to her destructive force, describing her morbid influence as inevitable, as in 'The Loves of Pola

Negri,' which quoted the actress as saying 'Always I have sought love, and always there have been disappointments. I am a fatalist. I believe in my star. It is my fate to be unhappy in love.' Statements such as these activated a number of different dimensions of the Negri persona; they added extratextual support to the filmic construction of Negri as fortune-telling gypsy and they also discursively reinforced her connection to Old World values. This association of Pola Negri with prophecy and with the past fed into her construction as the deep, eternal feminine. In terms of her vamp characterization, it also undergirded the notion that the Vampire is of the East, creating a web of associations around Negri's vamp that connected her to past, rather than present values. As Dijkstra points out, in vampire mythology 'to travel eastward is to travel into the past.'[59] Given that the vampire is a figure of degeneration, this kind of associative web may indeed have helped to craft a kind of self-fulfilling destructive prophecy around Pola Negri.

In any event, this sort of Old World fatalism that permeated press characterizations of Negri contrasted sharply with the energetic ideals of American capitalism. Interestingly, at the start of her American career, Negri was sometimes valorized in American capitalistic terms for her work ethic:

> Much has been written, still more talked of, concerning Negri's life before she became celebrated. Really the details are commonplace with a record of hard work and struggle for recognition. . .when the director said 'Go to it!' she went to it like one doing an honest day's job for a day's pay.[60]

Rose Shlusinger even looks forward to a conversation with Pola Negri by observing, 'Ah, one thought, there was a woman and a workman!'[61]

However when public favor turned against Negri, she was criticized for failing to meet these same standards of diligence. The problem, according to one writer, was that 'Pola came to the studio when Pola felt like it, and not one second sooner.'[62] In the last years of Negri's Paramount contract (1926–1928) there was a markedly unsuccessful attempt to reverse this impression – a trend exemplified in fan magazine pieces entitled 'How Pola Was Tamed' and 'The Transformation of Pola.' This latter was a remarkable series of sketches by Malcolm St. Clair (the actress's director for *A Woman of the World*) depicting first a disgruntled cast and crew awaiting the star's arrival on the set, and then the results of Pola's 'transformation:'

> Then Mal showed Pola how good she'd become. He showed her a picture of herself arriving, the first star at the studio . . . Somebody put her wise to the fact that friendliness gets you farther in Hollywood, and everywhere else, than frigidity.[63]

Despite their flair, such attempts at re-configuring Pola Negri's star persona seemed distinctly 'too little, too late' to reverse a trajectory of representation which emphasized her icy European reserve and deadly effect. Negri remained a remote figure, or as one contemporary reviewer of *Loves of an Actress* suggested, an 'acquired taste' too exotic for the American public at large:

> Pola Negri has always been an as-you-like-her star. Even the Negri fans, however, will look askance at the stellar assignment in a role which automatically suggests a Swanson or a Talmadge rather than the severer brunet personality of the Polish star.

In a remarkable conversion of the authenticity discourses of her early career, when Negri left Hollywood in 1928 to return to Europe, the failure of her American career seems to have been attributed (at least in the fan magazines) to inauthenticity. The implicit linkage here was between integrity and Americanization. In 'The Passing of Pola,' Leonard Hall wrote that 'Pola Negri's failure was a failure of the mind and spirit.'

> Stars are because film fans find in each one thing to love and cherish. In Jack Gilbert is a certain irresponsible, devil-may-care charm. Buddy Rogers and Dick Barthelmess are every woman's boys . . . Mary Pickford began to fade when she grew less the dimpled hoyden and more the First Lady of Filmdom and chatelaine of the Fairbanks manor. Pola Negri just neglected to be herself.[64]

Thus, in the Hollywood of the 1920s which prided itself on the range of its 'types,' any unclassifiable personality was judged to be a fraud. Since every type was representable in Hollywood terms, the public's rejection of Pola Negri had to be due to her failure to represent herself truthfully. Negri's 'inauthenticity' confirmed the authenticity of the star-making system – if she could be seen as lacking that authenticity associated with stardom, then Hollywood's failure to develop her talent could be explained away.

The fall of the femme fatale and the rise of the good girl were trends that went hand in hand with one another paralleled by the displacement of the immigrant Other by American purity. Both were part of a process of cultural displacement whereby one form of femininity was replaced by another. The vamp had to be discredited in order for the good girl to come in. The iconography of the ethnic vamp was a necessary counterpoint to the iconography of white female victimization coming to be popularized by filmmakers such as D.W. Griffith. In a sense the differences between the vamp and the modern girl were posited in terms of a nature vs. culture debate, with the kind of timeless Old World femininity embodied by Negri superceded by the tractable, modern femininity associated with such All-American actresses as Clara Bow or 'convertible ethnics' like Colleen Moore.

I am inclined to believe that Negri's career foundered for these reasons, but additionally and perhaps most importantly, because Hollywood had constructed two Pola Negris and they were fundamentally at odds with one another. The domesticated Negri was never as interesting to American audiences as her early persona of the exotic Other, nor was this earlier image ever entirely put aside in favor of the rather weak discourses of transformation and containment that particularly marked the late stages of her American career. Moreover, Negri's ethnicity was presented as timeless and eternal, incapable of conversion, and so her American-ness could never be definitively established. In short, Negri's vaguely Eastern European ethnicity was seen to be utterly resistant to attempts at Americanization. She could not be made to work effectively as an American cultural export, and for this reason, Negri had to be excluded from rather than included in such imperial ventures.

It is widely believed that Negri was among those foreign-born stars who did not survive the transition to sound because of her heavy Eastern European accent, when, in fact, Negri's Hollywood career ended before sound came in, and she had a successful sound test for Paramount in the early 1930s. Such accounts are nevertheless interesting, for they are fundamentally accurate in attributing the failure of Negri's career to an ethnic impediment. When the actress returned to Germany in 1935 to make films for UFA, there were persistent rumors in the American press that her European career was advancing due in part to a romantic relationship with Hitler. Despite the unlikeliness of an association between the German leader and a non-Aryan Pole, and Negri's own dismissal of the rumor in her autobiography, at the time of her death in 1987, obituary reports seized on this detail with relish, while stopping just short of confirming the affair.

The legacy of Negri's vamp persona seems to have pervaded even the critical reception of her memoir in which the author was strikingly and consistently characterized as untrustworthy. Other sorts of de-legitimizing discourses placed Negri as a symbol of the failure of Old Hollywood, wrongly reporting her as penniless, or working in low-status jobs. As would also be the case with another imported sex symbol, Hedy Lamarr, exaggerated accounts of the actress' fall from grace and glamour to more pedestrian pursuits suggest a continuing need to diminish her achievements. While acknowledging rather than extensively analyzing this dimension of Negri's later life here, I scrutinize this phenomenon in a more systematic fashion in Chapter 5.

The significance of Negri's failure to be successfully assimilated into Hollywood typology should not be under-estimated. In the context of the culture industries' normalizing, assimilative imperatives, Hollywood's failure to recuperate Negri's sexuality and ethnicity are striking. The significance of Negri's resistant role would have been strengthened by the tremendous fanfare associated with her arrival in the United States and her status as 'star' before she even arrived. Negri's positioning outside of the Hollywood cult of personality necessitated explanation and at the close of her American career, many such explanations were attempted on the pages of fan magazines.

The kinds of discursive tensions that permeated the fan magazine pieces on Negri in the 1920s persist in a certain confusion about how to consider her work historically. Positioned as resource both in terms of her gender and her ethnicity, Negri was never successfully exploited by the Hollywood system, and to that extent she continues to embody a certain slippage of categories, resisting classification as an actress and as a woman in ways that, for the feminist film historian, may be entirely satisfactory.

4

SONJA HENIE IN HOLLYWOOD

Whiteness, athleticism and Americanization

By all accounts Norwegian figure skating star Sonja Henie morphed relatively smoothly into a movie star for Twentieth Century Fox. Unlike her foreign-born contemporary Hedy Lamarr, who carried with her to Hollywood a scandalous past that had to be sanitized and recuperated, Henie brought to the screen a secure public persona founded on her three Olympic gold medals and her ten world figure skating titles. Her skating talent was the defining feature of her stardom; when she had the opportunity to commemorate her career in the cement outside Grauman's Chinese Theatre, she left impressions of her skate blades as well as of her hands and feet.

Nevertheless, when it came time to casting Henie in Hollywood films, the issue of her ethnicity proved as decisive as her skating talent. Accented and dramatically untrained, the skating star would have to be contextualized within fictions that explained her foreignness and did not make strenuous tests of her acting skills. Unlike many other ethnic stars whose all-purpose ethnicity could be directed toward characters of various national identities, Henie nearly always played young Scandinavian women. (Like Pola Negri who for Hollywood was not so much Polish as Eastern European, Henie was not so much Norwegian as she was Scandinavian). The skating star came to Hollywood with a fully-formed persona which Hollywood developed new methods to exploit, rather than crafting a persona for her from scratch, or modifying one that had been established in other national cinemas (as was the case for example with Pola Negri). Her films demonstrated her persona more than they invented it, and her evolution into the centerpiece of winter-themed light musicals in the 1930s and 1940s seemed an unproblematic extension into new realms of public knowledge about the star. The peak of Henie's film stardom somewhat overlapped the period of child star Shirley Temple's massive success; of the nine films in which Henie appeared for Twentieth Century Fox, her earliest ones (including *One in a Million* [1936], *Thin Ice* [1937] and *Happy Landing* [1938]) were the most successful. Her career, as Thomas Schatz notes, 'was winding down during the war'[1] though it was by no means concluded. In this chapter, I seek to track the question of what whiteness meant within Sonja Henie's celebrity and how it was nationalized.

Figure 6 Sonja Henie represented a benign internationalism in her Hollywood career

Henie's career was virtually entirely free of scandal, controversy, and sexuality (although she became a retroactively scandalous figure upon the publication of an unflattering biography late in her life). Her persona and the image of Twentieth Century Fox (a studio with a reputation for wholesome entertainment) appeared ideologically interdependent and mutually supportive. The trajectory of Henie's straightforward assimilation reflected in her biography became the defining feature of her star persona. Her Hollywood image is well summed up in a 1944 profile where she is described as follows:

> Experts in these matters will tell you that she most certainly *does* possess an extra something. It is, they say, an elusive quality known in the profession as 'wholesome charm.' This young lady from Norway, the greatest single attraction in the world of sports-entertainment today, possesses the smile of the pure in heart; the lingering touch of that most ingenious of accents, the Scandinavian; a little girl's head of curly blonde hair; dumpling cheeks. Altogether she is – for a hundred million movie fans – the epitome of innocence.[2]

Henie's tendency to be presented as sexually and ethnically innocent[3] and ideally white is well displayed in her third film, *Happy Landing* (1938), one which dovetails closely with her own star biography. Here Duke Sargent (Cesar Romero),[4] a suave bandleader billed as the 'flying maestro,' and his friend promoter Jimmy Hall (Don Ameche) stop unexpectedly in Norway as they travel from New York to Paris. This veering off course in a journey from one metropolitan center to another provides the opportunity to introduce Trudi Ericksen (Henie), a romantic young country girl who dreams of meeting someone from far away. When Duke twice invites Trudi to dance, he has (according to local custom) symbolically proposed marriage, and when the two men learn of the cultural faux pas, they flee, although Duke has been inspired by Trudi to write a song which becomes a hit entitled 'A Gypsy Told Me.' It soon becomes clear that Duke is a shallow, vain man who mines his experiences with women for story and song material, although he frequently distorts actual events to exaggerate his own involvement and (most distinctively) to underscore his role as a deliverer of exotic authenticity. When he introduces the song in Paris, he invents a story of a gypsy woman approaching him in Rome to tell him that one day he will find his true love. More remarkably, in an introduction of a later number, Duke describes a song that came to him 'on a night out West.' He then describes finding a warehouse of cigar store Indians and asks his audience:

> Have you ever paused to think what's become of the wooden Indian? Do you realize they're a vanished race? Ladies and gentlemen, we found their happy hunting grounds . . . And as the rain beat against the roof and the wind howled down the chimney, we saw what no white

man has ever seen before – the war dance of the wooden Indian. Hold
your scalps, palefaces, here we go again!

It becomes evident that Duke's musical numbers are thus largely geared to
nostalgic/romantic renditions of ethnicity and embellishments of whiteness that
showcase his role as an excavator of other cultures. He perceives Henie's ethnic
identity as unproductive for these purposes and so when she shows up at his
New York hotel sometime later it appears fitting that his response is to ask
'What'll I do with a Norwegian?' Although Trudie's stable whiteness is not
susceptible to the same kinds of exoticizing representations as the ethnicities
Duke sings about (Italian, Gypsy, Native American), it is nominated by the film
to anchor the numerous locations and characters introduced. When Trudie's
skating talent is discovered, Jimmy becomes her promoter, and Trudie is transformed into a skating star who fills halls around America. Celebrating their
success, he seeks to buy her an expensive piece of jewelry and asks her if there
is something she has always wanted since she was a child. When Trudie tells him
she's longed for a vacuum cleaner, Jimmy is delighted and assures her that she'll
'never make a golddigger.'

Happy Landing emphasizes Henie's girlishness, naivete and whiteness in rather
stark contrast to Flo Kelly (Ethel Merman), Duke's sometime girlfriend, who is
shown to be both mercenary and violent (though these qualities are temporarily
erased in her upbeat musical numbers). Although Jimmy warns Duke that Flo is
'strictly bad news,' the couple reunite late in the film, where the combination of
Duke's womanizing and Flo's jealousy produce violent altercations. When Duke
phones Jimmy to complain 'Why I'm black and blue all over – she beats me!'
we cut to the horrified face of a black waiter as Flo bursts into the room. It is
in moments such as these that *Happy Landing* gives away its gendered racial
politics, constructing inappropriate female behavior as racially transgressive action. Several times in the course of the film Duke and Jimmy ask about a
woman 'Is she a blonde or a brunette' such that, in effect, this becomes the
film's structuring question about femininity. Though shot in black and white
stock that cannot bring out these distinctions as forcefully as color, the film
wants us to know that the safely blonde Henie and the brunette Merman
represent starkly opposing images of female morality. In this way, the film
adheres to a broader pattern in the Henie films of nominating blonde women
for virtue. In the case where female co-stars or supporting players are also
blonde, Henie is emphatically costumed and lit to bring out her superior whiteness. Her appearance across her films bears evidence of the way that as Richard
Dyer has identified, 'the photographic media, the apparatus and practice *par
excellence* of a light culture, not only assumes and privileges whiteness, but also
constructs it. . . . Idealised white women are bathed in and permeated by light.
It streams through them and falls on them from above. In short, they glow.'[5]

Happy Landing nearly comes to closure on the image of a double wedding
between Trudie and Jimmy and Duke and Flo, yet returns in a brief final scene

to the foursome skating in Central Park, then elevates Henie to a position of prominence amongst a large group of skaters, leaving behind its image of coupling in favor of a deified image of Henie's individuality and an aesthetic view of her performing body as a white ornament. *Happy Landing*'s commitment to mounting a performance of whiteness is revealed in part through racially coded vignettes that although they take place at the margins of the film, in many ways give away its racial investments.

Whiteness, cuteness and national rejuvenation

Like Colleen Moore, with whom she shared a 'safe' ethnic status, Henie was frequently cast as a diminutive, performing doll. Because her whiteness was secure, it could be frequently referenced through a visual vocabulary that emphatically and simultaneously underscored her association with winter sports, her connection to a 'safe' white ethnicity and an unblemished sexual morality that served her casting as innocent girl-women on screen.[6] Whiteness was an ongoing thematic intertext for Henie's persona, referencing both the white accessories of her sport and her Nordic ethnic status. And indeed, even the star's fetish for material whiteness was a celebrated feature of her persona. A 1937 article reported that 'Sonja sleeps at least ten hours a night in a white bedroom, drives in a snow-white automobile, dresses in white. Carries a rabbit's foot for luck, although her own feet are luckier.'[7] When Henie campaigned to make herself known in Hollywood after screen tests had not materialized into parts, she effectively waged an exhibition of whiteness. Gladys Hall's account runs as follows:

> So it was that Sonja leased the white house. It must be white, she stipulated, the furnishings white, also. She bought a very de luxe and very streamlined car, also white. She rode about the boulevards in her white car, dressed all in white, young as the morning, seemingly as indifferent as a young winter moon, until she had the satisfaction of seeing heads turn wherever she appeared.[8]

Furthermore, those facets of her persona that might have proved 'unworkable' within the established Hollywood representational lexicon of femininity were effectively converted into qualities of ethnic and gender identity that were highly representable. Henie's foreign nationality was acknowledged but only insofar as it pre-narrativized and rationalized her coupling with or rescue by an American male. Henie's athleticism and skating prowess were also acknowledged by the films but were converted so that these talents could be pressed into service to demonstrate her fitness for companionate marriage and good citizenship. Further, Henie's sports skill and her foreign nationality served as mutually de-complicating explanatory features of her persona – her skating talent was merely a function of her Norwegianness, and her Norwegianness meant simply an affinity for winter sports.

Finally, and perhaps most importantly, the insistent positioning of Sonja Henie as a 'cute' performer mobilized a 'construction of cuteness as an aesthetic value that constitutes a marker of racial distinction.'[9] As Lori Merish has shown, 'Cuteness engenders an affectional dynamic through which the Other is domesticated and (re)contextualized within the human "family." Cuteness aestheticizes the most primary social distinctions, regulating the (shifting) boundaries between Selves and Others, cultural "insiders" and cultural "outsiders" . . .'[10] In other words, what we deem cute often occupies a liminal position, such as between human beings and the natural world (animals) or adulthood and infancy (children), and for Henie, her cuteness was an indicator of her status as both assimilated and apart. In the Henie persona cuteness was reflected by both the star's body and her language, for not only were her skating performances coded as innocent dance numbers on ice, but her rushed, accented style of speech also gave her the effect of a childlike lisp. Following closely upon the racialized performances of cuteness established by her contemporary at Twentieth Century Fox, Shirley Temple, Henie's persona offered cuteness as an interpretation of her foreign nationality and ethnic/racial status.[11] What I am suggesting is that both stars provided a forum in which admiration of the white, girl (or girlish) body became a way of speaking whiteness in ways that were otherwise unavailable, imagining national recovery as a reclamation of whiteness. And for Henie as well as for Temple their enunciative relationship to a nationalized whiteness was in part a function of their proximity to its borders. Where Temple mimicked the self-consciously racialized identity of African-Americans in film narratives that foregrounded the de-sexualized, performative child's body, Henie appears in a series of films in which her status as a foreigner demonstrated 'the social power of cuteness exercised as a drama of socialization.'[12] Thus, important differences between the two stars manifest themselves as well, for the childlike adult body of Sonja Henie serves functions that would not be possible for the child body of Shirley Temple.[13]

In many ways Henie and Temple shared status as icons of unfettered individualism at a time of national crisis, when collective values threatened to swamp the equation between initiative and reward so cherished in American social ideology. Amidst the economic threats of the Depression, their cuteness also structured an image of juvenile vitality that displaced the spectre of the wan, malnourished child of the Depression. Like Temple, who by Charles Eckert's acccount, represented an 'an appeal to universals,'[14] Henie incarnated the wondrous appearance of talent, diligence and transparent and spontaneous expression. Yet Henie's stardom engaged a level of ethnic specificity that must also be factored in.[15]

As an acceptable vision/version of white ethnicity, Henie deviated somewhat from the persona of her studio stablemate Shirley Temple, yet both stars incarnated the body in exuberant, individualist motion. In stark contrast to the early 1930s backstage musicals which prioritized the bodily collective, the Temple and Henie films acted to overthrow the residual effects of the Depression and to restore a sense of corporeal individualism. That both of these bodies were constructed as both female and innocent only furthers their contrast with the tarnished, debilitated male body of the Depression centralized in 1930s genres such as the gangster film, the biopic, and the horror film. For both Sonja Henie and Shirley Temple, the dominant discursive meaning of their whiteness may well have been recovery, an element that compensated for the sense of diminished national, white vigor in the 1930s.

To act as a tonic to the social and economic ills of the Depression, Sonja Henie was marked as particularly 'healthy,' and the equation between whiteness and health in her persona was figured both visually and narratively. In the publicity constructed on Henie by Twentieth Century Fox, she is presented as the bearer of an ethnic pedigree and a physical vigor that enable her to flourish in the Southern California paradise. In her studio biography, 'The Life Story of Sonja Henie,' she is described as a 'healthy, wholesome type of old-fashioned girl' who has fallen in love with Southern California, and her biography is replete with descriptive passages such as: 'This blonde Nordic girl from wintery Norway loved the sunshine of California and its perpetual semi-tropical climate.' Many of her publicity photos featured Henie costumed in white and enjoying the Southern California 'good life' as for instance in the photo shown, where she is presented walking off the tennis court, glowing with health. As a positive ambassador for skating, Henie's rationale for publicizing the sport is linked to the salubrious effects of practicing it, for 'she wanted to see children converted to its health-giving and body-building possibilities, as well as the fun derived from it.'[16]

Similar keynotes of health and fun are struck in *My Lucky Star* (1938) where Henie is introduced as Norwegian Christina Nielson, a young employee at Cabot's Fifth Avenue department store whose beauty and skating talent are discovered by the scion of the firm, an irresponsible playboy named George Cabot, Jr. (Cesar Romero). In this film as in many others (including *Second Fiddle*, *Everything Happens at Night*, and to a lesser extent *Happy Landing* and *Sun Valley Serenade*) the Henie character is the agent who converts an American male from artifice to authenticity. Discovered by George, and later wrongfully named in his divorce suit, Chris (Henie's character's name is colloquialized here to emphasize her fundamentally down-to-earth nature) will ultimately enable her mentor to pay off his wife in their divorce and repair his relationship with his father by seeming to prove his good business sense. As I have suggested, her role as the playful, pragmatic motivator in helping a male lead toward a more purposeful, meaningful existence overarches a number of the Henie films.

My Lucky Star simultaneously advertises winter fashions, winter sports and college camaraderie, doing so through a discourse of whiteness that involves careful handling of the structuring tension between exceptionalism and averageness in the Henie persona. Early in the film the executives of Cabot's Fifth Avenue hold a sales meeting in which they note the rising popularity of winter sports and identify the need to secure the sportswear market for college girls. Christina agrees to model women's fashions to a college community in

Figure 7 Publicity photos emphasized themes of health and vitality in Sonja Henie's
persona, while also perpetuating the use of white as the star's 'signature color'

exchange for paid tuition, and is sent off to Plymouth University where the film
shifts its emphasis to tableaux of camaraderie set in the outdoors (singing parties
on sleighs, skating displays on frozen ponds, walks through picturesque college
grounds, etc.). The collegiate setting rationalizes Henie's ongoing connection
to the values of youth and play, yet also serves as the backdrop for the star to
counterbalance her exceptionalness and her growing fame with reminders of

the importance of humility, as she takes lessons in being 'a good sport' and being 'regular.' When some of her fellow students mock her in the college's famed winter carnival, performing a satire called 'Fancy Clothes Chris,' in which she is accused of 'strutting around like a peacock,' Chris is abashed until the class president finds her and urges her to prove her 'regular' status. Chris returns to the ice, and performs a spectacular skating number that cements her re-integration within the group.

The scene thus reflects in miniature a dynamic that threads through the Henie persona as it was constructed in the late 1930s and early 1940s – Henie paradoxically proves how regular she is by displaying her exceptional talent. In this way she advocates for a consensus value system that establishes how even the most extraordinary member of a group is finally validated not by standing apart, but by standing amongst. Using a discourse of 'regularity' as a cover for a process of standardization over behavioral norms, fictions of this sort carried a great deal of weight in late 1930s America. This ideology of individual merit that reflects glory on the group was essential in a culture recovering from the Depression and girding itself for World War II. Accordingly, *My Lucky Star*'s closing image of vibrancy is central to the work performed by Henie across a number of her films in its emphasis on the star's performing body showcased within a group of her not-quite peers. Hoisted into place by her fellow Plymouth University students in the number that closes the ice show, Henie takes the place of the white body centered within a constellation of multicolored ones (the other students appear in variously colored costumes). The number gives vivid shape to what was often a more nebulous concept in Sonja Henie's star persona – a delicate negotiation and conflation of individualist and collective values.

Athletic agency and the mandate of whiteness: paradigms of containment and meritocratic myths

In this section I want to investigate how paradigms of containment and meritocratic myths were activated around Sonja Henie's persona in such a way that the more troublesome facets of her persona as a sports star and a foreigner were either set aside or made functional within Hollywood's ideological economy. I turn first to some of the strategies employed within Henie's films to defuse the potential power of the image of aggressive, competitive athlete in favor of an image of softened, playful femininity. In a discussion of the films of Henie and Esther Williams, Greg Faller has argued that 'although they embody an aggressive and god-like persona, an apologetic is offered for the triumphs; their athleticism becomes secondary as their true feminine nature is awakened by romantic love.'[17] In Henie's case, however, her essentialized femininity is significantly explained by her Scandinavian ethnicity and its connotations of a purified whiteness.

Characteristically, Henie is contrasted within the film narrative by a non-ideal female foil character who embodies the reverse of the idealized traits ascribed to

Henie: where she is idealistic, they are cynical, where she is romantic, they are jaded, where she is calm, they are anxious, etc. The stridency of the female foils is presented as ethnically and/or regionally suggestive (Ethel Merman [as Flo Kelly] fills this role for instance in *Happy Landing*, while in *Iceland* Joan Merill plays Adele Wynn, the male protagonist's old friend from Brooklyn). In *My Lucky Star*, as in nearly all of the Henie films, a contrastive female foil character is presented, though in this film there is no romantic rivalry operating, and consequently the portrait sketched is more benign, and is meant to serve for comic relief. Mary Dwight (Joan Davis) is Chris's college roommate whose brassy singing style, tall, gaunt figure and prominent nose suggest a physical and ethnic contrast to Henie. Thus, the diminished whiteness of the female foils serves alternately comic or dramatic purposes depending upon whether or not there is a romantic rivalry operating. In tying the resolution of the romance to the selective operations of the male protagonist and his differentiation between ethnic stridency and the largely mute, but positively valued ethnic identity of the Henie characters, the films look approvingly on Henie as the possessor of a higher grade ethnicity. In short, she is presented as literally and metaphorically whiter than her female rivals.

Henie's film career was well timed, for, as one contemporary writer put it, she 'bobbed up on the celluloid horizon at the exact moment when the country was in its wildest craze over winter sports.'[18] The productive conjunction of Henie's skating talent and heavily-accented English may also have mitigated against the casting problems of foreign-born actresses after the silent era. Though her films certainly required her mastery of English to the extent that she could clearly convey dialogue, they also could rely on set pieces in which Henie did not register as a speaking subject but merely a body in motion (although there is less need for this in Henie's later pictures, which see a distinct improvement in the quality of both her English pronunciation and her acting).[19]

As Faller has observed, male sports stars exhibit a more consistent pattern of crossing over to film stardom than do women.[20] (In a career whose duration closely resembles Henie's Olympic swimming champion Johnny Weismuller appeared in twelve Tarzan films for RKO and MGM between 1932 and 1948). Yet Hollywood long displayed a hesitancy to exploit the box office potential of well-known female athletes. Although Australian swimmer Annette Kellerman starred in *The Daughter of the Gods* in 1916, tennis star Helen Wills whose classical facial features would have seemed ideal for Hollywood, failed her 1927 screen test before producers apparently unready to fashion a cinematic icon from a sports star whose arms had been described as 'pistoning-columns of white muscle.'[21]

Although newspapers speculated openly during the 1932 Olympics about which of the female swimming competitors might be transformed into a film star, and Eleanor Holm, a swimming champion of the Games, was cast as Jane in *Tarzan's Revenge* (1938), her film career was short and unsuccessful. It was Henie (and subsequently swimming star Esther Williams) who emerged as the relative exception to the rule that female sports stars don't make good movie stars.

Thus, though it would appear difficult to reconcile the kinds of femininities constructed through female sports star personae with the narrative paradigms and modes of performance favored by Hollywood, Henie and Williams (whose career with MGM, as I have said, slightly followed Henie's) represent two exceptional cases.[22] While susceptible to cultural codes that link sport to 'masculine' modes of competition and aggression, both Henie and Williams seem to have incarnated (for Hollywood and its audiences) a qualified femininity, that is to say, they were judged feminine 'despite' their sports achievements. Discursive patterns in coverage of Sonja Henie reflect the care that was taken to feminize her disciplined approach to her sport. One commentator noted that:

> Sonja is marvelously coordinated in mind and body. Mentally and physically she has steeled herself to accept a rigorous regime, and she has done it since childhood. Ability plus an iron will has [sic] carried her far. Yet she's all woman and a sentimental softie at heart.[23]

In Henie's case her affiliation with a sport known for the 'feminine' qualities of grace and beauty would have greatly minimized the 'damaging' associations to the male realm of competitive sports. Both Henie and Esther Williams were also individual competitors, rather than participants in team sports, whose potential competitive implications would have been more difficult to suppress. Furthermore, any anxieties about an overly athletic body were put to rest by the kinds of reassuring accounts of Henie such as the one provided by Sidney Skolsky:

> Her legs are shapely, but they don't bulge with the hard muscles that are evident on practically every dancer or skater. She has her legs massaged daily. She is utterly feminine. The first word she learned when she came to America was 'okay.'[24]

While Henie's body was figured as safely feminine, and never masculinized by her athletic exertions, her Norwegian identity was similarly negotiated in order to retain only an enriching, vague flavor of difference. In accounts such as the one above, she is attributed with an accomodationist nationality (her first English word is 'okay') and that perspective is reinforced by a star discourse that harnesses her athletic skills to an agenda of patriotism and heterosexual romance.

Articles such as 'Entertaining Ideas,' domesticate and feminize Henie's ethnicity further by featuring a series of Norwegian-themed recipes including 'the Norwegian star's treasured version of an "old country" recipe for coffee cake.' In characteristic style, a 1938 series of promotional photos by Twentieth Century Fox feature the actress in front of a world mapped according to shipping lanes and holding a copy of the Rand McNally World Atlas. Such photos helped to communicate Henie's benign internationalism, illustrating that her Norwegian identity was entirely disconnected from any negative cultural, political or ethnic referents and implicitly celebrating the transfer of Henie (who became an American citizen in 1941) to the US.

Whiteness within the Sonja Henie persona tends to take a more literal, material form than it does for any of the other celebrities discussed in this book. Accounts of Henie's strenuous whiteness always abutted potential perceptions of a discredited Aryanness, and in certain respects, in the years leading up to World War Two, it is as if Henie functions as a shadow character for a Germanness that the culture doesn't quite want to speak. Henie's occluded Aryanness hovered just beyond reach in her star persona as an expression of her latent too-whiteness. First delivered to the American public through coverage of her victories at the Olympics, Henie was linked to an international sports contest that was largely constructed in the American press as a referendum on America's national vigor, for the Olympics acquired additional symbolic importance during the Depression and its accompanying crisis of national confidence. As David Welky has argued, 'the unofficial slogan of the 1932 Olympics was "America against the World."'[25] Henie's subsequent assimilation into American culture had the effect of demonstrating that on those occasions when superior talent emerged outside the US that its rightful place was within the nation. Yet Henie's victory in the 1936 Olympics was tinged with the spectacle of Nazi racism – as sprinter Jesse Owens' triumph forcefully rebutted Adolf Hitler's Aryanist agenda, Henie's success seemed to confirm it, as did her status as 'Hitler's favorite athlete.'[26] Well-circulated photos of a warm greeting between Henie and Hitler and subsequent press attention to the way that a prominently-placed autographed photo of the Fuhrer in her home in Norway saved it from being ransacked could de-stabilize the positive meanings of her whiteness.[27]

Films such as *Everything Happens at Night* (1939) siphon off anxieties regarding Henie's hyperwhiteness by situating her within a narrative of Nazi victimization and mitigating her agency through placement as the rescued object. Her nationality here unspecified, Henie's Louise Norden is the daughter of Hugo Norden, a Nobel prize winning leader of a peace movement, recently escaped from a concentration camp and now sequestered with Louise in a small village in Switzerland. News that he may still be alive is showcased in a large front page newspaper article, while another piece placed proximate to the headline notes 'European Clouds Grow Darker: War Seems Inevitable.' Two journalists, one American (Ken Morgan) and one British (Geoff Thompson) track Norden to St. Palo in Switzerland, and in the course of searching for his precise location, they meet his daughter. Henie's skating talents here are used only insofar as they showcase her beauty and grace to the smitten journalists. A conversation between Morgan and Louise foreshadows the close of the film and his rescuing role:

Morgan: Gosh, you're positively radiant.
Louise: Tell me about America. Is it really as wonderful as they say?

Morgan: Wonderful? Why, it's terrific. That's the greatest country in the world. Would you love America – and would America love you. Not, of course, that there's a scarcity of blondes or anything like that. But you're the most beautiful thing I've ever seen in my life. You're so alive.

Competing for the same story and unaware that it will endanger his life, Morgan and Thompson circulate the revelation of Norden's whereabouts, and in short order, the Gestapo arrive to seize him. After narrowly eluding their pursuers in a chase by sleigh to the train station, the two journalists and the father and daughter subsequently arrive at a port where the Nordens will set sail for the US. Here Henie's imminent immigration is tied to a decisive renunciation of color. She says 'The farther away from brown shirts,[28] purple shirts, pink shirts, green shirts, the happier father will be.' Morgan and Thompson engage in a bit of byplay over who will win Louise, yet it seems a foregone conclusion that Morgan's national credentials will prove decisive. He trumps his rival by declaring 'Well, you forget we have the Statue of Liberty. America, sanctuary of democracy. Haven for Europe's greatest minds – Toscanini, Einstein, Thomas Mann – and Dr. Hugo Norden.' Despite this declaration, the film's decisive interest is in the importation of Louise Norden, rather than her father. Framed as it is in the film's last scene, this dialogue enables us to read *Everything Happens at Night* as a narrative of acquisition in which Henie's exotic vibrancy is imported by an American male who sees her as carrying the right balance of ethnic similarity (as Morgan has noted, there is no scarcity of blondes in America) and difference (she is identified as being exceptionally alive – coded descriptive language expressing the values of vitality and cuteness that structured the Henie persona).

Wealth operated as another register in which Henie served American ideologies of work and its rewards. The star was the subject of occasionally ambivalent but mostly accepting discourses on her accumulation of wealth in accounts marked by an exceptional explicitness. Discourses on Henie's hard work and well-earned rewards acted to reinvigorate myths of meritocracy, and underscore her relationship to pluck as an ethnic/immigrant trait. By 1941 it was reported that Henie was the highest-paid female star in Hollywood (ahead of Ginger Rogers and Carole Lombard).[29] Henie's secure whiteness authorized unusual frankness in regard to the financial rewards of her skating and film careers. Typical in this regard is an article entitled 'Cash-Register Champion,' which reads in part:

> Miss Henie has shown determination and diligence equated only by the business acumen she displayed after turning professional in 1936. The arduous practice which won her three Olympic titles pays off today in her movie and ice-show routines. Hard work is still essential, though; six weeks of strenuous rehearsals for her next film, *The Countess of Monte Cristo*, are now in progress. Despite her sizable income from a variety of investments . . . she has no thought of quitting.[30]

During the peak of her popularity, Henie's accumulation of wealth was thus presented as fully compatible with her ethnic persona and Americanization trajectory. Indeed, the media occasionally referred to her as the 'US Mint.' Her publicity photographs typically presented her as a valuable commodity surrounded by other valuable commodities such as luxury automobiles, fur coats and elaborate jewelry. Such potentially excessive displays were invariably tempered by their status as evidence both of the star's assimilation and of a functioning meritocracy.

Second Fiddle (1939) provides a good example of the way that the meritocratic myths writ large within the pre-war and wartime Henie persona could be reduced to fit the shape of a film narrative. Much like *Ella Cinders* for Colleen Moore, this film operates as a kind of culmination narrative for its star, self-consciously engaging the process of celebrity manufacture, even while disingenuously modifying the actual circumstances of Henie's rise to fame in such a way that she becomes more fully endowed with her signature traits of innocence and diligence.[31] Drawing from the well-publicized attempts to cast the Scarlett O'Hara role in *Gone with the Wind*, *Second Fiddle* opens with a massive effort underway on the part of Consolidated Pictures to cast Violet Jansen, the protagonist of the celebrated novel *Girl of the North*. Just as the real-life effort to find the heroine of Margaret Mitchell's novel was controversially resolved with the casting of the British actress Vivien Leigh, this film too finds native femininity deficient for the adaptation of a bestseller which has taken on national status. It strongly suggests that no American woman is suitable for the part, as nearly every actress in Hollywood as well as Miss America, is tested for the role. Upon hearing that the film's director has vetoed yet another candidate, Consolidated publicity agent Jimmy Sutton (Tyrone Power) asks facetiously but pertinently, 'What does he think this is, a federal project?' Here, as in *Everything Happens at Night*, the film registers its awareness of the growing conflict in Europe alongside the process of nominating an idealized, Americanized female figure. Newspaper headlines detailing the ongoing casting effort are placed proximate to a story noting 'Riots mark European elections.' When the studio turns to its next candidate, 'Girl #436,' they find Henie as Trudi Hovland, a Norwegian-born schoolteacher in Bergen, Minnesota whose picture had been submitted, unbeknownst to her, in the national casting call.

As we first glimpse her, Trudi is leading her students in a musical number that showcases from the outset her role as a unifying, harmonious figure. Trudi, we learn, shares a home with her feisty Aunt Phoebe (Edna May Oliver), a convenient character who siphons off any toughness Trudi might need to express, freeing her to act exclusively the role of simple, humble ingenue. Modest, down-to-earth, and unswayed by the attractions of fame, Trudi considers the opportunity to go to Hollywood, decides that her chances of winning the role are probably not very good, and declines to go. When Jimmy finally talks her into it, she exclaims, 'I feel like Cinderella on her way to the ball.' Hustled through the departments of hair and makeup at Consolidated,

Trudi is shortly auditioning for the role, and when she wins it, a delighted Jimmy cries out, 'She made it – my little schoolteacher,' and makes her a mock patriotic salute. Altering the pedestrian details of Trudi's background (her father was in the fish business in Norway), Jimmy invents a romantic biography linking her to the Vikings, and conjures up a fictional romance between Trudi and the studio's male star Roger Maxwell (Rudy Vallee) and the celebrity production process is underway. A montage of headlines in French, Italian, and Chinese signals the reverberant announcement of Trudi's casting worldwide.

Second Fiddle presents Hollywood as positively impacted by Trudi, rather than the reverse, suggesting that she reads her new environment through a stable set of values grounded in her ethnic identity. Interspersed with short scenes of Trudi mastering her new craft, most of the lengthier sequences here focus on other characters who invoke Trudi, her value system and her frame of reference.[32] One evening as he and Aunt Phoebe survey the Hollywood skyline, Jimmy remarks on how beautiful it is. 'Oh yes, Trudi calls it the Hollywood midnight sun. She thinks it reminds me of Norway,' says Aunt Phoebe. Though Jean Varick, Roger's girlfriend is anxious and resentful about having her boyfriend billed as Trudi's true love, Jimmy (temporarily) reassures her, saying 'You've met Trudie – you think she'd try to vamp Roger? No, she isn't that kind . . . he's perfectly safe with Trudi, you can depend on that.' Similarly emphatic assertions are made throughout the film of Trudi's innocence and consequently her vulnerability. Unaware that Consolidated has manufactured the romance between she and Roger as a promotional gambit, and that the love notes she receives from him are actually authored by Jimmy, Trudi falls in love with Roger, and Jean confronts Trudi on the set, saying nastily 'Don't give me that innocent stuff.' When *Girl of the North* is released, Trudi's performance is celebrated, with her director calling it 'brilliant,' but Trudi, having learned that the romance with Roger is artificial, has fled back to Minnesota. In the moment of conversion from artificiality to authenticity that comes up so frequently in Henie films, Jimmy reveals that he's in love with Trudi himself, and tells Aunt Phoebe that 'I couldn't lie about a thing like that.' He returns to Minnesota and persuades Trudi to marry him to close the film. *Second Fiddle* thus certifies the values of authenticity even while it sketches a flattering self-portrait of Hollywood as a meritocratic system in which talented, hard-working 'unknowns' rise to the top.

The good immigrant: Sonja Henie and the wartime revue musical

As I have suggested, in important ways Sonja Henie's stardom rehearses the unproblematic character of uncontroversially white ethnic groups in the United States. Notably, Henie was not susceptible to the discourses of suspicion that marked the careers of other ethnic female film stars in the 1920s, 1930s and 1940s who were linked to Southern and East European ethnicities. In opposition to the discourses of transformation that marked the arrival of other immigrant stars such as Pola Negri and Hedy Lamarr, Sonja Henie's arrival in Hollywood was distinctive for the presumption that she did not need to transform, that assimilation required little adjustment on her part. The very stability of Henie's image was part and parcel of her whiteness for she seemed to epitomize the perfect conjunction of the disciplinary practises of whiteness and femininity.

Henie's stable national status is suggested by a variety of incidents in her films, including several in *My Lucky Star*. No explanation is provided by the film for why this young Norwegian woman has come to the US. Nevertheless, her role as the good immigrant is stressed in bits of comic business such as a scene in the college sweet shop where Chris and her male companion are aggressively urged to order ice cream with pistachio nuts from a Greek proprietor who pitches the nuts as a product from his homeland, and is nearly apoplectic when they decline, shouting, 'It's people like you what's wrong with this country!' This minor character's comic and hysterical assertion of his national interests is meant to contrast with Chris who is unencumbered by such concerns and can ideally pitch American-made women's clothing.

Reed Ueda has discussed some of the changing forces at work in wartime US culture regarding ethnic identity and citizenship. In his analysis, he demonstrates that naturalization became a major social movement in the US during the war years, with the war acting as a catalyst to redefine 'the social boundaries and qualities of citizenship.'[33] As the war began to loom, these changes impacted Sonja Henie's stardom, with films like *Everything Happens at Night* reflecting a narrative need to explain her presence in the US, and crafting scenarios that showcased her status as good immigrant; this trend would accelerate in Henie's wartime films. Coming from a nation whose position was neutral during World War II, Henie was in certain respects less well equipped than Hedy Lamarr (whose connections to wartime Europe are discussed in the next chapter) to figure in narratives of American patriotism. When themes of patriotism were activated in Henie's wartime persona, she tended to be figured as an American defense asset in ways that would be comparable to Hedy Lamarr's stardom. However, a slight sense of discontinuity is also produced in such accounts as they frequently offer apologetics for the star's lack of a more dramatic contribution to morale. The result is a mixed mode of discourse that includes such coverage as a 1942 article entitled 'Busy as a B-25!' linking the star's diligence to goals of wartime productivity, while another fan magazine piece tracks her appearances at wartime canteens and notes her apology for being unable to take her ice shows directly to the troops, 'I'd love to go overseas to entertain, but, well, if I haven't got an ice rink, I'm really not much good for anything.'[34]

The stringent efforts made to highlight Henie's Americanization tended to focus more often on her fulfillment of the contract of the American Dream. This trajectory was the most consistent feature of her celebrity in America. Indeed, even at the time of her death in 1969, obituaries contextualized Henie within this explanatory framework using descriptions such as 'Sonja Henie, who skated a gold-paved path from Norway to Hollywood,' phrasing that implicitly activates the idealized conception of immigrant belief in an America where the streets are paved with gold.[35]

This sense of Henie as 'good immigrant' would be heightened in the wartime phase of the star's career. Adjusting the 1930s persona that showcased her as a Depression therapeutic, a figure whose whiteness connoted health and vigor, Henie's participation in revue musicals linked her to themes of wartime courtship. In Henie's first scene in *Sun Valley Serenade* (1941) Ted Scott (John Payne), the manager of the Glenn Miller orchestra, adopts a war refugee who, he assumes, is a child.[36] Standing in place with a claim ticket for number 36, Scott and his friend Nifty Allen (Milton Berle) are stunned at the arrival of a fully adult (though still baby-faced) Henie as Norwegian war refugee Karen Benson. '36, there's something wrong,' exclaims Allen. 'That must be her chest measure.' Here, Henie's showcase arrival functions to resolve the threat of femininity as it was constructed in the Hollywood imaginary of the 1940s where displays of sexuality and glamour lapsed quickly into predatory eroticism and deadly agency. Sexual but innocently so, assertive but playful, Henie possesses a benign ethnicity linked to her status as a good immigrant figure responsive to latent anxieties that American women have been inappropriately disconnected from the domestic sphere during World War II. Henie's wartime films emphatically draw attention to her unthreatening sexuality and traditionalist qualifications for marriage. In *Sun Valley Serenade* Henie disparages her female rival by several times suggesting that she cannot cook. In *Iceland* (1942) she tells her GI boyfriend that she can prepare more than fifty different smorgasbord dishes, and they have the following exchange:

'Oh, a home girl, eh?'
'Yes, but I can be awfully good company.'
'I bet you can at that. You know, that's what guys in the service are always looking for, company.'

While moments such as this indicate Henie's functionality in the wartime gender economy, that sense of usefulness is strikingly absent from later coverage of her career as she largely stopped making films after 1943, and turned to traveling ice shows as her primary means of employment. In the waning years of her celebrity, discourses on Henie's wealth abruptly shifted so that it no longer symbolized the legitimate rewards of her work, becoming instead a suspicious sign of a powerful woman who was perhaps running amok. In this period, increasing attention (often obliquely critical) was paid to robberies of Henie's homes and jewels and to her appearances in court on matters of business. Unlike other female stars of the same era whose personae were actively eroticized, such that when they were no longer susceptible to sexual objectification they become grotesque, Henie's connection to the values of girlish play shifted the terms on which she was descredited. In her later star discourse metaphors of ice and wintriness lose their association to play and become descriptive of her personality instead. Accounts of her social life in the 1950s often criticized her self-glorifying behavior in this fashion as for instance in a blurb in a 1953 social column which noted that 'Miss Sonja Henie wears so much jewelry, or "ice," when she dresses up to go out in New York, that some folks mistake her for the Aurora Borealis.'[37] Similarly, a more recent article detailing the star's rejection of an ice sculpture presented to her alludes to 'Sonja Henie's icy heart.'[38] The rhetoric on Henie's business affairs seems to turn negative as she aged and her pre-war and wartime favor receded. A 1948 article, for instance, observed that Henie 'was known to be as cold at a business conference as the ice she skates on.'[39] In 1952, when a stand of bleachers collapsed at one of her ice shows injuring a number of spectators, suggestions were made that the star's thrift had motivated the use of substandard material.

After her death in 1969, discrediting anecdotes about Henie abounded, featuring revelations about her greed, alcoholism, selfishness, and crudeness.[40] What interests me about these accounts is less the issue of veracity than their adherence to a broader pattern of discrediting attention to the legacies of female film stars. In Henie's case, the negative claims about her tended to directly invert the positive attributes that anchored her star persona in the 1930s and 1940s. One telling account relates that during the filming of *Sun Valley Serenade* where choreographer Hermes Pan had created a black-ice ballet by flooding a skating pond with ink, that Henie was knocked over by a group of male skaters onto the dyed ice. According to Pan, when the star got up 'she was black. Her face and her costume were covered in it, and she went into her room with her mother snarling and screaming, and she refused to work for the rest of the day.'[41] Accounts such as this one notably turn on the suggestion that the star had lost her whiteness in more ways than one.

Conclusion

Most recently, the trend toward miniaturized, nationalized bodies in women's sport has found expression in both ice skating and gymnastics. Ann Chisholm's recent work on the cultural fascination with gymnastics and the promotion of the 1996 women's gymnastics squad as representatives of 'The Face of America,' provides insight into the use of sports stars as 'limit figures that mediate cultural anxieties and conflicting desires regarding national identity in the US popular imagination.'[42] For Chisholm, the acclaimed group of gymnasts was celebrated using a discourse of cuteness that served to cast them 'as figures that finesse antimonies between the aerial embodiment of (White, bourgeois) US citizenship and that which it ostensibly leaves behind.'[43]

The Nancy Kerrigan/Tonya Harding controversy of 1994 in particular illustrates how performing female bodies can powerfully incarnate notions of classed whiteness as spectators worldwide were cued to revile the unruly 'white trash'

Harding and revere the assimilated Irish-American Kerrigan. That episode, which took the form of a resonant contemporary 'mediathon' of celebrity scandal, lives on in widely circulated reports of Harding's involvement with domestic violence, and well illustrates the persistence of discourses of femininity and ethnicity in determinations of who qualifies to represent both whiteness and the nation.[44]

In this discussion I have sought to probe the socially conservative nature of Sonja Henie's American stardom in the 1930s and 1940s. Through her participation in a culturally verified category of women's sports, Henie attained fame, but in no way appeared to challenge conventional interpretations of athleticism as a loss of femininity. In her films as well as in other modes of star discourse, Henie is presented as an athlete who affirms female delicacy, rather than challenging it. Henie's potentially unproductive foreign nationality was emphatically connected to a visual, verbal and ideological category of whiteness that narrativized her athletic performances as expressions of heterosexual desire, American patriotism and immigrant success in a meritocratic culture.

In stark opposition to other stars discussed in this book, Henie's whiteness was guaranteed, though, as I have shown, it at times ran the risk of being overplayed and becoming dangerously Aryan. Indeed, it may well be the case that as American involvement in World War Two deepened, and public knowledge of the horrific consequences of the Nazi racial purification schemes expanded, that Henie's role as a border agent took on a new shape and her hyperwhiteness became problematic. Whether in this way the emphatic discourse of whiteness in the Henie persona catalyzed the dwindling of her film career as World War Two progressed is a matter of speculation. What is clear, however, is that the combination of Henie's accented, excessive speech with its characteristic rushed style and her silent, performing body produced a highly palatable vision of femininity in the late 1930s and early 1940s, one which explained away any associations of agency produced by her highly successful sports career. Finally, in the Henie films cuteness takes hold as a performance aesthetic, operating in the way Lori Merish has suggested, 'to mediate the subject's relationship to ritualized forms of social control; it can constitute a highly theatrical way of enacting familial allegiance and *choosing* the compelled, displayed, and [erotically] objectified body.'[45] The ingredients of Sonja Henie's persona cumulatively reflect the tendency to proffer national, racial and ethnic explanations for success in American life; taken together they worked to place Henie into a category of ethnic exceptionalism that freed her from the discourses of disparagement and suspicion that could (and did) accrue to other ethnic stars in Hollywood. In arguing that Sonja Henie's potentially challenging athleticism could be recuperated through a 'safe' mode of ethnicity, I have sought to provide a case study of the kinds of complex ways in which conventional understandings of gender and ethnicity interconnect to stabilize potentially unruly functions within a star persona.

5

ETHNICITY AND THE INTERVENTIONIST IMAGINATION

Domesticity, exoticism and scandal in the persona of Hedy Lamarr

Like Pola Negri, with whom she was sometimes explicitly compared, Hedy Lamarr epitomized the Continental exotic to a generation of moviegoing audiences. As Dorothy Kilgallen would write in 1952, 'Hedy Lamarr became this generation's version of the Vamp – a synonym for the woman who launches ships, wrecks homes and sends countless men to glory or to doom.'[1] Unlike Negri, Lamarr was established as sufficiently elastic to be claimed as an American – yet while fan magazine and other publicity discourses constructed a patriotic, domestic, maternal Hedy Lamarr, her association with a repressed exoticism and a scandalous European past kept Lamarr's 'good girl' status always slightly open to question. In this respect, the actress's Austrian ethnicity could be camouflaged, but never fully eradicated, an important fact when we consider the relation between ethnicity and gender in the studio era, where ethnic femininity seems increasingly capable of advancing a positive vision of American nationalism.

Lamarr's ethnicity could be partially but never fully re-made; at play in the actress's persona was an operative contradiction between her private domesticity and her association with public scandal and sexuality. This contradiction significantly complicated Lamarr's putative transformation from European exotic to simple American girl, but at the same time furthered her ideological usefulness in the wartime and post-war American cinema. Lamarr's Euro-American status made her a particularly functional icon in this period because she connoted the positive intervention of Americanism upon a European resource. Thus, despite some non-assimilable qualities, she remained a fundamental sign of American mastery over ethnic femininity. On slightly different terms, but in fundamentally the same ways as many other star imports, Hedy Lamarr became the embodiment of ethnicity invented in such a way that it communicated the desirability and validity of a set of values deemed 'American.'

Born into a prominent and wealthy family in Vienna in 1914, Lamarr (nee Hedwig Kiesler) was privately tutored and attended finishing school before enrolling as a teenager in Max Reinhardt's acting school in Berlin. Steadily broadening her range as an actress, Lamarr cultivated contacts in Central European theatrical and film circles and after appearing in films such as *Money on the Street* (Austrian, 1930), *Storm in a Water Glass* (Austrian, 1931), and *The Trunks of Mr. O.F.* (German, 1932), she was cast in *Ecstasy* (Czech, 1933), a film that would bring her international notoriety and remain a significant element in her star persona all her life. Portraying a young wife left sexually unsatisfied by her much older husband, Lamarr appeared in two particularly controversial sequences: a nude swimming scene, and a moderately explicit love scene. While celebrated in Europe as an art film, *Ecstasy* was banned in the US, and led to Lamarr arriving in Hollywood 'as a sort of prefabricated sex symbol.'[2] In 1937, Lamarr left her wealthy husband, munitions manufacturer Fritz Mandl, and negotiated a contract with Louis B. Mayer at MGM.

During the span of her American career, Lamarr was used chiefly to infuse exoticism into film narratives, often serving as a kind of 'display piece' and playing mysterious, deadly and foreign women. In films set outside US borders Lamarr often played women who were hypersexual, yet for the most part her characters in films set within the US were quite staid. The former set of films tended to emphasize her body, while the latter emphasized her face. From the late 1930s through the late 1940s, Lamarr was a major star, who though her films drew unevenly at the box office, was frequently showcased in a variety of forms of press coverage. Considerable press attention was given to Lamarr's private life – her children, her marriages (the actress was married and divorced six times), her interests, her home, etc. But by about 1953, Lamarr's film career had petered out partly as a function of industrial reasons that included changes in the studio system and the kinds of films being made in this period as well as undergirding ageist/sexist ideologies that deemed her 'over the hill' when she was in her late thirties and therefore 'irrelevant' to the new industrial climate.[3] Although these rough parameters enable us to understand some of the trends and transition points of Lamarr's career, it is important to note, however, that the star's film roles and fan magazine coverage seldom fully sustain this tidy linearity for reasons I discuss at the close of the chapter.

In the late 1930s, MGM had invested a good deal of time and money in cultivating Lamarr as a potential screen star. Nevertheless, the studio seemed a bit paralyzed in casting her, worried about the scandal produced by *Ecstasy* for which she had become well-known, and unsure what properties might suit the actress. It is clear that the re-naming of Hedwig Kiesler to Hedy Lamarr, and Lamarr's subsequent contract with MGM, marked a period in which the actress was viewed as an important new property in Hollywood.[4] In the absence of clear typological guidelines for casting Lamarr in the narrative of her own life, some writers pitched her as a sponsor of the return to 1920s film style. A certain number of fan magazine articles position her as a catalyst of nostalgia for 1920s Hollywood, explicitly comparing Lamarr to the European vamps. An article by Gladys Hall is worth quoting in this regard:

> Lamarr is making us remember. Old dreams and old delights are stirring in the hearts of women as well as in the hearts of men. She has brought

back a distilled quintessence, the lure that was the other ravishing Lamarr's; she has brought back the mystery and consciousness of sex that belonged to such women as Negri, Swanson, Naldi, the 'burning Sapphoes,' and the Salomes and Cleopatras and Helenas who have never died.[5]

It is clear that in 1938 imported European femininity signified the return of the vamp, although in terms of her role in *Ecstasy* and what was known about her private life, Hedy Lamarr had neither the appropriate filmography or biography to support such a characterization. As commentators scrambled to place Lamarr within the typology of female film stars, they also reverted automatically it seems to an equation between European-ness and quasi-aristocratic status and good breeding. For instance, Dorothy Ducas described Lamarr as:

> Young, well-rounded of figure, brunette, with mysterious green-gray eyes that have in them all the languidness and intensity of a well bred Persian kitten's, Hedy takes up where the sinuous heroines of yesterday's movies left off.[6]

The terms of such descriptions that implicitly asserted Lamarr's regal character and 'purebred' status would soon be converted as the actress was Americanized.

In the early days of her Hollywood career, Lamarr was subject to a starmaking process that openly exposed the need to conjure up a productive version of exoticism for her. At the same time, it was important to emphasize Lamarr's inherent desire for Americanization in order to set aside the toxic foreign femininity attached to the vamp archetype. An article by George Weller, a classmate at Reinhardt's acting school lays the groundwork for Hedy Kiesler's transformation into Hedy Lamarr by suggesting that she had always been an eager candidate for Americanization, even during the early phase of her career in Europe. Weller discusses performing in a play called *The Weaker Sex* in which he and Lamarr portrayed American characters:

> He [Professor Reinhardt] told me to teach her some American songs. I took this as a mandate to make an American out of Hedy Kiesler . . . The older and more reputable members of the cast, who in Vienna are supposed to keep the younger ones in line, never made any objection to Hedy and me spending so much time alone together harmonizing in the little property room. Before long, though, greasy electricians and scene shifters began dropping in to make it a chorus. They wanted to be Americans, too, not so much as Hedy Kiesler, perhaps, but as much as a stagehand would.[7]

Weller's claim that Lamarr was innately interested in all things American and uniquely facile in transforming herself into an American is supported by his account of the actress's fascination with the American tennis star Helen Wills and skill in mimicking her. He attributes a certain plasticity to Lamarr in descriptions that strikingly emphasize her ability to erase herself:

> Her egg-shaped visage would grow calm, expressionless and assured, her brow would clarify, and for a moment she would really become an American woman, the masterful, inscrutable American woman who has her shrine in the imagination of the Central European.[8]

Gladys Hall's earlier thesis, that Lamarr 'made women exciting to themselves again,' perpetuates the 1920s association between European exoticism and essentialist femininity but also implies that by this point in time, the exotic (now more processed and tamed than it had been in the 1920s) was something that could be acquired. Hall uses the persona of Hedy Lamarr to urge a regression to a more dependent mode of femininity.

> We have gone through an arid spate of years during which women have become economically independent and as flat, erotically, as the flat-soled shoes we wear. For in the pursuit of our comparatively new-minted freedom we have gone in for man-tailored suits, equal standards, straight-from-the-shoulder talk, shiny noses, rubbing elbows with men in business offices, cocktail bars, splitting the checks, standing on our own feet and *standing* there.[9]

Similarly, in other commentary the actress is represented as the exemplar of a reversion to earlier norms of gender behavior:

> If Hollywood's Great Era of Slap Happy Heroines is waning, thank a willowy Viennese beauty who has the most soul-stirring grey-blue eyes that ever gazed at you from the silver screen. For Hedy Lamarr's exquisite performance in *Algiers* has reminded the movie boys that a woman is something to be loved rather than to be socked on the jaw.[10]

With Lamarr figured as the catalyst for a re-mystification and de-familiarization of femininity, European exoticism is represented as something that can be procured. American women, even American movie stars, were urged to emulate the actress's glamorous style. For, as Hall wrote: 'We do not, I repeat, believe that Hedy has a corner on the glamour market. For there are others, home-grown . . . and although to be home-grown does seem to be something of a handicap to glamour.'[11] Established American movie stars such as Joan Bennett seemed to model the called-for transformation into European ethnicity. While numerous accounts detailed the influence of Lamarr's appearance upon Hollywood, and the widespread copying of her center-parted hairstyle, for instance, some specific articles detailed Joan Bennett's re-making 'into' Hedy Lamarr. For instance, a photograph of the actress in which she looks identical to Lamarr appeared in 1939 with the caption:

SIPHONED GLAMOR One of the many effects of Hedy upon Hollywood: The heretofore blonde Joan Bennett, bearer of a famous theatrical name and a star in numerous movies, dons a brunette wig and otherwise transforms herself into this startling copy of the Lamarr in order to energize her career.[12]

Articles describing a feud between Joan Bennett and Hedy Lamarr and comparing the relationship to the feud between Pola Negri and Gloria Swanson suggest a tendency to figure a rivalry between an imported female figure and an American counterpart. But the feud was also seen as another means by which Lamarr was reviving the norms and practices of the silent era. Barbara Hayes mused that: 'Actually Hollywood doesn't have many feuds any more, all things considered. Good old knock-'em-down, drag-'em-out fights such as Gloria Swanson and Pola Negri used to indulge in are all but outlawed today.[13]

What is especially striking about the mimicry of Lamarr's appearance and style among American actresses in Hollywood (particularly the quintessentially white Joan Bennett)[14] is that it suggests not only that feminine ethnicity was appropriable but also desirable as a de-politicized mode of sexual display. In other words, unlike the 1920s where female ethnicity often carried rather potent, fixed, and fundamentally serious ideological meanings, by 1939 it had become de-stabilized to the point that it could be seen as a beauty innovation. With non-ethnic stars impersonating ethnic ones, it appears that ethnicity took on positive connotations of transformation for both American and foreign figures in Hollywood.

Yet if in pre-World War Two Hollywood, Lamarr set the standard for exotic European style, in postwar culture the terms of such mimicry were strikingly reversed. By 1950, Sidney Skolsky would report that:

Hedy Lamarr says the American Girl taught her glamour. She bobbed her hair because they did. She wore it casually because they did. She learned to use make-up the way they did. Of course she had a beautiful face to start with.[15]

In the interventionist climate of postwar American culture, the notion that America looked outside its borders for an ideal, even in matters of beauty and appearance, became increasingly untenable.[16] In this chapter, I will demonstrate how interventionism served as a crucial thematic in Lamarr's biographical narrative and the film narratives in which she appeared.

American interventionism and ethnic femininity

Hedy Lamarr's American career significantly spans a period of comprehensive change in the way that America looked at Europe and the rest of the world. From the late 1930s to the early 1950s the historic ideal of American isolationism (the notion that America should look after American interests by developing itself in isolation from the wars and monarchies that disrupted the rest of the world) was displaced by a foreign policy that was bipartisan, aggressively anti-Soviet and distinctly interventionist in character. For most historians, this evolution can be traced to the intense social and military mobilizations of World War Two. For instance, Dewey Grantham has written that: 'No feature of the war years contrasted more sharply with the situation in the 1930s than the abandonment of isolationism in the United States.'[17]

For others, the period immediately following World War Two is also significantly determinative of the transition to interventionism. Eric F. Goldman notes that in 1946–1947:

> The more Americans fretted over home affairs, the more plain a fact of fundamental importance became. For the first time during an American era of peace, it was next to impossible to discuss domestic problems coherently without having the points become entangled in foreign affairs. To millions this was an intensely irritating fact. They felt, as generations of Americans had felt before them, that concern over international matters was to be confined to unfortunate periods of war. Foreign policy was something you had, like measles, and got over with as quickly as possible.[18]

A number of postwar developments suggest the extent to which the US had adopted a new posture in world affairs in the 1940s; the leading role taken by the US in advocating for and founding the United Nations which would be based in New York, the deep involvement of the US government in the formulation of peace treaties with the Axis powers, the administration of the Nuremberg trials, and the political reconstructions of Germany and Japan, and even the international context in which decisions about the regulation and surveillance of atomic energy were carried out in the late 1940s indicate the degree to which isolationism had been replaced by an ideology of global interdependency. As the US demonstrated its willingness to move militarily, politically and economically when it felt its interests to be at stake,[19] it adopted an increasingly anti-communist rhetoric. With a great deal of success politicians like Secretary of State John Foster Dulles championed the view that the world would disintegrate into chaos if the US did not undertake a global policing role. The economic toll of World War Two forced Britain and France to relinquish their hegemony in Africa and Asia; under intense pressure from its allies the US largely took over their roles as colonial supervisor and committed itself (in the name of containing communism) to its new interventionist agenda. In a famous speech in 1947, President Harry Truman outlined the new ideological mandate of American foreign policy, to 'support free people who are resisting attempted subjugation by armed minorities or by outside pressures.' Thus, in the increasingly polarized view of most postwar American leaders, American values, social institutions and mode of government had become the implicit international standard. Putting across and reinforcing this conviction to the American people as a justification for interventionism become a prime mandate of political and business leaders in the postwar era. They undertook the revision of American public policy in support of the establishment and maintenance of numerous international military installations – only the most visible sign of a vast network of global commercial interests fashioned by US corporations in the postwar period. Consequently, as John Quigley observes:

> Such interventionism became particularly frequent after World War Two, because of the political and economic preeminence the United States began to enjoy in the world as the French and British empires went into decline – a preeminence that this country has been resolutely prepared to maintain and to propagate as the stakes have grown steadily higher.[20]

Rationalizing interventionism as a new American policy in Europe and around the world entailed the ideological re-orientation of the US toward Europe, privileging a sense of American mission and supremacy. The national mission, according to one historian 'is the notion that the United States is an exceptionally virtuous country that has a crucial role to play in bringing the good things of American society and politics to the rest of the world.'[21] An insightful assessment of Europe's place in an American interventionist cosmology is offered by Edmund Stillman and William Pfaff:

> The interventionist sees Europe as a continent whose day in history is over. Gifted, resourceful, brilliant, but dangerous and, so long as it remains disunited, hopelessly outmatched by the superpowers, vulnerable to conquest unless protected. The interventionist seeks a united Europe, but ambivalently wants that union only under conditions which effectively institutionalize a predominant American influence over European external policy and military action. This desire to check Europe, even while defending it, has comprehensible sources in the experience of two world wars caused by European states; but the interventionist theory defines Europe's future in the language of a vague altruism, in schemes for a federal European community established on the American precedent which would function as an element in a larger association envisaged as a kind of next higher stage in the evolution of the American-led free world. Europe's dangers would then be ended by its assimilation to the larger grouping – in short, by its fundamental Americanization.[22]

Constructed as it was in an era of redefinition of the power balance between the US and Europe, Hedy Lamarr's stardom reveals some of the ways in which ethnic femininity can be deployed to build and sustain a sense of national mission. In much the same way that Pola Negri's persona took partial shape as an enactment of American imperialist desires, we may note that Hedy Lamarr's Americanization functioned in part to rationalize the transition to interventionism. This happened at a number of levels: first, Lamarr's biography was fictionalized in such a way that it served as an implicit argument for interventionism; second, the actress was framed in a number of film narratives where American interventionist moves were shown to be motivated by a benevolent national conscience (thereby disguising economic and political goals as moral imperatives); third, the scandal surrounding *Ecstasy* played out as a kind of interventionist drama of American regulation and surveillance over profligate ethnic female sexuality. Throughout her American career from the late 1930s to the early 1950s, Lamarr served as an implicit icon of the interventionist imagination – a symbol of what could be had and how it could be converted.

Hedy Lamarr and the management of exotic sexuality

Having consistently displaced sexuality and exoticism onto the Continental Other, Hollywood faced a particularly challenging task in remaking Hedy Lamarr from a woman associated with a scandalous film into a bankable MGM star who would be acceptable to the Hays Office and the American moviegoing public. MGM seems to have set about this difficult task by denying Lamarr's past (or Hedy Kiesler's past, for the actress's re-naming was of course partly inspired by the desire to disassociate her from *Ecstasy*). In some fan magazine articles, the actress's dark European past was represented as haunting her American present. Typical of such accounts was one that contrasts negative European history with the positive pastlessness of US culture:

> Only one thing will prevent the darkly tragic Hedy Lamarr from assuming her rightful place as a top-ranking star – the indiscretion of a sixteen-year-old whose only sin was ambition.
> 'Why can't I be judged on my present and future?' she pleads. The studio which holds her contract, has, ostrich-like, turned thumbs down on any references to the Ecstasy Girl in publicity releases. Hedy Lamarr must at twenty-three be reborn without a blemish on her reputation, without a history![23]

Such was the connection between Lamarr and *Ecstasy* that she was (despite the studio's preference) frequently known as 'the Ecstasy Girl,' as again in a 1936 article which noted that, '*Ecstasy*, naturally focused attention on her bodily charms. With these under Hays Office taboo, *Algiers* has to be content with her face.'[24]

Such accounts are significant for the way in which they reveal that throughout much of Lamarr's career, a disavowal of her scandalous body took place in favor of the actress's facial perfection. Lamarr was regularly assessed as 'classically beautiful,' and 'perfection,' sometimes in the context of her European ethnicity. Some descriptions condensed all three qualities as in a 1952 article which observed that 'the dark perfection of her beauty is classically European.'[25] In a few instances, notice was taken of the 'imperfections' of Lamarr's body which was judged to be somewhat excessive. Kyle Crichton offered this dispassionate (and disturbing) appraisal of the actress's figure, 'As a bit of consolation for the women of these United States, I must say that Miss Lamarr is extremely tall and has a figure that could be better. She is rather large of limb and has somewhat too much in the rear and somewhat not enough in the front.'[26]

In addition to figuring Americanization as a diminishment of Lamarr's bodily European 'excess,' one means for containing Lamarr's threateningly exotic sexuality was to figure her beauty as utterly natural – the result of fate rather than the actress's design. Such representations implicitly sharpened the distinction between Lamarr's screen roles and her real life, thereby fictionalizing her role as the exotic temptress.

The cover photo of Lamarr in *Life* magazine on June 1, 1942 tellingly illustrates the shifts in Lamarr's persona that took place coincident with America's involvement in World War Two. Here, Lamarr's glamour is strikingly tamped down, as she appears in what the cover blurb refers to as a 'plain and simple portrait.' Lamarr, costumed as a Mexican Dolores 'Sweets' Ramirez for the film adaptation of John Steinbeck's novel *Tortilla Flat* (1942), wears her hair in braids, with gold hoop earrings and a white lace blouse. She is posed in front of a simple chipped, white-washed wall, and in her right hand is a limp rose. Imaged in this way, Lamarr is no longer a symbol of forceful, European exoticism, but a quite different symbol whose distinct non-threateningness is signified by the wilted flower she holds. In casting Lamarr as a Mexican girl, the actress's national identity is diffused, shifted from the central European context to a marginal national location that disengages her from whiteness, thereby suppressing any link to images of Austrian identity. It seems likely that this discursive transition was designed to steer her away from a strong, Central European ethnicity, re-situating her accent and foreign Otherness in the safe representational terrain of the Spanish-speaking peasant girl. Such efforts to neutralize Lamarr's ethnic threat would ultimately be displaced as her own ethnic identity acquired an increased ideological functionality. By 1950 in *Lady Without a Passport* the actress would play a Viennese woman and would be publicized as wearing 'Austrian peasant dirndls' around the house.

In general, the discursive thread of Lamarr's association with foreign exoticism ran quite separate from attempts to domesticate and reduce her sexuality (discussed in the next section). And it should be noted that Lamarr's version of the foreign exotic certainly changed over time. Lamarr came to Hollywood at a time when a number of movies were directly and indirectly hyping entry into World War Two. Americans were uneasy about domestic security at this time, and there was a widespread perception of threat among Americans who were uneasily watching the escalating conflict in Europe. Although Lamarr's publicity packaging reflected ambivalence about her European identity, associating it sometimes with classical authenticity and at other times, with a negative past, the actress's early film roles showcased her as a non-dangerous import at a time of intense concern about the security of US borders.

Early confusion over how to cast Lamarr had been resolved when MGM loaned the actress to United Artists in 1938 for *Algiers*, in which she appeared as Gaby, the protagonist's Parisian love interest. The film's success seemed to open the door for the actress to then be cast in similar roles. In *I Take This Woman* (1940) she plays Georgi Gragor, a Russian woman raised in Paris, who works as a model for a New York-based couture house. Openly preoccupied with the question of how Lamarr could be assimilated, the film introduces her as the love interest/reward for the dedicated American physician Karl Decker (Spencer Tracy). While Georgi's employer Madame Maresca asserts that Georgi 'was made for luxury,' Decker argues that 'She's too useful a citizen to go to waste,' and acts as the negotiating figure in Georgi's transformation from aristocratic hauteur to public-minded benevolence. The film stresses that assimilation entails the rejection of any signs of aristocratic privilege and at the close, Georgi is happily installed in her husband's Lower East Side clinic, catering to an assimilating population.

I Take This Woman established a pattern which would continue through much of Lamarr's career in which she is placed as an exotic reward for a virtuous, white American male. Yet a more complicated and ambivalent film like *Ziegfeld Girl* (1941), a musical co-starring Judy Garland and Lana Turner, represented Lamarr as a virtuous and innocent immigrant, even while it registered some uncertainty about the starmaking process. The film's most startling moment of rupture takes places where its subtext on assimilation breaks out into the open and in a most unexpected place, a musical number performed by Garland, in which Lamarr herself does not appear. In 'Minnie from Trinidad,' Garland recounts the story of a girl from a small village in Trinidad, who is 'discovered,' and brought to Hollywood and her last name changed to Lamarr. The number provides a strikingly self-reflexive moment of ambivalent commentary on the importation of foreign female stars even while it tropicalizes Hedy Lamarr just as did many of her other films (*Lady of the Tropics* [1939] and *White Cargo* [1942] in particular).[27]

In films of the late 1940s and 1950s, Lamarr loses a certain degree of ingenue innocence. In many of her film roles, Lamarr is hyperbolically predatory in settings carefully distanced from contemporary American culture. Lois W. Banner has aptly noted that:

> Alongside the adolescent, asexual models of beauty existed the voluptuous earthy one. As Ava Gardner, Dorothy Lamour, and Hedy Lamarr portrayed them, their sensuality was so florid that their films were often

set in foreign climes, where they could portray fallen women outside the bounds of society.[28]

Even on such careful diegetic terms, some of Lamarr's films generated controversy, as it seems that the star's exotic sexuality was always threatening to slip out of bounds. The actress herself recalled that in *White Cargo* strategic editing choices minimized the display of her eroticism on screen: 'I was proud of my authentic African dance, which I rehearsed for weeks, and which gave me splinters in my feet. It was done with a bed showing in the background, and it was so sexy almost all of the scene was cut.'[29]

David Savran contends that:

> In dominant representations of gender from the '40s well into the '60s, femininity was squarely positioned on the side of 'nature,' sexuality, and irrationality, whereas masculinity was equated with 'culture,' intellect and reason. According to the logic of Cold War culture, it was the task of men to control, domesticate, and rationalize women and their dark sexuality, to ensure that 'feminine' would forever remain a synonym for 'submissive.'[30]

The Lamarr films of this period actively attempt to fulfill the cultural mandate Savran describes, but they seldom do so with complete success. A number of Lamarr's screen roles for MGM reference her exotic sexuality, staging it as a threat to whiteness. Lamarr's appearance (in dark body paint) in *White Cargo* presents an especially useful case study of the dynamics of this process. In this film Lamarr plays Tondelayo, a woman believed to be half African/half Caucasian, but who, it is revealed late in the film, is in fact half Egyptian and half Arab.[31] The film's trailer gives strong evidence of Lamarr/Tondelayo's liminal narrative role in the film, promoting her as 'Tender . . . and treacherous! Delightful . . . and deadly! Romantic . . . and ruthless! The most intriguing enchantress in the world of entertainment.'

The principal story unfolds in flashback from the perspective of present time, as two white male narrators reflect on their experiences on an island rubber plantation in the Congo in 1910. In its prefacing dialogue, the film engages issues of whiteness from the start and demonstrates that international economic competition and the demand for wartime productivity necessitate encounters with exotic cultures. 'A white man can't take this African culture as a steady diet,' says Jim Fish. But Worthing, a veteran of the rubber trade in Africa, tells him, 'With the Japs in Malaya, we need rubber, more rubber.' Thus, by demonizing the Japanese and establishing the Anglo-American cause as a necessary response to Japanese imperialism, *White Cargo* sets itself up as simultaneously an enactment and a disavowal of American interventionism as a rationale for economic exploitation. It camouflages Anglo-American imperial interests (differentiating 'our cause' from that of the war-mongering Japanese imperialists) and uses ethnic femininity as the catalyst for the Anglo male's descent into nativism.

As Worthing begins to reminisce, we flash back to the plantation of 1910, a grim locale whose residents include a leader, Harry Witzel (Walter Pidgeon, the film's co-star), an alcoholic doctor, and Langford, a worker who is to replace Wilbur Ashley, whose experience in the tropical heat of the Congo has driven him mad. (The film's trailer makes clear the nature of the real threat, however, sensationally announcing that 'It wasn't the heat that drove Ashley crazy. It was Tondelayo!') In this atmosphere of fading gentility and rampant alcoholism, Langford comes to embody the decadence that can come about when whites are removed from their governing cultural context.

Witzel, judging from appearances, has 'gone native.' Unshaven and unkempt, he complains ceaselessly about the rigid and overly civilized ways of the men who are sent to assist him, and is immediately antagonistic toward Langford, whose constant refrain that '[he'll] be all right once he's had a chance to get acclimatized' infuriates Witzel, who hears the remark as a too revealing insight into his own adaptations to jungle culture. Witzel can also communicate with the natives where the less adept whites cannot. Despite his sharp wit and veteran status, however, Witzel remains at best an ambiguous hero in a community marked by physical and social 'damp rot.' When Langford is immediately apprised of this condition in the walls of the plantation's structures, it is clear that the 'damp rot' serves as a metaphor for the community's decaying whiteness. Although the doctor advises Langford to 'take no notice of them – they're all sunbathers,' Langford closely attends to Witzel's advice for living successfully on the plantation, namely to avoid the local women.

When Langford retires to his cabin to reflect, Tondelayo appears, an incarnation of the possibility that whiteness can go native (for as we learn, she has previously qualified as white). Intrigued by her beauty, Langford is strenuously warned away by the other whites in a conversation that reveals the true stakes of the film: the struggle to keep to the rituals that hold whiteness precariously in place in a threateningly foreign setting. A visiting missionary, Reverend Roberts, begins the conversation by telling Langford of the dangers Tondelayo represents.

Roberts: It's the hardest fight we have. As soon as we teach a few women to cook and sew and speak a dozen words of our language, some white tries to turn it to his own advantage.

Langford: Why shouldn't he?

Witzel: Because the end is always in the beginning. It's always the whites who become the more degraded.

Langford: It's ridiculous to blame her for every white man who loses his balance.

Roberts: With all her faults, she has an innate morality.

Witzel: She's too high and mighty for the natives, and too smart for the white man.

With this, the group begins to sing 'There's No Place Like Home,' until a somber fade-out signals the end of this grim ceremony of resistance before the advances of ethnic femininity, and this short-lived episode of male camaraderie is never repeated. The film will shortly demonstrate that these tenuous loci of social stability are illusory, revealing whiteness to be not innate, but socially constructed, as Langford falls victim to the predatory advances of Tondelayo.

Enamored of the silk and beads Langford can buy her, and apparently having exhausted other male resources in the area, Tondelayo schemes to seduce Langford and he is soon asking the Reverend Roberts to marry them. The other whites are scandalized. 'Even out in this country we live up to certain stand-ards,' the doctor tells him. At this point the Reverend reveals that Tondelayo is not the half-breed they had presumed, but is, in fact, at least marginally white, and a shameful example of the failure of the white religious education system. (She has rejected her convent teachings). He had concealed her true ethnic status, the Reverend admits, because 'Tondelayo could only mean another ex-ample of our failure.' On this basis, however, he is obliged to honor Langford's request for him to preside over a marriage ceremony. Jubilant, Langford taunts Witzel, 'Get that? I'm marrying one of us!' to which Witzel replies 'What difference does that make? I'm not arguing about geography, it's what she is that counts.'

Langford's marriage to Tondelayo predictably proves his ruination. After Tondelayo finally catalyzes a physical argument between Witzel and Langford, Langford develops a fever, enabling Tondelayo to replace the quinine pre-scribed by the doctor with a jungle poison. When Witzel discovers the ruse, he administers Tondelayo's poison to her, whereupon she runs screaming into the jungle and dies. Langford is shipped back to civilization (becoming the 'white cargo' of the film's title) and Worthing, Langford's replacement, arrives to close the flashback.

White Cargo thus narrativizes the effective management of ethnic female sexuality, retaining a contemporary (1940s) resonance, yet through the struc-turing use of flashback, managing to convey a 'here's how we dealt with these problems in the good old days' flavor. However, by representing the film's hero (an anti-social outcast) as the only character empowered to extinguish the threat to whiteness, the film raises certain questions with respect to the capacity of a white community to protect itself against the threat of ethnic femininity, and Tondelayo's status as marginally white is the film's most uncontained and potentially most subversive element. Furthermore, our return to the frame story of Worthing and Jim makes clear the impossibility of viewing the 1910 events through the lens of seamless nostalgia, for as Worthing concludes his reminscence at the point of his own arrival, his companion prompts him, 'And you became acclimatized?' Worthing's sharp and sudden reply, 'Don't you ever use that word to me!' suggests that he has been reproduced in the mode of Witzel, a capable guardian of white purity whose knowledge of ethnic femininity has contaminated his own whiteness.

Consequently, the film's linkages between whiteness and rigidity and boundary definition perfectly accord with Richard Dyer's insights into the narrative function of whiteness in a number of Hollywood films.[32] In this film, Lamarr/Tondelayo functions to literally 'color' whiteness; not only has she had her own whiteness symbolically compromised through the application of body makeup, it is her influence that leads the civilized white men to engage in the kind of violence culturally associated with blackness. As Dyer points out, 'The implication is that the situation evokes in whites the kind of irrational violence supposedly specific to blacks. Of course, being white means being able to repress it . . . such repression constitutes the stoic glory of the imperial hero.'[33]

The key feature of the ending here is the representation of a possibility of rupturing the heroic repression into which Worthing has been schooled by Witzel. In this regard, then, *White Cargo* represents whiteness as contested and only ambivalently re-established. In coming to a conclusion which amplifies, rather than eradicates white trauma, the film thus interrogates the terms of white dominance and purity it apparently rehearses. In registering the vulnerability of the white interventionist cause to the lure of ethnic femininity, *White Cargo* represents an early use of Lamarr as an obstacle to American global hegemony. In the period after World War Two, she would become less an obstacle and more an accessory for such enterprises.

'Hedy is really a homebody:' domesticity and motherhood

After achieving box-office success and cultivating a more sanitized brand of sexuality in such films as *Algiers*, Hedy Lamarr was successfully incorporated into the Hollywood ideological system, at this stage of her career increasingly figured as the stay-at-home type. Such domesticating strategies enabled Lamarr to be converted from an impediment to interventionism to a participant in the interventionist cause. As if to counteract the notoriety of the actress's role in *Ecstasy*, numerous articles carefully delineated between Lamarr and her film roles and provided strenuous insistence that she was a dedicated wife who eschewed an active social life. The ongoing discursive thread underscored the fact that, in the words of one writer, 'Hedy is really a homebody.'[34] As early as 1939, domesticity was a dominant discourse in fan magazine treatment of the actress, with Gladys Hall assuring her readers that:

> If, therefore, you are under the impression that marriage and Hedy Lamarr are incompatibles, you are completely mistaken. If you imagine that the rich oil of orchid which you think is Hedy and the bread-and-butter commonplaceness which you think is marriage don't mix successfully – you don't know Hedy as I know Hedy.[35]

That Lamarr's domesticity should be emphasized when she was frequently divorced and re-married is particularly striking, and underscores the ideological imperatives that drove such accounts. Reading fan magazine articles on Lamarr in the 1940s, the name of her husband changes, but the discourse on her commitment to a stable and quiet home life never does.

Some fan magazine pieces crafted a quasi pastoral narrative of Lamarr's life in California, representing her as a country girl rather than an urban sophisticate. Gladys Hall wrote of Lamarr and husband Gene Markey:

> They hope, in time, to add ten acres to their land and they plan, then, to have chickens, cows, ducks and all the farmyard animals with their sleepy, homey noises, their substances of milk and butter and eggs. No longer need Hedy, bejewelled, magnificent and mask-like, preside over dinner parties which are affairs of state. Now, wearing the Austrian peasant dirndls she loves, she entertains Gene's bachelor friends and often their closest friends Myrna Loy and Arthur Hornblow.[36]

Other accounts took care to stress Lamarr's hyphenated ethnic identity. As Sara Hamilton wrote in 1938, 'Hedy, who has applied for her first papers, is rapidly becoming a full-fledged American with Continental "umph."'[37] Such descriptions hint at the liminality at the core of Lamarr's persona, and the way in which she came to serve as a testament to the positive outcome of interventionism by embodying a kind of productive tension between Americanness and Europeanness, between 'classical' or natural beauty and the transforming work of MGM.

While being depicted as a neutralized European threat, Lamarr was also represented as positively connected to a praiseworthy European heritage. Indeed, a number of references directly or implicitly praise Lamarr for sincerely retaining non-threatening European attributes while transforming herself to accord with American norms.[38] While it was reported that Lamarr had appropriately socialized herself by learning English from American films, a 1945 article, for instance, praised, 'this beautiful woman who goes about the business of life with Old World simplicity and common sense.'[39] Another attributed Lamarr's domestic frugality to her national background, observing approvingly that, 'Hedy is economical, too. These middle-European women are amazing, the way they mix elixir of passion flower with the good brown flour of common sense, as deftly as any house-wife tossed together a batch of shortenin' bread.'[40]

Thus, when Lamarr's perceived European attributes are mentioned, it is frequently in the context of domesticity and non-aristocratic class positioning. Strongly disassociating Europeanness from any type of power position, Lamarr becomes a 'peasant' in such accounts.

Significantly, during World War Two, magazine and newspaper coverage of Hedy Lamarr emphasized her dedication to the wartime cause, and filtered her behavior through the dual lenses of patriotism and productivity. Accounts of Lamarr's pregnancy in 1945, for example, stressed the actress's matter-of-fact approach and enumerated her daily routine of housework, quoting the actress as saying 'I am having a baby. Certainly. Who can't? The wives of your 120,000 soldiers have babies.'[41] A 'Truth or Consequences' style interview with Lamarr included such questions as: 'How much sugar did you have on hand during ration time?' 'Which is the blackout room in your home and how is it fixed?' and 'What are you doing for national defense?'[42] A captioned photo layout even mapped Lamarr's home largely according to a geography of patriotism, informing readers of facts such as: 'The patriotic color scheme of red, white and blue is the keynote of the dining room. The wallpaper is the American Beauty Rose pattern.'[43]

Some articles attributed Lamarr's patriotism to her good fortune in escaping an oppressive European past. One piece in particular represented the actress's work at the Hollywood Canteen in this light:

> She is lovely to look at. There's no argument about that. The movie fans will tell it to you, and so will the soldiers, sailors and Marines who visit the Hollywood Canteen. For this glamour girl, who used to eat from gold plates, now serves food to American service men at the Canteen on paper plates. She had her meals on gold plates when she was married to Fritz Mandl, millionaire munitions manufacturer. They lived in luxury, entertained foreign notables and resided in a castle.
>
> But she was virtually a prisoner there. She was not permitted to go about as she pleased. Then late one night in 1937, she ran away.
>
> And because she realizes what that freedom means, and because she wants to protect it, she is doing all she can to aid in the war effort.
>
> She has gone on Bond tours, she has played Army camps and she is at the Canteen every Friday night.[44]

Also indicative of Lamarr's conversion to American ideological norms and usefulness in propagandizing American nationalism were a remarkable series of news accounts in the fall of 1941 about the actress's 'secret weapon' for US defense. While these accounts suggest in rather evasive terms that Lamarr's sexuality was the 'secret weapon,' more recent articles indicate that apparently her invention was quite genuine. (A 1990 article alludes to Lamarr collaborating with another person on an idea for a sophisticated antijamming device for radio-controlled torpedoes).[45] Yet a 1941 piece described:

> Hedy Lamarr – screen siren and inventor.
>
> The film favorite yesterday for the first time was portrayed in this dual role.
>
> Her invention, held secret by the government, is considered of great potential value in the national defense program.

This was disclosed by Col. L.B. Lent, chief engineer of the National Inventors Council, now in Los Angeles on government business.[46]

Other articles complicated the distinction between Lamarr's defense 'secret weapon' and the actress herself, coyly commenting, for example, that 'Appropriately enough, her invention is listed as a "red hot prospect" in the files of the council.'[47] Although the tone of these news accounts is not entirely serious – mention is made that one as yet uninvented defense device of great value would be the death ray – such articles nevertheless conferred a strong degree of realism on Lamarr's persona as a model American by linking her explicitly to the serious subjects of technological prowess and wartime mobilization.

In this way, Lamarr's World War Two stardom exceeded the role that was assigned to her contemporaries, wartime 'pinup girls' such as Rita Hayworth and Betty Grable, but in certain respects came to resemble the actual roles undertaken by American women whose work in the technical wartime industries has been well documented. In a trenchant examination of the ways that women functioned as objects of obligation in World War Two, Robert B. Westbrook suggests that the image which has come to signify the end of the war, that of a nurse being passionately embraced by a sailor in Times Square, is altogether fitting for it portrays 'the consummation of the bargain between protector and protected'[48] that structured both the US interventionist stake and the mobilizing rhetoric soliciting American men to fight on behalf of their loved ones. The European emigre and implied victim status of Hedy Lamarr equipped her well to play a role as motivating icon of defense in wartime national mythology, yet there are suggestive flashes of agency that exceed that position as well.

'I knew you'd come over to my team:' Hedy Lamarr as interventionist accessory

As I have suggested, in the middle phase of her career, Hedy Lamarr frequently functioned as an ethnic woman who was acquired by a deserving American male protagonist. This is much the case in *Come Live With Me* (1941) in which the actress appears as Johanna Janns, a refugee having an affair with Barton Kendrick (Ian Hunter) an older, wealthy, aristocratic publisher. Learning that she is to be deported, Johanna arranges to marry Bill Smith (Jimmy Stewart), a struggling writer. Bill is fascinated by her, and writes his first successful story about her life (it gets sold to Kendrick's publishing house), and at the film's conclusion Johanna gives up Kendrick for Smith. In this film, then, the quintessentially American Jimmy Stewart acquires Lamarr as an icon of ethnic desirability from an implied European patriarch (his professional superior) in a process that mimics a broader shift in political and cultural power. In the process, Stewart is able to profitably exploit ethnic femininity (by narrativizing her life as a story he sells) uncannily enacting Hollywood's relationship to Lamarr as a star property. Similarly in *Dishonored Lady* (1947) Lamarr plays Madeleine Damien, a magazine editor whose suicidal tendencies are quelled through her involvement with two American men, effectively narrativizing the importance of guardianship over ethnic femininity. In this sense the film exemplifies the kinds of dramatic scenarios into which Hedy Lamarr was placed in the mid-1940s.

By 1951, Lamarr's representational function had shifted to better accord with her wartime and postwar domestication and the consolidation of American interventionist ideology. In films like *My Favorite Spy*, a Bob Hope comedy, Lamarr serves not only as the reward for a male protagonist's patriotism, but as an active agent of the interventionist agenda upon her conversion to American norms and values. Nevertheless, closure was necessarily linked to an insistence upon American male heroism even when the contribution of the ethnic female character was considerable. In this section, I want to provide a reading of the film that sees it as engaged in comedic interventionist propagandizing.

My Favorite Spy really stages two conversions – that of Hedy Lamarr as Lily Dalbray, a member of an international spy ring who transfers her allegiance to the Americans, and Bob Hope as Peanuts White, a burlesque comic who becomes a patriot. It is this latter transformation which opens the film when American government agents discover that White bears an exact physical resemblance to Eric Augustine, a foreign spy and the link to a German scientist who has developed a short cut to the hydrogen bomb now contained on a piece of microfilm. The government agents treat the rambunctious White with intense seriousness (at one point they are framed against a backdrop of a world map, a sign of the crucial need to maintain and defend American global interests)[49] and induce him to impersonate Augustine by appealing to his innate patriotism. (The unruly White turns instantly serious when the President calls him, removing his hat and noting soberly, 'I hold the fate of the whole world in my hands.)'

The film is structured as a fantasy that even the average American male can glorify himself through the international defense of American interests. By using Bob Hope in a fundamentally comic role, however, the film carefully differentiates between humane American masculinity and the exploitative cruelty of the European male. Eric Augustine serves as the film's representative of misogynistic, deadly cosmopolitanism. One government official previews Lamarr's entrance in the film by alluding to her past relationship with Augustine as follows: 'And women? He was irresistible, a magnet for international beauty that could lead him to more funding. He exploited them, slapped 'em around, and threw 'em away like matches.'

Sent to Tangier to recover the crucial microfilm, White soon meets Lily Dalbray who comments, 'You're here for a purpose,' to which he responds (in an assertion of the American interventionist mandate), 'I'm everywhere for a purpose.' White's cosmopolitan masquerade is both comical and significant, indicative of the requirement to shift cultural identity in order to negotiate global terrain. Impersonating Eric Augustine, White mimics aristocratic condescension, ordering wine for all the diners in a restaurant, and telling the wine steward, 'If there's not enough to go around, have the peasants jump on some more grapes.' Although White is able to recover the microfilm from a sinister band of Germans headed by Herr Koenig, matters are significantly complicated by the intervention of Karl Brubaker, the head of the international spy ring. As Brubaker, Lily Dalbray, White, and even Eric Augustine (who has managed to flee the US), all contend for the microfilm, Lily falls in love with White and transfers her allegiance to his cause. 'I thought I hated you, but I don't. You're an entirely new person. You're sweet and warm and not like the old Eric at all,' she tells him. White exhorts her, 'Lily, you've got to change your whole pattern of living. Give it up – we both have to.' Possession of ethnic femininity empowers the clownish White to accomplish extraordinary feats, but it is Lily who starts a fire to deter Brubaker at a crucial late point in the narrative. As the two make their escape, White tells Lily happily, 'I knew you'd come over to my team.'

In the film's conclusion, which stages interventionism as a circus in which Peanuts can perform, Lamarr and Hope engage in further transformative antics, camouflaging themselves as firefighters to escape detection. Although Lily is a significant participant in helping to contend against the international threat as the two join forces to retrieve the microfilm and bring about the arrest of Brubaker, it is White who garners credit for the mission. When he is congratulated by an American governmental official, who tells him, 'You've done a great service for your country' he responds, 'I haven't done badly for myself either' (indicating Lily). Thus, *My Favorite Spy* concludes by equating patriotism with the acquisition of ethnic femininity, a move which entails the reduction of Lily to the status of a possession or token of international service.[50]

The repressed Nazi past and fantasies of rescue

As the earlier account of Lamarr's volunteer work at the Hollywood Canteen suggests, throughout the actress's career, surprisingly frequent mention is made of her first husband, Austrian Fritz Mandl, who circulates through the narrative of Lamarr's life as a kind of incarnation of a grim European past. Described variously as a 'munitions magnate,' a 'munitions king,' and a 'munitions czar,' Mandl is invoked time and again as the sinister figure who catalyzed Lamarr's flight from Europe. By resorting to a discourse of aristocracy to allude to Lamarr's past (Mandl as 'king' or 'czar'), these accounts sharpened the distinction between America and Europe, suggesting that Lamarr's past was synonymous with anti-democratic oppression.[51] Hedda Hopper provided a typical characterization of Mandl, calling him 'the wealthy, powerful, sinister munitions manufacturer who fled Europe as it toppled and is now piling up new wealth in Argentina.'[52]

Gossip columnists such as Hopper forged a fictionalized biography for Lamarr which narrativized her choice to leave her husband and come to the United States as a story of flight and salvation. In such a narrative, Mandl became the symbol of a war-making patriarchal culture (which is one reason why it is endlessly repeated that he was in the munitions business), and indeed is rendered a figurative Nazi through his association with the provision of arms, his 'sinister' nature, and his flight to Argentina. (One account even transformed Mandl into a 'German munitions magnate').[53] Here is Hopper's succinct account of the events that led to Lamarr's contract with MGM:

> She had everything in the world that money could buy, but not a penny in her purse and no happiness. I got a mental picture of him [Fritz Mandl] as a cross between Napoleon and Mussolini. What a combination that would be to live with! Hedy escaped him twice. The third and final time was when she was lucky enough to get on a boat coming to America, which also contained Mr. and Mrs. Louis B. Mayer and Benny Thau. They met when they were half across and a film contract was offered her. She has divorced her husband since coming to America.[54]

Eliding a tour through Europe taken by Lamarr which led her to London, Paris and the Riviera among other destinations before heading to the US, this history strains credulity somewhat in light of the fact that although fleeing for her life from an oppressive tyrant, Lamarr was able to book passage on a luxury ocean liner. More significantly, this fictional version of Lamarr's private history de-emphasized her agency in choosing to come to the US, re-orienting the terms of that decision to position Lamarr as a victim and Louis B. Mayer as her rescuer. As I have suggested, these elements of Lamarr's biography propounded an implicit interventionist argument which centered on the placement of Lamarr as a beautiful victim in an inferior, bellicose nation (embodied here by Fritz Mandl). Lamarr's placement in a rescue fantasy whose structuring terms are a malevolent European past and a benign American present would recur not only in her publicity but in the film narratives in which she appeared. It is in this context of Lamarr's fervent patriotism and fictionalized flight from European oppression that I want to turn to a discussion of *Lady Without a Passport* (1950), a film made late in Lamarr's career, which forcefully engages the interventionist rescue fantasy which I have suggested was a structuring element of Lamarr's persona.

Lady Without A Passport strongly thematizes issues of American border regulation, from the very opening of the film which features prominent acknowledgement made to an Assistant Commissioner and Investigator at the US Immigration and Naturalization Service.[55] The film's real-world connections seem to have been implicit in the review discourses on *Lady Without a Passport* as well. One reviewer warned that:

> Any foreigner thinking of sneaking into the US without a passport had better take a look at 'Lady Without A Passport,' opening yesterday at the Orpheum and Hawaii Theatres. Uncle Sam has many eyes, all peeled, for such . . . US immigration methods are all shown, plus romance, thrills and Hedy Lamarr.[56]

Interestingly, MGM's press book for the film seems to overstate Lamarr's narrative agency, implying that her role is that of a predatory woman, when, in fact, the film quickly shuts down Lamarr's agency, reducing her to the status of a victim contested over by the INS agent hero and sinister ethnic villain, and literally led about through the last third of the film. The narrative action begins with the killing of an illegal alien, Ramon Santez, in an urban milieu where space is ethnically charged. (The film opens with an extended tracking shot of Santez walking past an Italian grocery store toward a Chinese restaurant, which serves as the backdrop for his dramatic death.) When the local police are unable to find any record of Santez, they conclude that it 'looks like a job for the Immigration boys,' and refer the case to the INS, instigating the heroic interventions of the immigration agents which structure the film.

An INS Inspector, Pete Karczag (John Hodiak) tracks Santez's course through Miami to Cuba, where he soon learns of the Gulf Stream Cafe, run by the sinister Palinov, who assists aliens in getting to the United States. Karczag decides to masquerade as Joseph, a disgruntled Hungarian seeking entry to the US, and he goes to the American Embassy where he stages his own refused admittance, and loudly airs his complaints to catch Palinov's attention. As Karczag walks through the streets of Havana in the white suit he wears throughout the film, he is framed in low-angle shots that emphasize his superiority to the local population. In one telling instance, a small boy runs into the street only to be guided back to the sidewalk by Karczag, with a fond pat on the head that drips of colonial condescension. When Palinov approachs Karczag, his villainy is marked by his ethnic fluidity – he greets the INS agent in fluent Hungarian.[57] At the Gulf Stream Cafe, Karczag meets Marianne Lorress (Lamarr), a Viennese woman whose father has been illegally residing in the US for ten years. Turned down at the American Embassy, Marianne has been forced to seek Palinov's help in getting to the US. Later that evening, Karczag finds Marianne (who has been thrown out of her apartment) in a nightclub where the police have been called due to her refusal to work in the flimsy costume she has been assigned as a cigarette girl. Karczag intervenes, and takes Marianne to his hotel where a besotted bellboy testifies that 'That girl could sell me cigarettes, and I don't smoke.'

Upstairs Marianne forestalls Karczag's advances in a speech that articulates one of the strongest critiques of law and authority in a film which otherwise reveres such institutions. 'For ten years, they've driven me and everyone like me across the world. You can't stay here. We have laws. Get out! But where? Where can I go? Now I'm in Cuba. I may stay, but I can't work. The law says don't earn your living or you'll be deported. Earn your bread on the street!' In the midst of this speech Karczag notices a tattoed number on her arm, and Marianne adds bitterly, 'Another souvenir of the law – Buchenwald!' The revelation that Marianne is a Holocaust survivor is not only profoundly disruptive to the narrative flow (for a contemporary spectator the moment is deeply disquieting, although it is difficult to know whether the information would have been as shocking to an audience in 1950), it also significantly re-orients Marianne's status in the film, altering her from an autonomous, decisive woman to a victim. By invoking Nazi oppression, however briefly,[58] the film is able to contrast European imperialism with American democracy more forcefully and engage a fantasy of rescue whereby Marianne's grim European past qualifies her for the benevolent intervention of the American INS inspector.

From this point forward in the narrative, Marianne is a passive object contested by Pete Karczag and Palinov. She remains on the margins while Pete realizes that she is innocently unaware of Palinov's schemes and the stakes are raised in terms of the conflict between the two men. When Marianne tells Karczag, 'you know what it means to me to go to America,' he rebukes her saying 'Some are not so impatient, they wait to enter legally.' The two fall in love, however, and for the sake of their being together, Marianne agrees to stay with Karczag in Cuba. The INS agent demonstrates his integrity by preparing a letter to send to his supervisor, indicating that he may stay in Cuba and resign from the service. When Palinov exposes Karczag's real identity to Marianne, however, she leaves and joins the group of European aliens he is smuggling into the US. As Karczag dictates to the Cuban police how to handle the situation, and relays the information about Palinov's activities to the INS, Marianne and the others are provided with forged documentation papers and board a secret plane bound for Florida.

Frank Westlake, Karczag's INS supervisor, meanwhile receives the information from Karczag and pores through the files of the alien group. We learn that one of the aliens has turberculosis and so falls short of immigration health standards, another was previously naturalized but deported, and one greedily plots to avoid paying duty on the jewelry she brings into the country. (Although why paying a large sum of money to Palinov instead is a better option is unclear). The aliens further demonstrate their ineligibility for the privileges of American citizenship by complaining to one another. 'What kind of a country is this? Even in the air in the United States police follow,' says one. Throughout all of this Marianne stays quiet, just as when the INS officials scan the files of the other aliens, she is represented only by a sketch of her beautiful profile, rather than a thick dossier on her history. In place of the damaging information we learn about each of the other members of the group, the film substitutes Marianne's beauty as her qualification for citizenship.

As the INS agents obsessively map the American coastline wondering where the alien group will land, Palinov's pilot decides to make a re-fueling stop in Jacksonville, and when he sees a posted warning with their plane number on it, and noticing a technician on the phone, he panics and draws attention to their whereabouts. The INS sends up navy planes, and we experience the ensuing action through the aerial camera motivated by one of the navy pilots who also provides accompanying commentary as the alien plane makes a crash landing. When Palinov takes Marianne and the pilot into the small lifeboat, and sends the remaining aliens into the woods, the pilot helpfully mentions such details as the presence of alligators and water moccasins. The INS agents mobilize to provide assistance, and when protocol dictates that they go after the group in the woods, Karczag insists on searching for Marianne, telling Westlake, 'One of the people in that boat is an alien, and I want to go after her.' He shortly catches up with the group on a dock where Palinov tells Marianne she can make her choice, and though Karczag tells her he would have to arrest her, she chooses to stay with him anyway. Karczag sabotages Palinov's getaway boat, and confident in the knowledge that he will shortly be in INS custody, strolls with Marianne along the dock. 'Millions of people right now are pretty happy to be right where they are,' he tells her. 'But when someone wants to go somewhere else so badly that they'll risk their lives, then it's time for me to help them, not turn them away.' Marianne calls Karczag Joseph, the name by which she has known him, and he corrects her, to close the film as follows:

Pete: Not Joseph, Karczag. Pete Karczag.
Marianne: Karczag? Pete Karczag – A real American name.

The complexity of *Lady Without a Passport*'s representation of ethnicity lies in part in its somewhat ambivalent championing of the absorptive capacities of American culture. Though this is put across straightforwardly in the film's conclusion, other narrative elements would seem to counter the invocation of assimilation through coupling as a method of closure. It is through the relationship to ethnicity that the film distinguishes its villain (who is engaged in false ethnic impersonation) from its hero, who legitimately retains elements of an ethnic past. Although the film never says it outright, Karczag is marked by name and his fluent and convincing adoption of the persona of 'Joseph' as a Hungarian-American. In one remarkable exchange, he even suggests a critique of the American myth of social incorporation:

Marianne: Havana does look lovely.
Karczag: It's a way station – the last one. Then the United States.
Marianne: Is it everything people dream about?
Karczag: I don't know. It is what many have dreamed. But others whose dreams have edges which are too round, colors too bright, they are disappointed.
Marianne: Oh, I'm not looking for streets paved with gold. A home, respect, freedom, and neighbors who want the same thing.
Karczag: Marianne, don't hope for too much.
Marianne: I'm just beginning to hope.
Karczag: Even if things go as you expect, I've been to the United States; a little thing like an accent, a foreign name can set you apart.

Despite such critique, *Lady Without a Passport* largely stands as a drama of social incorporation founded on the sanitization of the sexualized European exotic in

the context of a struggle for control of ethnic femininity between two competing masculinities: that of the unscrupulous ethnic and that of the heroic and
virtuous American. As we have seen, by 1950, this film narrative would have
born a strong intertextual resemblance to Hedy Lamarr's biographical narrative.
Furthermore, as the notion of Marianne's redemption through naturalizaton is
the unspoken center of the film, with her Nazi past powerfully invoked, then
instantly put aside, certain implicit links may have been suggested between
Palinov and Fritz Mandl as dual representative incarnations of a threatening,
contentious European past, and the misuse of ethnic femininity whose true
value could be accessed only through American interventionist maneuvers.

Ethnic femininity and scandal

Hedy Lamarr was imported from Europe after a European film titled
'Ecstasy' exposed her briefly, out of focus and nude. Around Newark,
N.J., in the mid-1930s, and probably throughout the rest of moral
America, 'Ecstasy' was considered such vicious temptation to the libido
that it ran for months in little out-of-the-way theatres.[59]

Despite a large body of work in Hollywood films, Hedy Lamarr was inextricably
linked throughout her career to *Ecstasy*, the obscure Czech film made in 1933.
The film's notoriety, as I have suggested, was tied to a sequence in which the
actress appeared nude (although by contemporary standards, the scene would
be judged only minimally explicit). The history of *Ecstasy* provides an illuminating case study of celebrity production and control activities relevant both to
Hedy Lamarr and to stardom in general. In the first wave of connections
between the actress and the film at the time of her arrival in Hollywood, *Ecstasy*
was figured as a 'mistake,' an inappropriate display of sexuality associated with
the culture she was leaving behind. In the second wave of linkages in the 1950s,
the film was cited as titillating proof of Lamarr's essential erotic nature. Particularly when Lamarr's role as an icon of interventionist attainment dwindled,
interest in and (it would appear) circulation of *Ecstasy* was heightened, re-
activating discourses on a sordid European past and an ungovernable sexuality.
Relatively late in Lamarr's career, consistent mention was made of the film –
Americans learned, for example, of Fritz Mandl's extensive (but ultimately unsuccessful) efforts to purchase every existing print. Even in contexts in which it
was apparently not relevant, reporters and others sought to contextualize the
actress's real-life activities through the film. For example, a brief article noting
Lamarr's honeymoon with Ted Stauffer in 1951, read as follows, 'Black-haired
Hedy Lamarr, whose film fame began when she swam in the nude in *Ecstasy*,
today was honeymooning with her fourth husband, Ernest (Ted) Stauffer,
Acapulco night club operator, after a surprise ceremony last night.'[60]

Mention of the film could also disrupt the kind of standard adulatory feature
articles which helped to implant a sense of Lamarr as safely sexual. In May

Figure 8 The Breen Office's photograph of the Rialto Theatre's lobby display for *Ecstasy/ My Life* with Hedy Lamarr.

1951, for instance, it was reported that 'Hedy Lamarr blew her top yesterday when she caught a look at a pre-publication copy of *Look* magazine for June 5, with a picture of the star "swimming in the nude."'[61] The accompanying still, of course, was from the notorious swimming scene in *Ecstasy*. This debate over the *Look* article instantiates the seemingly irresistible attraction presented to Hollywood commentators by the film, and this attraction is worth considering in depth. The scandal associated with *Ecstasy* was the defining element in a continuous scandalous subtext in Lamarr's persona, keeping her dark European past always hovering at the margins while Lamarr was superficially domesticated.

Before going on, a brief plot synopsis of the film is in order. *Ecstasy* details the tragedy inspired and suffered by a young bride named Eva, who is married to an older and apparently sexually incapacitated man. A tellingly prominent photograph of the man's mother, which he gazes at on his wedding night, hints of excessive maternal devotion as the implied source of difficulty. Eva returns to her father's house when she perceives the constraints of her marriage. When her father urges her to return to her husband, telling her, 'You have your whole life before you,' she tells him, 'Exactly, that's just it.' Lonely and bewildered, Eva rides her horse to a nearby pond one day. While she is swimming her horse gallops away in response to a mating call, taking her clothing with it. The horse and the clothes are retrieved by David, an engineer whose virility is presented as an obvious contrast to the shortcomings of Eva's husband.

Eva and David spend an evening together at his cabin, and make plans to meet again soon at an inn. When Eva returns to her father's house, she finds that he and her husband have been waiting for her. The husband argues for a reconciliation, but Eva declines. As he drives away, he slows the car down to pass through an engineering site, and it so happens that he gives the engineer a ride to town. Already distraught over Eva's refusal, the husband recognizes a necklace as the young man puts it into his pocket, and the realization drives him to suicidal ends. The three protagonists converge at the inn, where Eva and David enjoy a happy reunion. As they celebrate with music and dancing, the husband sees them from above, and apparently disgusted with his own incapacity, writes a short suicide note to his mother. The festive music downstairs is dramatically interrupted by a gunshot, leading the couple to go upstairs together where he recognizes his companion and she her husband. David says the suicide is terrible for the older man may have loved someone, as they do. Eva rather ambiguously refers to the man as being in love with her, but the conversation is abruptly ended, and the couple leave for the train station. Waiting for the train to Berlin, David falls asleep. Eva gently kisses him goodbye, then steps into the path of an oncoming train. At the conclusion, the engineer re-visits the countryside where he first saw Eva, surrounded by lush images of springtime, and fantasizes about the children they might have had together.

Controversial from the start, *Ecstasy*, inspired debate in Europe well before it ever had any exhibition in the United States. Fred Stein observed that:

> Having won the Prague State Prize for Excellence, the film was exhibited at the International Exposition in Venice in the summer of 1934, where it attracted the biggest crowds and became the object of furious praise and blame. *L'Osservatore Romano*, official organ of the Vatican, denounced it and deplored its popularity. The fame of the picture spread to all the nations of the world, and in nearly every country it has been banned. The Nazis displayed a degree of originality when they stated in *Der Angriff* that it was suppressed in Germany because Hedy Kiesler is Jewish.[62]

Ecstasy was also strongly associated with scandal in an American context. Before it was shown in the US, the *Hollywood Citizen* noted that 'a film, *Ecstasy*, which deals so frankly with a young girl's emotions that Germany banned it, is now shocking blase Paris – in defiance of the French government's ban.'[63] Not surprisingly, *Ecstasy* was viewed as morally and socially anathema by the newly-formed Hays Office, responsible for administering the Production Code, that mode of self-regulation which had been adopted by the Hollywood film industry. Indeed, it appears that the film's timing was quite disadvantageous, for it appeared in a period when the Motion Picture Producers and Distributors of America (MPPDA)[64] through the Hays Office was taking a strong stance against films which were perceived to be immoral or indecent.

Based on the Motion Picture Association of America (MPAA) Production Code Files, it appears that the Hays Office (only nominally overseen by Will Hays and run in detail by Joseph Breen) kept close tabs on *Ecstasy* from the start. A short article on August 8, 1935, noted that the only print of the film in the United States had been burned on July 27 by agents of the government adhering to an order by Federal Judge John C. Knox.[65] However, a report dated July 21, 1936, by Charles R. Metzzer of the Production Code Administration Office (submitted to Hays with a covering memo from Breen) makes clear not only that illicit screenings of the film were ongoing, but that the film's banned status was being used as a promotional ploy. Metzzer refers to the film as 'highly – even outrageously – indecent,' and describes the film's reception at a screening in New Jersey as follows:

> The picture is rather delicately done. There was a packed theatre to witness it and the audience was very quiet and orderly, and the few comments by persons sitting near the reviewer indicated that many of the people did not understand the picture very well, but had come out of curiosity due to the sensational ads in the lobby which indicated that this was a banned picture by the federal government which was the last word in sensational nudity, and suggestiveness.[66]

A letter dated May 26, 1937, to William G. Smith at Jewel Productions (representing the interests of *Ecstasy*'s importer, Samuel Cummins) from Breen leaves little room for doubt as to the unacceptability of the film. The head of the Production Code Administration wrote that:

> It is our considered, unanimous judgment that the picture is definitely and specifically in violation of the Production Code. This violation is suggested by the basic story and by a number of the details, in that it is a story of illicit love and frustrated sex, treated in detail and without sufficient compensating moral values.[67]

Further communication from Breen to Hays on May 31, 1937, confirms that, 'Along with three other films, which were rejected for such reasons as depictions of veneral disease and white slavery, *Ecstasy* was rejected for its "improper treatment of illicit sex." '[68]

Ecstasy appears to have maintained a marginal but nearly continuous presence (mostly without PCA approval) in American film exhibition through the 1940s and 1950s while Hedy Lamarr was a major Hollywood star. Debates about additions and deletions to the film were ongoing, and Production Code Administration files suggest that the two most problematic sections of the film were the nude swimming scene and close-ups of Lamarr's face as she makes love with David. Significantly, in the version released for American consumption, a scene was inserted just before Eva and David spend the night together which tells us that Eva has received a divorce. The PCA, however, also mandated the addition of a further scene showing the marriage of Eva and David, and the re-titling of the film, to downplay its notorious history. Apparently, by the mid-1940s, negotiations had successfully concluded between the PCA and the film's American importers. But at this juncture, *Ecstasy* seems to have slipped further out of PCA control, as the film went through a confusing series of name changes and various versions of the film with different additions and deletions went into circulation. The agreed-upon title *Rhapsody of Love* was in some cases replaced by exhibitors with *My Life*, a title seemingly designed to punctuate the connection between the content of the film and the star biography of Hedy Lamarr. The American version of the film replaced 'Hedy Kiesler' with 'Hedy Lamarr' and gave her name top billing over the title, using sensationalized looking credits out of keeping with the tone and narrative style of the film to promote the movie as a scandalous text (or at least to frame what was by now a rather mundane film through a scandalous intertext). The *Motion Picture Herald* reported on Feburary 4, 1951 that a film entitled *My Life* was in exhibition but was disingenuously preceded by the title *Ecstasy* in large letters.[69]

A memorandum from Gordon S. White to Breen on January 27, 1951, registered great alarm at an unapproved version of the film being shown at the Rialto Theatre in New York. White presented a strong case for immediate action:

> We are presented with a very serious worry in the Rialto Theatre's exploitation of the picture *My Life* (formerly *Rhapsody of Love*).

> You are, of course, familiar with the record of the prolonged negotiations which preceded the granting of a Code Certificate of Approval for this picture, which is the revision or adaptation of the old picture *Ecstasy*, containing much new footage, complete new dialogue, and also eliminating the worst of the footage of the original *Ecstasy*, which produced such bad reaction generally.

> This picture is now being presented at the Rialto Theatre, with promotion which is completely false and misleading. The displays in front of the threatre and in the lobby and the newspaper ads which began to run today certainly would give the theatre patrons the idea that they were going to see the picture *Ecstasy*. The pictorial displays in the lobby are based on the still pictures from the original and on sensational news stories about the controversies over the original picture.[70]

White's memo concludes urging strong action to shut down the Rialto's exhibition:

> If we permit this Rialto display to get by, this type of exploitation will continue all over the country and we will be put in the most ridiculous position possible. This would appear to be one of the most flagrant double crosses in all the history of our dealings with difficult pictures, and definite and positive action certainly seems to be indicated.[71]

Photos of the sensationalistic promotional display in the foyer of the Rialto Theatre accompanied White's report.

A further memorandum from White to Breen on January 31, 1951, documented the film's transfer from the Rialto to the Times Theatre at 42nd Street and Eighth Avenue, noting that the version being exhibited did not contain the required scene of the marriage of Eva and David and that a display in front of the theatre touted the 'complete version' of the film. *Ecstasy*, it seems, never did come fully under Hays Office control, and managed to circulate as long as that office had any significant regulatory function. As a consequence, the film exemplified an omnipresent discourse of scandal that weighed against attempts to recuperate Lamarr's exotic European sexuality. Clearly, the intense surveillance and suppression campaigns conducted against *Ecstasy* reflect fundamentally similar strenuous attempts to keep positive meanings of ethnic femininity in place. Whereas for Fritz Mandl this positive meaning was the non-eroticized image of his trophy wife, for MGM and the Breen Office it was the bankability and ideological functionality of the Americanized post-scandal Hedy Lamarr. Nevertheless, these two attempts to erase Lamarr's scandalous history and transgressive display of eroticism were contrasted in press accounts and biographies of the actress, such that Mandl's campaign to purchase all the prints of *Ecstasy* was characterized as an example of his megalomaniacal quest for power while Hollywood's suppression of the film was seen as a justified and reasonable intervention.

Cheapening the value of celebrity: auction sales and shoplifting

> And of all the glamour queens, surely none was more glamorous than Hedy Lamarr. She seemed the definition of the word. Of all the stars of the forties and early fifties, she was probably the most classically beautiful, with those huge, marbly eyes, the porcelain-skin, the dreamy little smile, and the exotic voice that was an artful combination of Old Vienna and the MGM speech school.[72]

In articles such as the one cited above, Hedy Lamarr is warmly remembered using those transformative discourses which we have seen to be typical of virtually every stage of her career, represented as simultaneously American-produced and yet fundamentally European. There is, however, an almost chilling quality to the foregoing description, for although meant as a testament to the actress's beauty, the account reduces Lamarr to a doll-like figure frozen in time (or at least in the writer's memory). Other more recent public discourse on Hedy Lamarr runs strikingly counter to such dreamy recollections, however.

From the 1960s to the 1990s, Hedy Lamarr drew consistent press attention for shoplifting and for her litigious propensities (she seemed to be continually engaged in numerous lawsuits). Throughout much of her career, but especially after the 1950s when her career was perceived to be waning (or over), Lamarr was associated with a recurrent pattern of inappropriately exhibitionistic behavior in relation to commodities. The negative commentary surrounding this behavior suggests that stars are fundamentally authorized to engage in one kind of economic relationship (they sell themselves) and are not to be associated with low-level commerce. Two of the most consistently publicized forms of behavior were Lamarr's choice to hold auction sales of her possessions on several occasions, and her arrests for shoplifting of cosmetics and other items. Attention to these events took place in tandem with a certain stripping away of the positive dimensions of Lamarr's persona – emphasis on *Ecstasy* as a suppressed pornographic film, and suggestions that Lamarr was neither intelligent nor particularly charming pepper later accounts of her life and career. In some of these, as well, the actress increasingly became a blank. In 1952, Dorothy Kilgallen reported that a number of Lamarr's divorces were due to sheer boredom on the part of her husbands, and painted the actress as a dull and disappointed woman behind a glamorous facade. Writing about Lamarr's autobiography, *Ecstasy and Me*, in 1966, Myron Roberts stressed the 'waste of life' that he felt the actress's story communicated. 'Beauty is obviously to be seen, admired, even worshipped. Miss Lamarr, particularly, has been seen, admired, even worshipped by millions and yet there is a sense of terrible loss.'[73]

Press coverage of Lamarr's auction sales tended to be overtly or implicitly critical, conveying a sense that the actress had been indiscriminate and haphazard in the organization of her possessions for sale, or that Lamarr was not conforming to the market logic behind celebrity. In this sense, Lamarr's 'overexposure' may have punctured her remote desirability. Even the most sympathetic accounts of the auctions were tinged with a tone of nostalgic regret, seeming to suggest that an auction was an inappropriately public display. The *Saturday Evening Post*, for example, assigned the same reporter who had written a 1944 article on Lamarr describing a staged shopping trip with the actress, which implicitly praised her (wartime) display of moderation and sound economic sense to cover the 1951 auction. Punctuating the actress's fall from grace through the regretful tone of the demystified author, the piece even describes him finding a pair of pajamas Lamarr had purchased on their shopping trip together amongst the items available for purchase.[74] In an article summarizing Lamarr's career, Dorothy Kilgallen assessed the actress's periodic propensity to hold auction sales as either a bizarre personal trait or a publicity stunt.[75] A piece by Burt Prelatsky entitled 'Hedy . . . Going, Going, Gone' is typical of this sort of commentary (and also seems titled as a mean-spirited reference to Lamarr's waning fame). Prelatsky describes one of the auctions as follows:

> Much there certainly was, but crammed together as it was, you had the feeling that for $100 you could take the whole kit and kaboodle home with you . . . It all may have been glamorous in its accustomed sur-roundings, but here, as a solid mass of slightly erotic statuary, prints, candelabra, Christ figures, Passover plates, clocks, dishes, chandeliers, silverware, bottles, bric-a-brac by the ton and 16 mattresses, it looked like the result of the world's most ambitious scavenger hunt.[76]

What is particularly interesting in such accounts is the indirect criticism of Lamarr, for, in effect, demystifying her star persona. Prelatsky and others suggest almost that the actress gave away the tokens of her celebrity too cheaply, and by electing to hold an auction sale demonstrated a distorted relationship to commodities.[77] This may have been in part due to the frustrating illegibility of the possessions sold by Lamarr – why did she have both Christ figures and Passover plates, for example? Buyers and the general public could not glean any helpful information about Lamarr's private life from such an undifferentiated collection of items. Furthermore, by occasionally holding such auction sales throughout her career, Lamarr indirectly (but transgressively) intervened upon one of the foundational pleasures of stardom – the creation of a linear narrative about the star. Rather than building that narrative through accretion, Lamarr's periodic decision to sell her belongings at auction ruptured the continuity of her evolving persona, severing links to her own history.

Coverage of Lamarr's arrests for shoplifting appeared in the press as recently as 1991.[78] Interestingly, in Lamarr's first arrest for shoplifting in January 1966 (where she was charged with taking cosmetics and clothing from a May depart-ment store), her son and others defended the actress by citing her patriotic de-votion to the US. Christopher Young reports that, 'Her son Tony told reporters, "For the past thirty years my mother has been doing a great deal for the United States and the people in it and in return she has received a slap in the face – for nothing."'[79]

Similarly, Lamarr's daughter Denise pointed out that in just one day during World War Two her mother sold more than seven million dollars' worth of bonds. Why it was thought to be useful to invoke Lamarr as a 'good American' at this point is not fully clear, but it is certainly noteworthy that to counter any criticism of the actress, her publicists and family called upon her status as a contributor to American national mission.

Most reports of the shoplifting charges took note of the fact that Lamarr had numerous large checks in her purse at the time of her arrests, making it clear that it was not financial desperation that drove her to take the items. Reporting the arrest in August of that year, Lamarr was referenced as follows: 'The film siren – whose most famous quote was "Any girl can be glamorous; all you have to do is stand still and look stupid." '[80]

This quote is not altogether a random choice, for it suggests not only the kind of demystification shown to be associated with Lamarr's auctions, but the same kind of discrediting press attention shown to earlier ethnic 'sex goddesses' such as Pola Negri.[81] Not only were their later lives represented as the outcome of a fame that did not buy them long-lasting success or genuine personal fulfillment, but they were held as publicly accountable throughout their lives, whereas Colleen Moore retired into an untroubled privacy.[82] One potential explanatory frame for this would surely have to do with Negri and Lamarr's status as vamps whose sexualized ethnicities were, at some level, more disruptive than assimilative. In this context, the possibility of their converting from public to private life was seen to be impossible.[83] Colleen Moore is the distinctive exception here because her public tenure, as I discuss in Chapter 2, was limited by her positioning as a child – because her public life was constructed as asexual, her conversion to private status was sanctioned. For Negri and Lamarr, once sexualized in public, it seemed they could never go back. While it would be undoubtedly reductive to decisively establish a single explanatory paradigm for the hostile, largely condemnatory discourse applied to these actresses in full or semi-retirement, it seems likely that they hold in common an assertive sexuality that has made them perpetual public property, mystified in such a way that their aging or their mundane activitites are narrativized as a form of public punishment.[84]

In the specific case of Hedy Lamarr, we may note that such captious discourse emerges quite specifically in the late 1960s, at the historical moment when many Americans first became disenchanted with interventionism as a result of the high costs of involvement in Vietnam. As Lamarr shifts in this period from a productive icon (contributing to national defense, etc.) to a wasteful one (squandering her life, indiscriminately selling off her possessions, etc.), it appears that she is still so intensely linked to the interventionist agenda that when that policy was cast in doubt, her celebrity became suspect as well.

Hedy Lamarr's career in many ways is reflective of a fundamental cultural ambivalence about assimilation. In her screen roles and in press accounts of her career and private life, she is continually represented as neither fully Austrian nor fully American. If she was, as a caption to a publicity photo claimed in 1944, 'the toast of two Continents,'[85] she seemed to belong to neither. Somewhat in the tradition of Pola Negri, Hedy Lamarr was seen by the studio as a valuable resource, but one whose precise use value was unclear. John Kobal sums up the problem as follows:

> During her years at MGM, the challenge, the opportunity her mesmerizing appearance offered as a catalyst – if not for art at least for compelling drama – was continually fumbled. Confronted by a priceless object, everybody wanted her, but having got her they were at a loss to know what to do next, which may have been why the powers at MGM kept

casting her as kept women, repeating her first successful role until inspiration might strike. When she wasn't kept, she was being miscast – as a Russian street conductress; as the 300th actress to play Tondelayo, the copper-toned African man-killer, as 'Sweets' Ramirez, a fiery Mexican fish cannery worker.[86]

My analysis of Lamarr's celebrity seeks to show that Kobal's summary overlooks one crucial dimension of the actress's stardom – her utility in helping to advance an inteventionist narrative which served American political and economic goals. While we might contrast accounts of Pola Negri's reported sponsorship by Hitler to Hedy Lamarr's flight from oppressive Nazi types in Europe as a sign of their respective relationships to American culture, it is also important to consider the differences of timing in their careers. At least one commentator has termed the period from 1943 to 1958 (which significantly overlaps with Lamarr's career) 'a culture of outsiders' in America, and indeed the period is marked by distinctive achievements by immigrant, racial and religious Others in US culture. In 1955, for instance, Ralph Ellison (a black man), Vladimir Nabokov (a Russian immigrant), and Saul Bellow (a Canadian Jew) were major forces in American literature. In art, two dominant figures were Jackson Pollock (from a poor, non-religious family) and Willem de Kooning (a Dutch immigrant of questionable legal status).[87] This would seem to suggest a higher degree of receptivity in American culture to the ethnic 'outsider' as an emblem of American achievement and capability in the period of Hedy Lamarr's stardom than in Pola Negri's.

The narrativization of Hedy Lamarr's personal life took shape around a governing distinction between European and American culture that sought to hold Lamarr's European past as false and wasteful, and her American present as an authentic realization of her potential. From this we might extrapolate that one of the paradigmatic assumptions of Hollywood as an expression of American culture is that America is the place where everyone reaches their fullest potential or finds their most authentic, best self. As one of the ways by which stardom works to hold a hegemony of American values in place, this phenomenon bears noting, for it would seem to suggest that one stock narrative scenario for ethnic female stardom showcases the interventionist maneuvers of Hollywood upon the development and refinement of ethnic femininity as a resource. Yet while the interventionist theme tried to lineate the narrative of Lamarr's Americanized ethnicity, her star text was never completely linear.[88] In fact, it was increasingly characterized by a kind of 'return of the repressed' in which the presumption of a sordid past operated as a recurring and disruptive element to depreciate her celebrity.

6

MARISA TOMEI AND
THE FANTASY OF ETHNICITY

This project has conceived of ethnic femininity as both shifting and multiple, yet in its various incarnations bearing an important relationship to the way a nation sells itself and manufactures nationalist mythologies. Seeing film and film culture as important registers for our collective cultural unconscious, I have sought to examine the significance of the popularization of ethnic female star personae as a partial index of the way in which American culture wants to envision itself. In this respect, ethnic femininity has a long representational association with fantasy. In this chapter, I explore the notion of fantasy in more detail via a consideration of a contemporary star persona.

In previous chapters, I have worked to establish an understanding of the ethnic female film star as a figure crucially linked to the complexities of American social history and myths of cultural inclusion during the silent and classical eras of Hollywood history. Because this chapter's focus on actress Marisa Tomei is considerably more contemporary and therefore less grounded in the kinds of established understandings distance and time provide, it will require an adjustment in terms and a corresponding turn toward more provisional conclusions. While discourses of ethnicity continued to be exerted in 1990s Hollywood with both frequency and flexibility, in newer films and in the personae of some newer female stars we can track both the perpetuation of fears of ethnic agency and a topical cultivation of ethnicity as a positively valenced reversion. It will be my project to demonstrate how Tomei, an Italian-American, simultaneously maintains both of these modes of ethnic identity in her persona, in some sense continuing the legacy of the vamp as the embodiment of ethnic threat while also being narrativized as productively in touch with her own ethnic past. As we shall see, Tomei's most consistent ongoing role is as the American woman who re-discovers and employs her ethnic heritage. In this way, her stardom sustains sociologist Richard Alba's point that in contemporary culture:

> Ethnic identities have become ways of claiming to be American, and this is a profound change from the past. Ethnic identity can be a means of locating oneself and one's family against the panorama of American history, against the backdrop of what it means to be an American. No

longer, then, need there be any contradiction between being American and asserting an ethnic identity. Increasingly, they are accepted as the same thing.[1]

Marisa Tomei (an Academy Award winner for *My Cousin Vinny* [1992]) certainly doesn't have the career longevity or the sharply defined persona of the actors and actresses most frequently discussed in the domain of star studies. In the peak phase of her visibility in the mid-1990s, she appeared chiefly in ensemble films, not star vehicles. This certainly modulates her celebrity; yet as I will show, Tomei is a star whose films provide a rich field for posing questions of ideology, ethnicity and gender. Press coverage of Tomei's ethnicity, her status as an 'accent specialist' and her appearance in a number of films that overtly and implicitly engage issues of contemporary ethnicity make her an ideal case study as a contemporary incarnation of ethnic femininity. Most particularly, her stardom well reflects late twentieth century tendencies to promote the re-discovery of ethnicity as a source of vitality.

All press and publicity materials on Tomei invariably mention that she is from New York and that she is of Italian descent. As a freshman at Boston University in the late 1980s, Tomei was offered a part in the soap opera *As the World Turns*. Parlaying that experience into additional soap opera and sitcom parts on television, Tomei appeared in her first significant film role in the Italian-American comedy *Oscar* in 1992.[2] While frequently appearing in stage productions in New York with the theatre group Naked Angels, Tomei continued to make movies, most significantly *My Cousin Vinny*, followed by *Untamed Heart* (1993), *Chaplin* (1993), *Equinox* (1993), *The Paper* (1994), *Only You* (1994) and *The Perez Family* (1995). In 1996, she appeared as a guest star in a special one-hour episode of the NBC sitcom *Seinfeld*.

As we shall see, Tomei's affiliation with structures of fantasy is nearly continuous in all of her filmic and extra-filmic roles: in *Only You* and *The Perez Family* she plays women who actively fantasize; in *Untamed Heart* and *Only You* she appears in romance fantasy films; in *The Paper* and *Seinfeld* Tomei is situated as an object of male fantasy, while ongoing rumors about Tomei's Academy Award subject her to fantasies about the disempowerment of ethnic femininity. Yet Tomei's fantasy status also transcends these rather literal forms – since fantasies are also concerned with the traces of a lost object and often rooted in enigmas of origin, we may observe how her persona operates as a form of retrieval and device for stabilizing those forms of ethnic identity contemporary culture fears lost.[3] Throughout this discussion, I conceptualize fantasy in line with the emphases of psychoanalytic theory, seeing 'the supposedly marginal operations of fantasy to be constitutive of our identity and to be at the centre of all our perceptions, belief and actions.'[4]

As I discussed in Chapter 1, a number of developments in contemporary Hollywood suggest a general re-invigoration of whiteness through the discovery of ethnicity, and this phenomenon is particularly perceptible in stardom. Marisa

Figure 9 Tomei appears as a fantasy vision of empowered transformation for George
Costanza on *Seinfeld*

Tomei is one example of a current star whose ethnicity can be usefully invoked
to stage American myths of individuality and positively reference ethnic history.
As Tomei's character name in *My Cousin Vinny* (Mona Lisa Vito) suggests, the
actress's stardom is predicated on a balance between European classicism and
the energies of the unruly ethnic woman. While continually threatening to
expose the excessiveness that marks cultural fears of ethnicity, she also invokes a
positive legacy of ethnic femininity. In the narrative of her own life and family
background and in a number of the film roles in which she appears, Tomei
personifies ethnicity as a potential solution to broader issues of cultural crisis.
Thus, even in the relatively short span of Tomei's celebrity, we may track four
explicit levels of ethnic meaning with which she is associated. While not entirely
distinct or chronological, these levels do generally play out as somewhat of an
evolutionary trajectory in the actress' film roles, promotion and publicity. These
categories of ethnic meaning are as follows:

1. Ethnicity as excess;
2. Ethnicity as the sign of sincerity and/or authenticity;
3. Ethnicity as a restorative response to the evacuation of
   contemporary culture;
4. Ethnicity as individual empowerment.

138

An ingenue (one reviewer characterized the actress as 'a surprising talent capable of holding an entire movie with her bright eyes and unspoiled manner'),[5] Tomei's vivacious style enables her to be positioned as an ethnic antidote to contemporary American cultural exhaustion. Straddling a line between ethnic excess and ethnic vitality, she remains a potent and highly charged figure in relation to American fears and desires about ethnicity.

Cultural exhaustion, ethnicity and contemporary Hollywood

Complementary to these readings of the Tomei star persona is an understanding of American culture in a vacuum in the mid-1990s. Tomei's peak popularity came at a time when the nation was rocked by divisive public events that symbolized enduring racial inequities including the Los Angeles riots and the O.J. Simpson trial, and in the midst of an economic recession. These factors contributed significantly to a broadly-felt, pre-existing sense of cultural malaise. After World War Two and the inauguration of a new posture involving a permanent global base structure and presence initiated with 'national security' as its legitimating metaphor, some commentators have written of the contemporary national mood as a new kind of 'security crisis' characterized by a broad-based psychological uncertainty and anxiety in relation to American productivity and achievement. Miles Wolpin, for instance notes that, 'One of the ironies of late twentieth-century America is that despite the enjoyment of impressive material wealth and military capabilities, in the psychological realm – particularly with respect to nuclear proliferation, terrorism and, until recently, Soviet capabilities – the nation is experiencing unparalled levels of insecurity.'[6] Wolpin further notes:

> The superior economic performance, unsurpassed living standards and societal cohesion which underpinned American hegemony after World War II have been seriously attenuated if not lost. The dollar has been totally divorced from the gold standard; trade imbalances have become chronic; unemployment levels have continued their secular rise, assuming structural significance; and transit deterioration, urban decay, and high crime rates have taken on an endemic character. The rapid post-war rise in the American standard of living – which supported the historical expectation undergirding traditional American optimism – fell off and then ceased in the late twentieth century.[7]

Making use of a broad set of indices to gauge national social health, Marc Miringoff and Marque-Luisa Miringoff have argued that in many respects, social health declined in the 1990s, even while, for much of the decade, economic health appeared to be robust.[8] Robert Crunden has similarly referred to this cultural climate as a zeitgeist of 'exhaustion:'

American culture entered the middle 1990s with an air of exhaustion, of ideas that had run their course. Radicals had felt defeated since 1968 and post-modernists since the late 1980s. Liberals had nothing new to offer after 1965, and although Bill Clinton seemed liberal during the 1992 elections, he offered nothing creative in a cultural sense, only a new face and a semblance of energy after two consecutive presidents who seemed managerially fatigued. In their turn, the conservatives were no better, having nothing substantive to offer beyond calls for experience and suggestions of an unpleasant nature about the character of their opponents . . . the situation in employment, in medical care, in rebuilding the infrastructure of the nation, seemed close to desperate, even as the levels of decay in the cities and of violence everywhere seemed to rise inexorably with every day's news.[9]

Crunden's observations suggest the problem of cultural rejuvenation faced by the US in the mid-1990s – if at various times the US has colonized foreign cultures to enhance its own sense of identity, we seemed to have now reached a point of exhaustion of global resources. World culture having become increasingly homogenized and Americanized, it appeared that we now faced a depletion of global cultural resources to plunder. Yet economically and culturally, it seemed impossible to retreat to an isolationist stance. In fact, our very economic system necessitates the continued search for new markets. Lacking a representational forum that is expressive of this dilemma, and in the absence of other cultural territories to encroach upon, we naturally turned inward. In mid-1990s American culture, popular fictions were very much shaped within a crucible of barely-disguised 'white panic'[10] and one way to detour around the problematic status of whiteness was to take evasive action by claiming ethnicity. Kathleen Neils Conzen and her co-authors have explored this phenomenon in their research on American ethnic culture, noting that 'particular moments of societal crisis, such as wars and economic depressions, have been periods of intensified inventions of ethnicity.'[11]

The advent of such inward-looking, nostalgic impulses in the New Hollywood can be traced to one significant point of origin in the financial and cultural success of the blockbuster *Godfather* franchise of the early 1970s. *The Godfather* (1972) is the film which Thomas Schatz has associated with the reversal of the American film industry's decline after a period of stagnation following the 1948 Paramount decree, the displacement of film by television as the pre-eminent culture industry, and the success of the international art film in the American market. It is of interest to note that Hollywood's first important successful response to these internal and external threats was a film that also marked the contemporary American cinema's discovery of ethnicity and its marketability in the New Hollywood. Schatz aptly notes that:

By the time of its release, *The Godfather* had attained 'event' status, and audiences responded to Coppola's stylish and highly stylized hybrid of the gangster genre and family melodrama. Like so many 1970s films, *The Godfather* had a strong nostalgic quality, invoking the male ethos and patriarchal order of a bygone era.[12]

In addition to these elements, *The Godfather* most importantly invokes a nostalgic conception of ethnicity which can be traced to the historical specificities of its production and an increasing cultural desire to return to an ethnic past. Released just two years before Congress would pass the Ethnic Heritage Act, the film notably sustains much of the same logic about the need for ethnic preservation. *The Godfather* marks a cinematic shift in thinking of ethnicity, where assimilation is now linked to sterile bureaucratization and the preservation of an ethnic past to vitality.

As the blockbuster film has taken on increasing significance in the New Hollywood, we may note the way in which ever more grandiose spectacle productions correlate to an increasingly diminished sense of national value and positive self-identity. In some cases, the amount of ideological work such films have to accomplish is more awe-inspiring than their filmic special effects.[13] In the section to follow, I will argue that in smaller scale films we may chart the same kind of impulse to recover family and national identities.

Ethnicity as potentially disruptive excess

In certain arenas, Tomei's Italian ethnicity is represented as a form of excess, and correlated to an underlying exoticism which may be suppressed, but is always present at some level. A 1994 article for instance, disregards the fact that Tomei was on a weight-gain diet for her role in *The Perez Family* and represents her appetite as natural and inherently quasi-sexual:

> What an appetite this Marisa Tomei has. Her tight black bell-bottoms hit the Naugahyde, and instantly an old Greek waiter is taking orders. Swiss-cheese omelette with onions and bacon. Bagel with butter and jelly. Big vanilla milk shake. If this isn't enough to convince you that Tomei is exactly the kind of woman you dream about meeting in a joint called Kaps Coffee Shop on a rainy winter afternoon in New York City . . . midway through her meal, she slips out of one shoe and sock to reveal fire-engine-red toenails and a tattoo of a giant Egyptian eye on her right instep.[14]

Tomei's connection to excessive sexuality is also suggested in press accounts of her role as Faith in *Only You*, a film which downplays the character's original ethnicity in order to narrativize her acquisition of Italian ethnicity while visiting Rome and Tuscany. According to one writer, the actress struggled to 'project an All-American kind of pretty' in the film, and felt herself to be 'a little bit too earthy' for the role.[15]

Sartorial excess is also filtered through the lens of Tomei's ethnicity. One article noted that 'Young Hollywood stars like Marisa Tomei and Dweezil Zappa often wear unfashionable clothes.'[16] Named to a 'Worst-Dressed' List in 1993, the actress's 'style weakness' was evaluated as a tendency to 'swing from excess to ennui.'[17] The article went on to comment acerbically, 'Though she deserves credit for trying to avoid a standard Hollywood basic-black wardrobe, the Brooklyn-born Tomei, 28, who is single and nests in both LA and New York City, should save her comedic spins for the screen.'[18]

Similarly, when Tomei is criticized for her performances (which is not often) she is referenced as being too over the top, too excessively energized. Tom Gliatto has provided:

> Some notes for those keeping track of the 30-year-old Tomei's development as an actress:
>
> 1. Accents aren't a strong point. Playing a party-loving Cuban boat-lifted to Miami in 1980, she sounds uncomfortably close to Charo. 'I am like Cooba,' proclaims Tomei. 'Used by many, conquered by no one!'
> 2. In rare moments of repose, Tomei's face can be sad, winsome and touching. Maybe someday she will stop being cast as a vivacious cupcake. Meanwhile, the icing is getting stale.[19]

Such discourses illustrate residual cultural anxiety about sexualized ethnic femininity (as this is seen to be expressed through appetite, dress, etc.). In similar fashion, in *My Cousin Vinny* ethnic femininity remains associated through its female protagonist (Tomei's Mona Lisa Vito) with excessive physicality, ambitious drive and 'unfeminine' knowledge. Accordingly, her agency must be subverted and expressed through the achievements of her fiance. At the start of the film, as she and Vinny Gambini (Joe Pesci) arrive in a small Southern town, distinctly out of place and marked as New York Italians through dress, speech, and dramatic body language, the couple have the following exchange:

Mona Lisa: What?
Vinnie: Nothin'; you stick out like a sore thumb around here.
Mona Lisa: Me? What about you?
Vinnie: I fit in better than you. At least I'm wearing cowboy boots.
Mona Lisa: Oh. Yeah. You blend.

With this, Tomei (whose all-black ensemble and red lips are reminiscent of the signature style of the vamp) takes a photo of three elderly black men sitting on a nearby bench, and comments, 'I bet the Chinese food here is terrible.' The conversation about the inability to effectively assimilate hints at the film's rich subplot about incorporation and community, setting the stakes for the action to follow in which Vinny, and Vinny's two young clients (one his cousin) are gradually accepted by the local townspeople. Thus, the film plays actively with the problem of coming to terms with the otherness in our midst, smoothly concluding with a vision of superficial harmony and promoting the notion that 'we can all get along' in the same year that Rodney King made his famous plea with respect to contemporary American racial strife. And yet to accept this version of narrative closure, the film asks us to accept the resolution of racial conflict on ethnic terms, proffering ethnicity as discursive camouflage for the race issues implicitly activated by the film's depiction of the Southern town as anachronistic space.

Yet Mona Lisa Vito, the film's hyperbolic embodiment of ethnic femininity, remains always to some degree outside of this incorporative ideal. She has played a key role in establishing the case to exonerate the boys, yet when the district attorney announces he will drop all charges, Mona Lisa and Vinny emerge from the courthouse, where he tells her, 'We have to get out of here by three. Make sure all the bags are in the car.' While Vinnie shakes hands all around on the steps of the courthouse (with the male judge, his male clients, even the male prosecuting attorney, who tells him, 'You got an open invitation any time you want to come down here,') Mona Lisa is bringing the car around. Clearly, the maintenance of cultural order depends upon the preservation of certain proprieties with respect to channels of male power, and in the social world depicted in *My Cousin Vinny* ethnicity is less of an obstacle than gender to assimilation into the most 'foreign' of settings (the small Southern town being represented as an anachronistic outpost of provincialism).

Tomei's first film role in *Oscar* (1992), a clumsy ethnic comedy starring Sylvester Stallone, references a similar concern about the management of ethnic femininity. Like *My Cousin Vinny*, the film also strikingly casts Tomei in the role of the florid but profoundly good-hearted ethnic woman. As Angelo 'Snaps' Provolone, Stallone plays a 1931 crime boss who has promised his dying father that he will become 'an honest man.' All of the action takes place on 'the day that Snaps Provolone goes straight' with the protagonist attempting to transform himself to enter into business with a group of WASP bankers. This transformation largely entails the suppression of the signs of ethnicity in himself and in his associates, an endeavor the film will show to be futile, seeing ethnicity as something which cannot be evaded. *Oscar* represents Italian ethnicity as on the one hand profoundly comic, yet ethnic identities are endowed with an authenticity shown to be lacking in the film's two primary groups of non-ethnic characters, the bankers and a squad of federal agents.

Snaps Provolone's plan for a smooth transition into the realm of 'legitimate' business collapses early on as he is confronted by his accountant Anthony Rossano (Vincent Spano) who asks him first for a raise, then his daughter's hand in marriage. Snaps storms upstairs to confront his daughter Lisa (Tomei) who is reclining in a lavish pink boudoir, reading *Lady Chatterley's Lover* and smoking. When she asserts her independence, telling him, 'I'm a modern thirties woman,' he insists that she won't marry Anthony, but instead, the man he has picked out for her, Bruce Underwood III. Nora, the family's Irish maid, advises Lisa to claim she is pregnant to force her father's hand, a ploy that works perfectly. The confusion deepens as a poor girl appears at the house to tell Snaps that she has been passing herself off as his daughter Theresa Provolone (this is the woman Anthony has met), while Lisa is in love with Oscar, the family's chauffeur. Nora soon announces that she is quitting to marry Bruce Underwood herself, prompting Snaps to lament, 'Great! The maid gets a millionaire, my daughter gets a chauffeur.'

Learning that Oscar has fled the country, Snaps tricks Anthony into signing a statement that says he is the father of Lisa's child, while Anthony returns fifty thousand dollars he had embezzled from Snaps in exchange for permission to wed his daughter. The money is returned in the form of an expensive collection of jewelry hidden in a black suitcase. As Nora packs her bags to marry Bruce Underwood her valise is mistakenly substituted for the bag of jewels, and the ensuing confusion structures the film as other ethnics (the Irish maid, a German chauffeur) take brief, unrightful possession of the treasure. By this point in the film, it becomes evident that Snaps Provolone will never assimilate into white business ventures, as he can't even get out of his own house (and never will, throughout the course of the movie). Instead, his fated role is that of the ethnic patriarch attempting to establish order in his squabbling kingdom. Complicating Snaps's attempts to find a husband for his daughter and regain his money from Anthony are a number of other farcical elements including a variety of inept ethnic minions, the Fanucci Brothers, tailors who Snaps represents as Sicilian hitmen,[20] and Dr. Thornton Poole (Tim Curry), Snaps's elocution teacher. When Anthony meets Lisa and learns that she is the only Provolone daughter, he contrives for her to meet Dr. Poole, telling Poole and Lisa that each is in love with the other, and the pair are soon exchanging compliments. 'Your diction is surprisingly good, considering your genealogy,' says Poole, to which Lisa replies, 'That's the sweetest thing anybody's ever said to me, Thornton.'

As Lisa falls in love with the character who superficially appears best suited to facilitate her assimilation into 'white' culture,[21] Theresa re-appears, and shortly thereafter a replacement maid for Nora, a woman named Roxanne who had once been involved with Snaps. Roxanne reveals that Theresa is, in fact, their illegitimate daughter, and with this, Snaps decisively broadens his reach as an ethnic patriarch, establishing a family connection to virtually everyone in his domain, as Theresa becomes his daughter and Anthony and Poole his sons-in law.

Meanwhile, the activities in the Provolone household are being monitored by a group of Federal agents determined to prove Snaps's criminal status, and the white bankers plot to disenfranchise Snaps in their business deal together. As the bankers arrive at the mansion and the federal agents raid the house, colorful, positive ethnicity is visually contrasted with the staid brown suits of the agents and the gray-suited bankers. The bankers immediately deny any connection to Provolone, as the senior banker, Kirkwood[22] argues, 'You don't really think we're in business with these people, do you officer? We're only here because he threatened us.' 'That's right,' another chimes in. 'He threatened to put the arm on us.' The agents, convinced that the comings and going of the black bags must mean something suspicious, seize the bag, and dump Nora's lingerie out on the table. Toomey, the head agent, leaves the house discredited while one of the bankers surreptitiously steals a piece of lingerie. When Kirkwood reflects that 'That's what we get for going into business with a crook,' Snaps makes the speech that establishes the film's conclusion as ethnic exoneration, saying, 'I'm a crook? You come into my house with your fine print and addendums and try to con me out of my dough? Gee, I'm used to dealing with mobsters, bootleggers and gunsellers, but you bankers – are scary.'

Snaps renounces his plan to assimilate into white business culture, and at the close of the film, his business family and his work family are jubilantly reconstituted. *Oscar* thus narrativizes family solidarity through ethnicity and safely contains the sexual energies of ethnic femininity when Snaps is able to marry off his daughter. Part of the comedy, however, is based on the assumption that ethnic female sexuality is free-floating and attachable to any available male object, as Lisa is paired with Oscar, Anthony and Thornton. This dimension of ethnic adaptability will be important in a number of subsequent narratives, from *The Perez Family* to *Seinfeld*, as a means by which the dilemmas of male protagonists are enacted through actual or fantasized coupling with the ethnic female as a reward or restoration.

Ethnicity as classical authenticity

In his analysis of the production and reception of stardom Joshua Gamson investigates authenticity as the drive to discover the 'real person' behind a star image. While clearly remaining an unresolvable issue, in Gamson's view, the drive to discover the authentic remains one of the key pleasures of our engagement with stars. Gamson asserts that:

> Despite their different approaches to star/audience distance, in fact, both fantasy and identification activities require a resolution of the question of truth. In order to get pleasure from the activity, these audiences need to be reasonably certain that what they are getting in each particular case is the real thing. The question of who and what celebrities really are must be answerable.[23]

Whether or not we find Gamson's assertions applicable to all stars, they are aptly born out in the persona of Marisa Tomei. In this section, I want to consider the ways in which Tomei's ethnicity serves as a code for authenticity, carrying with it a kind of truth value that is discernible in both physical and emotional registers.

Naturalness and authenticity are often posited as dimensions of Tomei's physical attractiveness. A 1996 photo of the actress, for instance, is captioned with the sentence, 'Marisa Tomei's barely made-up complexion is naturally dewy.'[24] In addition, Tomei's Italian ethnicity is sometimes offered as the explanation for her physical expressivity in both diegetic and extra-diegetic contexts. Alyssa Katz's description of Tomei as Mona Lisa Vito describes the actress physically communicating the role as a function of her familiarity with the bodily ethnic vocabulary of Flatbush, 'through a complex but subtle vocabulary of subtle neck thrusts, precisely calibrated eyebrows, and I'm-pissed loose lips . . . Flatbush-reared Tomei's regional ties helped ease her into this high-pressure role.[25]

Similarly, Tomei is identified as 'the twentysomething actress – who used her Brooklyn heritage to great advantage in *Vinny*.'[26] Through descriptions of this sort, she is associated with a kind of bodily authenticity, where her performance amounts to a staging of her ethnic identity. In some sense, Tomei then serves as a conduit to a romanticized ethnic past, epitomized by her connection to a 'neighborhood.' That such a connection should be frequently mentioned in the actress' press coverage is therefore not surprising. In 'She's Straight Out of Booklyn,' Joel Engel notes, 'For Ms. Tomei (pronounced Toe-MAY), the character's geographic roots were familiar. "I really knew the neighborhood," says the actress, who comes from the Flatbush section of Brooklyn.'[27] Similarly, in a review of the film *Untamed Heart* (1993) Jami Bernard compares Tomei to Latina star Rosie Perez, linking both actresses to an ethnic authenticity in part derived from their origins in urban neighborhoods. Bernard classified Tomei and Perez as 'two of the new crop of sassy, streetwise, borough-accented, ethnic leading ladies who are galvanizing the screen.'[28] For Tomei, a superficial streetwise quality masks an identity grounded in innocence, in a way that updates the ethnic innocence embodied by Colleen Moore and Sonja Henie.

A cinematic category of authentic heritage meanings also accrues to Tomei's persona. The actress's appearances in a number of films that reference generic nostalgia reinforce her status as an icon of classical authenticity. In 1994, for instance, she appeared in two movies which clearly evinced nostalgia for an older kind of American film; Ron Howard's *The Paper* is a film whose frantic pace and journalistic setting mark it as an homage to such classical newspaper films as *The Front Page* (1931) and *His Girl Friday* (1940), while Norman Jewison's *Only You* takes shape as a nostalgic romance. Of the latter film, one reviewer wrote, 'From the beauty of Venice by moonlight to the luxury hotels of the seacoast village of Positano, Jewison creates an atmosphere of European romance and beauty similar to films such as *To Catch a Thief* (1953) and *Roman Holiday* (1953).'[29]

In other contexts, Tomei's ethnicity serves as an implicit explanation for her spirituality and groundedness. For instance, in an interview conducted by the actress with Rosie Perez (which is as revealing of Tomei as her ostensible interview subject) Tomei reports that the last question she asked was 'What is the last thing you do before you go to bed at night?' and when Perez reported that she prays, Tomei said 'Me too.'[30] A 1993 article further noted that 'Tomei attributes her success to what she calls her spiritual connection.'[31] In a 1994 article the actress discussed her closeness to her Italian grandmother, 'Grandma Rita,' who is constructed as an icon of ethnic domesticity:

> Marisa found her soul mate in Grandma Rita, the domestic matriarch . . . 'I go to her when I want to feel the simplicity of life. It's a real freedom, and it's a girlie thing. I love sitting down havin' a talk, havin' a cup of coffee, dunkin' some cookies together and shootin' the breeze.'[32]

In all sorts of ways, press coverage of Tomei credits the actress with a reverence for the past. Whether she is confessing a 'love for show-girl clothes of the 1920s'[33] or testifying that 'I'm nostalgic and sentimental about everything,'[34] a public perception has been built of the actress as appropriately appreciative of the values of the past. Linking ethnicity to genuine communication and a fidelity to lost values, descriptions of the actress frequently allude to her self-consciously old-fashioned views on gender roles. In 1994 the actress was quoted as follows:

> 'I think men need their girlfriends or wives to believe they can do whatever they want to do,' she says. 'Everybody needs that, but men need it more. I don't know whether it's planted in their genes or some myth they psychologically live up to or just the way society is, but they're the ones who go out and quest. So they need us cheering them on, 'cause' – her voice goes into singsong – 'we're the ones who have the babies.' She laughs. 'I can't *believe* I just said that.'[35]

All such discourse takes place in the context of Tomei's ethnic family values, thereby reinforcing the actress's connections to heritage. That heritage is represented as a kind of primitivism, in keeping with Allen Woll and Randall M. Miller's observation that representationally 'Whatever their occupation, sex, or locale, Italian characters seemingly dealt with the world in a primitive way.'[36] In Tomei's case, such primitivism is figured positively for holding a contemporary functionality. Joanna Powell offers one of the most straightforward descriptions of Tomei's ethnic persona: 'Tomei is a sweet patootie from Brooklyn, and very Italian: warm, sexy, strong, and above all, family oriented.'[37]

Two of Tomei's mid-1990s film roles illustrate the extent to which she is associated with the thematics of family and ethnic heritage. One film, *The Perez Family* (1995) narrativizes Tomei's purification as a Cuban prostitute who in the US renounces sex for family and embraces the values of capitalist enterprise.

The second film, *The Paper* (1994), places Tomei as the spiritual center of a close-knit work family at a New York newspaper. In this section I provide achronological readings of the two films as a means of considering the ways in which they fit together as linked narratives of immigration and regionalism and exemplify Tomei's ongoing association with the resolution of family crisis.

Tomei's decision to undertake the role of Dorita Perez in *The Perez Family* engendered a certain amount of controversy over the non-politically correct casting. One review of the film alluded to the issue of Tomei's Italian ethnicity being seen as substitutable for Cuban ethnicity, noting:

> No doubt there will be complaints about Tomei's performance. She's not Cuban (though she worked on her tan), and she has added a good twenty pounds of flesh, which she swings around with abandon, her hips and breasts floating up and down like a raft on a boiling sea . . . It takes us a while to see who Dottie is; ruby-lipped and dreamy, she's less a whore than a woman in love with the idea of herself as a freedom-loving hot tomato.[38]

Whether or not the debate over the film's casting explains its commercial failure, I think what is most important in this context is that the casting and/or the controversy detracted from the ethnic authenticity that I have argued to be so central to Tomei's star persona.

The Perez Family focuses on two sets of Cuban emigres to the US separated by a twenty-year interval. The family of Juan Raul Perez (Alfred Molina) made up of his wife Carmela (Anjelica Huston), daughter Teresa, and brother in law Angel have settled in Florida, while he has been jailed in Cuba for burning his sugar cane fields rather than surrender them to Fidel Castro. As the film begins during the Mariel boatlifts of 1980, Juan has been released from prison, and leaves Cuba to reunite with his family. During the trip he meets Dorita Perez (Tomei), a former prostitute and sugar cane cutter whose anachronistic conception of American culture is strongly tied to her reverence for John Wayne and Elvis Presley. Shallow and vain (Juan and Dorita first meet when she hands him a mirror so that she can apply her lipstick), Dorita is nevertheless positioned as an example of steadfast ethnic femininity. As she quits her job at the Matanzas Sugar Cane Farm, she proudly tells her lecherous boss that 'I am like Cuba. Used by many, conquered by no one.'

Early sections of the film are laden with such apparently paradoxical constructions of Dorita. Clearly, she associates American culture with consumerism (whether of screen images or other commodities); her first purchase in the US is a bottle of nail polish. Dorita's crass, materialistic vision of American culture (suggested by such comments as, 'When we get to Miami, I will have a gold compact with little shells on top') is designed to contrast with Juan's stoic endurance as a political prisoner and noble quest to reunite with his family. In one early scene, Dorita's finger rubbing lip gloss onto her lips is visually rhymed with a nearby soldier caressing his weapon. Yet at the same time, Dorita's innocence and probity are suggested by her choice to anglicize her name to Dottie, her exuberant Cuban dance that rouses the weary boat passengers, and her jubilant dive from the boat to swim to shore upon arrival in Florida. With some irony, the film stages a vision of America as a glorious refuge as the boat finally docks and the passengers descend toward an ebullient, American flag-waving crowd. Scenes of Dottie and Juan arriving in the US are intercut with information about the lives of Carmela and Teresa Perez and Carmela's brother Angel Diaz. We learn of Carmela's intense devotion to the memory of her husband and her hope that he will return to his family, of Teresa's Americaniza-tion, and of Angel's success in a furniture business oriented toward a Cuban clientele. Assimilation into US culture has, it seems, distorted the Perez family solidarity into hysteria about self-protection as Angel ceaselessly urges new security innovations upon his sister. When a mix-up occurs with a new security system, Carmela meets Federal Agent John Pirelli (Chazz Palmintieri) and it appears that for the first time in twenty years, she is considering extra-marital romance.

Entry into the US for Dottie and Juan is complicated by the fact that each is traveling singly (fearing an uncertain welcome and worrying about how time and imprisonment have diminished his looks, Juan decides to say nothing of his family). When an immigration official informs Dottie that single Cuban men are seen as possibly gay, and single Cuban woman as likely prostitutes, she deter-mines to form a family with Juan (since they share the same surname) to facilitate their legal entry into the US. Housed in a makeshift camp for Cuban immigrants at the Miami Orange Bowl, Dottie is also able to fabricate a 'father' (a mentally ill man named Armando Perez whom they call 'Papi') and a 'son,' (a boy named Felipe Perez). During this period of time, many of Dottie's anach-ronistic and naive illusions about American culture are punctured. She makes the traumatic discovery that John Wayne is dead, then in the midst of a screen-ing of a John Wayne film the picture breaks up. At that moment Dottie updates her fantasy American male with a passing blond American security guard whom she refers to as 'My United States freedom hero.' Though Dottie had hoped her first sexual experience in America would be with John Wayne, she transfers her idolatry to the security guard. At the end of an evening with him, he attempts to put money down her dress, and she rebuffs him, devastated.

From this point forward in the narrative, Dottie is a changed woman. Her commitment to her newly-constituted 'family' is no longer self-serving, but sincere. Juan, Dottie, Papi and Felipe are sponsored by a local church and begin to work selling flowers at an intersection as a family. When Felipe is killed by an American gangster, Dottie mourns as if he were her own son. Though Juan tells her that 'He was from the street, mixed up with bad people – gangsters,' Dottie insists, 'He had no family. He wanted to change to be with us.'

Meanwhile, Juan's nervous attempt to visit his wife ends disastrously when he triggers the alarm system and runs away, prompting Carmela to begin shooting practice at Angel's urging. When Juan asserts his identity to Angel at his store, Angel is enraged, asking, 'Who gives you the right to come in here asking questions about my family?' More and more in the last third of the film, it is the Americanized Angel who is represented as the villain of the piece. His ostentatious display of nouveau riche values and self-aggrandizing hucksterism are increasingly emphasized as we see that his business ads feature Angel as the face on a one hundred dollar bill, and we learn that his steady stream of bribes to the prison guards inadvertently provided the incentive for keeping Juan in jail. When his brother-in-law chastises Angel for his self-important attempts to advertise his own wealth, his criticisms seem entirely valid. Dottie falls in love with Juan, and through him rejuvenates her Cuban identity. 'My name is Dorita,' she asserts shortly after they make love for the first time. Meanwhile, the relationship between Carmela and John Pirelli deepens, and as the film moves toward a finale, we are thoroughly confused about who belongs with whom. Indicating her conversion from self-absorbed hedonist to selfless martyr, Dorita agrees to give Juan up for the sake of his family. All the principal characters wind up at a festival, where Juan and Carmela finally meet, though she nearly shoots him, recognizing him as the attempted burglar, but not as her husband. In the ensuing melee, the American security guard shoots Angel in the hand, and the real Perez family is ambivalently re-constituted as Dorita and John Pirelli nobly retreat. Juan and Carmela immediately realize that they are no longer in love with one another, but he warmly thanks her 'for keeping our family together.' At the film's conclusion Dottie's reversion to Dorita is very much in evidence as she is back selling flowers in a bright orange dress, long dangling earrings and flowers in her hair. When Juan returns to her, their reunion is structured in ethnic and national terms. (Dorita tells him, 'You taste like sugar cane,' when they kiss.)

While we might see Tomei's role as Dorita Perez in *The Perez Family* as a kind of updated Tondelayo – indeed Tomei wore dark body paint for the role, just as Hedy Lamarr did in *White Cargo*, and employs a strong Cuban accent comparable to Lamarr's imperfect English – this film has considerably different ideological investments. While *White Cargo* is fundamentally designed to stave off the threat of ethnic femininity, *The Perez Family* valorizes ethnicity as signifying a nobility of spirit underneath a colorful exterior. Tomei's role is that of the restorative and primordial feminine. In this regard, one reviewer referred to Tomei's part as that of 'a sensuous Latino earth mother,' going on to note (in a remarkable catalogue of comparisons):

> Dottie is the Ava Gardner of the nineties, a barefoot contessa, a woman whose sexuality is integrated and fully realized. We see such a woman in Melanie Griffith whose passion and depth remind us of Marilyn Monroe, the quintessential feminine spirit of yet another era. In Italian cinema, Dottie is Anna Magnani and in France, Simone Signoret. Carmela is Greta Garbo in Queen Cristina and Ninotchka, Grace Kelly

in High Society, and Audrey Hepburn in Robin and Marian. These women and the characters they portray represent the eternal feminine spirit which inspires and matures masculine energy.[39]

Clearly, as in *Oscar*, Tomei's role as an icon of ethnic femininity signifies the easy and straightforward transference of her affections (from John Wayne, to the security guard, to Juan Raul, she gradually abandons her desire for a non-ethnic romantic partner). Additionally, in a quite striking fashion, Dorita's discovery of ethnic heritage endows her with immediate sincerity and the ability to catalyze family formation. In *The Perez Family*, characters are seen as progressively losing touch with core values the more they are Americanized. In the end, the extent of Americanization matters more than history and family ties in deciding coupling issues, and American identity seems to correlate inversely to 'freedom' as an ideal. (Seeing Dorita dance at a disco, Carmela comments, 'I was never that free,' while Dorita says that she wants to be with Juan because 'I want a man who is free. The way I thought the United States was free.') As an unconverted ethnic, Dorita is represented as the ideal figure to rehabilitate Juan's damaged masculinity, and the conclusion of the film plays out as a restorative assertion of heritage.

Tomei's off-screen role as the guardian of old-fashioned morality is replicated in her role as Martha 'Marti' Hackett in Ron Howard's 1994 film *The Paper*. Playing the young, pregnant wife of a New York newspaper editor, Tomei embodies the anchoring influence of ethnic femininity in a frenetic, destabilized urban environment marked by social, racial and gender conflict. Through the opening and closing device of a radio broadcast, *The Paper* reifies regionalism as a stable value counteracting broader global chaos. A WINS radio broadcast, which promises 'you give us twenty-two minutes, we'll give you the world,' marks the beginning and end of the narrative, but strikingly avoids any attention to the world outside of New York. Similarly, in an editorial meeting at *The Sun*, the newspaper where Henry Hackett (Michael Keaton) works, an international editor evaluates global news stories only in terms of whether people from New York were involved.[40] If there is a local connection, then the story is deemed newsworthy. While Tomei's ethnicity is more intertextually than textually determined in this film, it nevertheless strongly connects to *The Paper*'s key thematic of regionalism. In this context of regionalism as legitimate community, Tomei's New York accent, colorful mannerisms and 'street smarts' signal the kind of ethnic vibrancy the film represents as valuable.

The Paper opens with the murder of two out-of-town white businessmen in Williamsburg, Brooklyn, designed to look like a retaliatory killing for the prior murder of a black teenager. (The car containing the bodies is spray-painted with graffiti reading 'Whitey' and 'White Ghosts'.) When two black teens pass by the car, they are falsely accused of committing the crime. The film's first image after the crime prologue is of Marti Hackett's pregnant body as she stretches beside the bed where Henry is still sleeping. Henry, we learn, has an interview that day for a job at a more prestigious newspaper, *The Sentinel*. As he gets ready to leave for work, Marti tells Henry, 'You know those days that can change your life? This is one of them for us.' Marti thus functions in the narrative as the positive sign of Henry's family responsibility.

In the frenetic environment of the newsroom, Henry, the Metro Editor and a dyed-in-the-wool newspaperman, is in his element amidst a group of contentious, raucous reporters. The co-workers at *The Sun* are depicted as an unruly, but fundamentally good-hearted and dedicated work family.[41] The one distinct exception is Managing Editor Alicia Clark (Glenn Close) whose icy demeanor and distorted sexuality mark her inappropriate attempt to seek inclusion in a community that is prohibited to her on the basis of gender.[42] While Henry shares a father/son closeness with Editor-in-Chief Bernie White (Robert Duvall), Bernie chides Alicia for committing adultery when she comes in to ask for a raise. Henry and Bernie are further linked because they struggle with similar dilemmas – Bernie is trying to reconcile with his estranged daughter, while Henry is trying to be a good husband while meeting the extraordinary demands of his job. While Henry's professionalism is pure instinct (he can 'feel' the presses at work downstairs when others cannot) and he will later embark on a noble quest for the truth, Alicia has more mercenary motivations and adheres to traditional news standards. When Alicia at one point tells Henry, 'Those are union drivers waiting out there, Mister,' he imitates her with a John Wayne accent and exaggerated swagger. Thus, while the newspaper business is shown to be made up of hardworking men trying to reconstitute the families threatened by their legitimate dedication to their profession, Alicia is represented as out of bounds due to her usurpation of male professional authority and lack of commitment to her marriage. For these reasons, Henry occupies the moral high ground in his power struggle with Alicia.

Henry's possible move to *The Sentinel* is figured as 'going uptown' to a more cosmopolitan setting and more corporate organizational style. Thus, one of the questions that drives the film in its early sections is the issue of whether Henry will stay with *The Sun* (whose fundamentally democratic mission is suggested by its slogan 'it shines for all') or 'trade up' to the more elite newspaper.[43] When, during his interview, a senior editor there refers to *The Sun* as 'a cute little paper,' Henry is enraged by the condescension, and illustrating the triumph of news instincts over careerism covertly steals information from the editor's desk related to the Williamsburg murder case. Learning that the police are investigating the businessmen, even while they hold the two African-American teenagers, Henry sets out to establish a new angle on the story. Marti, who has taken leave of absence from *The Sun* during her pregnancy, secretly taps a contact at the Justice Department, and provides the key break in the case when she learns that the murder victims had unwisely invested money belonging to the Mafia. Revealing this link between criminality and Italian ethnicity, she says to her husband triumphantly, 'Dumbfellas, huh? Un-Wise Guys.' Unlike Alicia, who plots to use her sexuality for professional gain, Marti's professional accomplishments are naturally eroticized. Learning of the Mafia connection, Henry tells Marti, 'Oh honey, you are so good . . . What are you wearing?'[44]

Based on the information provided by Marti, Henry acts to secure a quote to back up the story that he hopes to run on the front page. If there was any question of his defecting from his community at *The Sun* such fears are quickly put to rest, when he receives an irate phone call from the editor at *The Sentinel*, who has learned of the stolen information. When he admonishes Henry, 'You just blew your chance to cover the world,' Henry explodes in a tirade that asserts his regional and class identity over the snobbery of *The Sentinel*: 'I don't fuckin' live in the fuckin' world. I live in fuckin' New York City!' Alicia, meanwhile, tries to sexually manipulate *The Sun*'s publisher Graham Keighley (Jason Robards) who calls her behavior 'cheap.' Henry and a *Sun* reporter extract the quote they need from a police detective in a precinct men's room, making it clear that there are gendered networks of power from which Alicia is excluded.

In possession of the quote he needs to run the story, Henry returns to *The Sun* to find that Alicia has ordered the presses to start running with a sensational, erroneous story on the arrest of the two black teens for the Williamsburg murders. Refusing to curtail production due to expenses, Alicia tells Henry, 'We only have to be right for a day,' to which Henry protests, 'People will read this, Alicia, and they'll believe us.' The argument between them pulls out all the stops in terms of gender stereotypes as Henry shoves Alicia, then immediately goes to see if she is all right. When he does so, she trips him, then tries to spray him with mace. Complaining to Henry that she knows how he and his cronies talk behind her back and never include her in gatherings at the Bear's Head bar, Alicia insists that they run her headline, and wins out. Henry returns home to find that Marti had started to hemorrhage and is being rushed to the hospital for an emergency caesarean section. In so directly using Marti's sexualized body as a register for the crisis signified by the breakdown of truth, the film also reinforces Marti's function as domestic inspiration for her husband's noble quest. In this respect, Tomei is placed in the narrative to restore white male heroics, a role for which her star persona seems ideally suited. Here as elsewhere in the ensemble films in which she takes part, Tomei's role is to facilitate the restoration of order by incarnating essentialist values.

In contrast to Marti's incorporative function, Alicia is linked to excorporation, and at the only moment when she approaches insider status in the film, she is violently punished, accidentally shot in the leg by a disgruntled man who had been criticized in another reporter's columns. Marti and Henry learn they have a son and immediately put aside their arguments about his work schedule, Bernie White looks in on his daughter at home, and the WINS broadcast returns to assert the primacy of regionalism to close the film.

It should be evident that where *The Paper* engages volatile issues of race from the outset through its representation of the Williamsburg murders, ethnic regionalism serves as the mechanism to evade that racial conflict. The film's vision of a functional New York diversity (microcosmically rendered in *The Sun*'s newsroom) is used to overcome the reality of the more troubling issues of racial discord and police brutality and inequity. In this context, it is significant that the narrative problem that drives the surface plot originates with the 'out of town' businessmen, and is resolved through local ingenuity.

The thematic of regionalism (at work, as I have argued, in the narrative of Marisa Tomei's life as well as in the film) should be read as a response to the homogenization of contemporary American culture, and in tandem with the invocation of ethnicity, as another method of claiming differentiation. It is part of a process in which 'ethnic identities are continually being reinvented to ful-fill our longing to feel anchored to a secure, harmonious, and localized past, although we are living amidst the vast and chaotic landscapes of consumption that characterize the present.'[45] In his study of American regionalism, Michael Bradshaw observes that there was a certain 'oneness of life in the US' in the late twentieth century. He writes that:

> Many features of human interaction are becoming similar across the nation and are reflected in common artefacts – buildings, advertising hoardings, recreation facilities . . . To accompany this attention of the commercial world to cultivating similar tastes in the whole population across America, there has been a convergence of values, economies and experiences for individuals.[46]

Within this framework of the 'flattening out' of difference in American culture, I suggest, those regions that evince ties to European ethnicity are reified as 'pockets of authenticity.' As the national becomes either a blank space dominated by commercial trademarks and logos, or, conversely, a space which has become too heterogeneous and fractured to be located for some Americans, the regional takes on increased importance as a comprehensible, definable level of community. In this respect, *The Paper* deploys Tomei as a sign of ethnic heritage in asserting regional coherence over national chaos.[47]

Thus, in both *The Perez Family* and *The Paper* the energy of Tomei's ethnic persona is fundamentally directed toward the establishment of a micro-community in opposition to a broader American social chaos. Whether that community is overtly or implicitly ethnic, it is inevitably constructed as a functional alternative to a discredited American culture characterized as disabled or damaged. The formation or re-formation of an ethnic subculture is thus posited as a means of evading the dysfunctionality of contemporary American culture, and ethnic femininity serves as a kind of anchor in film narratives designed to suppress anxieties related to American cultural crisis.

Ethnic femininity and the nostalgic romance

Nostalgia is another important mode of fantasy activated by the Tomei persona. The actress's appearance in a number of romances demonstrates not only the degree to which her persona is in keeping with dominant American morality, but the usefulness of ethnic femininity in staging romance as a conduit to the discovery of the past and family values. In *Untamed Heart* (1993) Tomei plays Caroline, a working-class waitress who has just concluded the most recent of a series of romantic relationships where her emotional demands are considered excessive. However, Tomei is loved from afar by Adam (Christian Slater), a dishwasher at the diner where she works. Adam, so smitten with Caroline that he follows her home from a distance every night to ensure her safety, has a heart condition from which he dies at the end of the film. He expires, however, at the moment that his narrative purpose – to put Caroline in touch with the basic values of home and community – has been served. In narrativizing Caroline's vulnerability in public space, the inability of her family to shield her from danger, and the romance as a means of discovering an alternate, intact community, *Untamed Heart* plays out some of the themes I have cited earlier with respect to the failings of contemporary culture, and Tomei's placement in film narratives that posit evasive solutions.

The hero's nostalgic function is made evident throughout the film in an accumulation of references to the past. Adam is intensely devoted to a set of old records which he uses to block out the present through fantasies of the past. He tells Caroline 'when the rain is falling, I put them on, and it stops.' (Upon his death, he significantly leaves the records for her). At one point, Adam endears himself to Caroline by his ability to activate her fantasy of the past. When she complains that her family now uses an artificial Christmas tree and expresses her desire for a live tree – because 'it brings back memories, you know, when life was simple' – he brings her a real tree and sets it up in her bedroom.

In *Untamed Heart* the hero enters at a moment when a kind of crisis of guardianship is occurring in relation to the heroine. Caroline turns to her romantic relationships to provide the support of family roles left unfilled – her father has left the family, and her mother and stepfather are barely present. This broken family is the film's metaphor for the broader failings of contemporary culture. When a younger brother leaves Caroline without transportation at the end of her work shift, it is because no family member is available to give her a lift that Caroline walks home through Minneapolis and is nearly raped. In a number of other ways, the film strongly problematizes its heroine's relationship to home. In several of its major sequences, *Untamed Heart* treats the issue of Caroline's attempt to leave or return to her parents' house. The first present-day image of the film (after a flashback sequence of Adam's childhood at an orphanage) is of Caroline walking into the house, then hurriedly racing through it in preparation for a date. She then joins her boyfriend in his truck where he informs her he wants to break things off. She runs quickly back into the house, and this initiates a series of returns to the 'safe space' of home. From this point on in the film, Caroline's attempts to return home structure the narrative. The axis between the diner where she works and the house where she lives is strongly charged and represented as a kind of gauntlet. The first time Caroline travels this route, her best friend warns her to be careful, noting 'there are a lot of crazies out there.' The near-rape occurs the next evening, although Caroline pleads with her attackers, 'I just need to get home.' When Adam foils the attack, he carries her to the front porch of her house and sits with her until dawn when she awakes. (He has already proved his worth as a chaperone, by following her home every evening to make sure she gets home safely. He even admits to sneaking into the house to watch her sleep, suggesting that Caroline's home and family are insufficiently protective and secure). *Untamed Heart* would appear to be one of a number of newer romance narratives that place little faith in the stability of childhood homes and the continuity of family.[48] Caroline's 'real father' (as she puts it) has left the home, and the existing family structure appears to be minimal, with family members disconnected from and out of touch with one another. Nevertheless, in *Untamed Heart* the space outside of the home is even more traumatic than home itself.

At its conclusion, *Untamed Heart* employs Adam's death as an object lesson for Caroline in a reverential sequence of memorialization and familial reconstitution. The film is unable to completely salvage the idea of the restored nuclear family, but at Adam's funeral, Caroline stands beside her brother and is surrounded by the members of her 'work family.' After the service Caroline seeks out her friend Cindy to tell her, 'I love you. We're family.' She then goes to Adam's apartment to find that he has left her the box of records from his childhood, and the film closes with Caroline in a reverie as she plays one of the records for the first time, enacting a double-layered nostalgic scenario.

We can better understand the complex terms of the nostalgic trajectory in *Untamed Heart* by referencing Freud's notion of the family romance, a fantasy structure whereby the developing child learns to channel dissatisfaction with his/her parents into desires that lead beyond the family.[49] Through this wishing process, the child imaginatively substitutes non-family members for one or both parents, psychologically initiating hopes for the future that contain within them desires to return to the past. Functioning as a psychological lever between the past and the future, the family romance checks family-oriented nostalgia and the impulse to preserve the past in favor of moving toward a future which the child imagines can be just like the idealized past.

In *Untamed Heart* the traditional desires that drive the family romance fantasy are mobilized, but only in order to serve new ends. The film's awareness that an ideal family past has broken down and that forces outside the family have become more threatening cast the substitution process that drives coupling into doubt. As a result of this, the psychological trajectory designed to facilitate socialization out of the family must be re-worked, and in this film, the goal is to repair and maintain existing families rather than authorizing the creation of new ones. For if the family romance has usually worked to channel family-oriented nostalgia and the impulse to preserve the past into future-oriented choices about coupling, here the terms are reversed. Whereas the family romance is designed to exploit the desire for an idealized past so that it serves as a lever to the future, this film presents a hero whose limited historical connections cause him to embody an idealized future presented as a way of recovering the past.

Tomei's intertextual associations to restorative ethnic femininity lend the film a stronger sense of narrative purpose. While she is not directly ethnicized in this film role, she is once again marked as regional (Tomei won praise for an uncanny midwestern accent she adopted for the part). In this respect, *Untamed Heart* represents a moderate departure from Tomei's body of work as a whole, yet the film's stress on nostalgia and the recovery of family make it ideologically consistent with the central facets of her persona.

The ethnic female star and the fantasy of escape: Tomei on *Seinfeld*

Marisa Tomei's guest appearance as herself on the long-running and highly successful NBC sitcom *Seinfeld* on February 8, 1996, was distinctive for its activation of Tomei's persona in the context of ethnic fantasy. The use made of Tomei in the show offers an excellent case study of some of the contemporary representational possibilities of ethnicity, now flexible enough to serve as a solution to cultural dilemmas of racism, family disintegration, and even as a fantasized escape from the protocols of dominant culture. On *Seinfeld* Tomei incarnates ethnicity as empowerment – one indicator of this is the frequency with which her Academy Award is mentioned in the episode's dialogue.

In one of the primary storylines of the show's 1995 to 1996 season, George Costanza (Jason Alexander) has impetuously committed himself to an engagement with Susan, a wealthy woman he does not love. In this special hour-long episode, George anguishes over his entrapment in the relationship when Katie, a friend of Elaine (Julia Louis-Dreyfuss) tells him he is exactly the sort of man her friend Marisa Tomei finds attractive. In one of the show's stock settings, Monk's restaurant, George, Elaine and Katie have a conversation which places Tomei into circulation within the episode as the fantasized solution to George's perceived domestic entrapment:

Elaine: Oh, you know what? He got engaged.
Katie: Oh, you did, oh.
George: Why, is that bad?
Katie: I actually would have set you up with a friend of mine.
George: Oh, yeah?
Katie: Yeah, you'd be perfect for her. She loves quirky, funny guys.
George: Bald?
Katie: Loves bald.
George: Loves bald? (laughs) Who is she?
Katie: Marisa Tomei.
George: The actress?
Katie: Yeah.

George: You're friends with Marisa Tomei?
Katie: That's right.
George: (growing increasingly agitated) That's incredible! *My Cousin Vinny* – I love her. She was fantastic.

Adhering to the show's stock formula of information repetition and reaction within the ensemble, George immediately reports the breaking news to Jerry, who commiserates with him over the constraints that make it impossible for him to consider a date with Tomei:

George: So she said that she could have fixed me up with her.
Jerry: What do you mean, could have?
George: Well, you know, if I wasn't engaged.
Jerry: (winces) Ooh.
George: She could have fixed me up with Marisa Tomei. She said I was just her type.
Jerry: Really.
George: Yeah, yeah, you know the odds of my being anyone's type? I have never been anyone's type. But apparently this Marisa Tomei loves funny, quirky, bald men.
Jerry: You know she won an Academy Award.
George: Like I don't know that. *My Cousin Vinny* – I love that! I, George Costanza, could be on a date with an Oscar winner. An Oscar winner, Jerry. Do you know what that's like? It's like if fifty years ago, someone had fixed me up with Katharine Hepburn, same thing!
Jerry: Now there's a match. You and Katharine Hepburn.
George: You've seen her, right?
Jerry: Katharine Hepburn, oh yeah.
George: Marisa Tomei!
Jerry: Yeah, yeah.
George: She's beautiful, right? She's just my type. The dark hair, the full lips.
Jerry: You like full lips.
George: Oh, I love full lips. Something you can really put the lipstick on.
Jerry: Mmm. Too bad you're engaged.

In addition to aligning Tomei with ethnic exoticism and fantasized sexuality, this exchange is significant for the way in which it fetishizes the actress ('the dark hair, the full lips') and suggests her transparent construction as an object of male desire ('something you can really put the lipstick on'). At a more complex level, it is important to note Tomei's status as an outlet for the anxiety and dissatisfaction George attaches to heterosexual coupling in marriage. Here, Tomei serves as a placemarker for George – referencing the themes of empowerment and ethnicity in her persona, she becomes the figure whose arrival signals the killing off of his domesticated WASP wife. The exchange above illustrates the way in which both George and Jerry associate Tomei with what George's life would be like if he weren't engaged. Feeling himself to be trapped in a stultifying domesticity (an entrapment that in earlier episodes is suggested representationally as his fiancee forces him to sit around the house and watch episodes of 'Mad About You'), George stages a fantasy of escape through representational means as well, renting a video version of *My Cousin Vinny*. When Susan returns home to find him watching the film she strikingly compares herself to Tomei, asking George, 'Did you know Marisa Tomei won an Oscar for that? She's beautiful, don't you think? I wish I looked like that.' As George rolls his eyes in a long-suffering fashion at the camera, he apparently resolves to pursue the opportunity to meet Tomei. Although Katie has been hospitalized for a heart arythmia, George visits her bedside to attempt to get Tomei's number. When this fails (the unconscious Katie never responds) George coerces Elaine to obtain her phone number. Meanwhile, George rents *Only You* and this time Susan asks him, 'Do you have a thing for her?' to which George replies, 'Yeah, I have a thing for Marisa Tomei. Like she would ever go out with a short, stocky, bald man. Like that's her type. She's an Oscar winner!'

As Susan exits to the kitchen (looking bewildered and mildly suspicious), George fantasizes her re-entrance in the form of Tomei. The set is suffused with dreamy white light and Tomei enters, reviving Continental glamour in a black evening dress, to tell George that she loves him and to urge him to get ready for 'the premiere.' As George and Tomei kiss, his fantasy is abruptly punctured when Susan re-enters looking quizzically at him now embracing a pillow. However, shortly thereafter, George has his sought-after date with Tomei, and we see them in a brief scene on a park bench, the 'real' Tomei here no different from George's fantasy version as she laughs at his jokes, and finds him witty and charming, telling him, 'It's hard to believe anyone could be so spontaneously funny.' However, when she asks him, 'How is it you're not taken?' he confesses his engagement and she punches him and storms off. This action is then repeated by Susan when Elaine misses a detail in George's complex alibi, and Susan suspects him of cheating on her. In the season finale of *Seinfeld* broadcast on May 17, 1996, the Marisa Tomei gag was followed through as the last bit of season-ending business (although the actress was not seen again on-screen). With Susan dead from toxic glue poisoning (triggered by licking wedding invitation envelopes), George calls Tomei and attempts to set up a date after the funeral, but she hangs up on him.

While on the one hand entirely in keeping with the show's typically misogynist treatment of major and minor female characters, the usage made of Tomei in these episodes of *Seinfeld*, is distinctive in characterizing her as an ethnic icon for a particular purpose. As the fantasy embodiment of George's desire, Tomei appears here to reference all four major dimensions of ethnic meaning in her persona: she is physically excessive (dressed glamorously, possessing 'full lips you can really put the lipstick on'), she is represented as authentic (an 'Oscar winner,' 'like Katharine Hepburn'), she facilitates recovery (in George's imagination she saves him from the wrong marriage), and lastly she appears as a figure of ethnic empowerment (foreshadowing the means by which George will solve his dilemma by eradicating Susan).

De-legitimizing ethnic femininity

In the beginning of Chapter 1, I noted that monuments such as 'Gateway to Hollywood' work to ossify ethnic femininity as a formulaic ingredient in the narrative of Hollywood's past, relegating ethnicity itself to the status of a no-longer-operative category. A similar sort of denial about the ethnic female's prominence in public life can be seen to be at work in a persistent urban legend featuring Marisa Tomei. The impulse to reject the contributions of present-day ethnic women in Hollywood is born out in the rumor that Tomei had won her Academy Award by mistake. In a March, 1995 column Steve Harvey alluded to the rumor as follows:

> With Oscar time approaching, we're reminded of the strange urban folk tale involving Marisa Tomei. You may recall she won for Best Supporting Actess in 1993 as the wisecracking girlfriend in *My Cousin Vinny*. The rumor, as detailed by the *Hollywood Reporter* a year ago, was that Tomei had 'received her Oscar statue by error' because presenter Jack Palance 'hadn't been able to read the name written in the secret envelope' and had 'arbitrarily' called out her name.[50]

A similar account tacitly contended that the reasons behind the rumor were legitimate, alluding to the story as, 'the terrible rumor that won't go away . . . Some people believe she didn't deserve the award,' says a filmmaker who worked with the actress. 'And some people aren't ready for this type of recognition.'[51]

In an episode of the NBC live comedy program *Saturday Night Live* originally aired in March, 1996, a parody performance of Tomei by one of the show's ensemble members also obliquely referenced the rumors that her Oscar was not rightfully hers. In a recurring sketch entitled 'The Joe Pesci Show,' which lampoons male Italian ethnicity as hyper-aggressive gangsterism and cartoonish sub-par intelligence, Tomei was represented as a guest in a special Oscar tribute show. Tottering onto the set in high heels and mini skirt, the actress playing Tomei snapped her gum and spoke in heavy Brooklynese, leaving a distinct lipstick print on the cheek of 'Pesci' as the host. Seated next to guest host John Goodman as Robert De Niro, 'Tomei' was quickly interrogated about her Oscar, with the implication being that she had traded sexual favors for the award. Goodman as De Niro says that 'I heard things' about Tomei's winning the Oscar and 'Pesci' complains that he should have been nominated as well. The skit quickly takes on the terms of a gendered ethnic rivalry as 'Pesci' whines about his exclusion and 'Tomei' asserts, 'I guess I was better than you.'

160

As 'Tomei' is then verbally attacked by 'Pesci' and 'De Niro' and ultimately walks off the set in tears, one has the sense that what is being produced here is a very anxious comedy predicated on broad-based notions of intra-ethnic competitiveness and a suspicion of ethnic femininity. Tomei's portrayal as a smug award-winner, may well operate as a kind of backlash response to the most recent phase of Tomei's ethnic trajectory – the empowered ethnic woman.

Understanding that urban legends take shape as fantasy solutions to cultural anxieties, one can easily read the anecdote about Tomei's illegitimate Oscar as expressive of cultural concern about her status as an unruly ethnic woman. As an indirect means of articulating anxiety about Tomei's 'premature' admittance into an elite group of performers at the top of the industry (not to mention an almost guaranteed substantial increase in the salary that she would be paid for films) the rumor siphons off fears that power in Hollywood might be in the process of re-distribution. Tomei's status as one of a number of younger actresses with unproven and somewhat unknown ethnic backgrounds made her difficult to pin down, and therefore threatening. Her ability to personify a threat to white, male powerholders is hinted at in the use of Jack Palance in the rumor. As an embodiment of a stock Hollywood male type (and a strong symbol of endurance as a function of his role in *City Slickers*, his performance of a series of push-ups in the preceding year's Oscar ceremony, and the homage being given to him by Billy Crystal and the film industry at large) Palance was an ideal figure to make the fictional 'error' that led to the 'false' recognition of a young, female ethnic actress. Palance's intertextual relation (through the Western genre) to the threatened white community and the rejuvenation of white male heroism in *City Slickers* made him a potent star indeed to figure in such a rumor, which implicitly narrativizes the loss of power by a white male leading to the illegitimate attainment of power by an ethnic woman. Were Palance's role in the story not sufficient evidence of Tomei's role as a threat to white male power, it was also reported at one point that the sportscaster Frank Gifford (a television star whose rugged, male machismo is similar to Palance's) had repeated the rumor by way of opening banter at an awards ceremony for sports broadcasters, warning his audience that if Tomei came to claim any awards that evening, 'someone had better tackle her.'

Further reference to the illegitimacy of Tomei's Oscar win was made in a broadcast of NBC's *Suddenly Susan* on October 10, 1996. The sitcom starring Brooke Shields was at that point the third highest rated television show in the country, sandwiched between NBC powerhouses *Seinfeld* and *ER* in its 'Must-See-TV' lineup. In the episode in question, Shields unsuccessfully attempts to persuade a police officer that she is being systematically harassed by the power company. In response to her pleas, the officer skeptically rejoins, 'Lady, I gotta tell you. The Kennedy conspiracy I can buy. Marisa Tomei wining the Oscar – maybe. But the power company turning your lights on and off? Come on!' After the line about Tomei is delivered, it is punctuated by the loud laughter and appreciative applause of the studio audience.

I cite the wide circulation of discrediting rumors about Tomei to underscore my assertion at the beginning of the chapter that anxieties attached to the display of eroticized ethnic feminine power remained very much in evidence in the mid-1990s.[52] At the same time, however, many of the actress's film roles and much of her extra-filmic publicity indicates that European ethnicity increasingly factors as a fantasy solution to cultural crisis. In addition to being thoroughly imbricated with the thematic of escape or denial through fantasy, Tomei strikingly epitomizes ethnicity's capacity to act as a sliding signifier, pointing toward but finally veiling over zones of cultural crisis. Her regenerating role in response to a perceived sense of cultural exhaustion stands at the heart of many of her films and anchored her star persona throughout the mid-1990s. While examples of positive depictions of feminine ethnicity linked to the assertion of American nationalism extend as far back as Colleen Moore's declaration in 1925 that 'there's no place like home,' or Hedy Lamarr's wartime service and vehement denial of invitations to leave the US in the 1940s, Marisa Tomei represents a somewhat different case. Whereas Moore, Lamarr, and others embodied the idea that ethnicity could be productively converted into Americanism thereby demonstrating the nation's assimilative capacities, Tomei is aligned with the conversion of American culture into ethnicity as a means of recovering a past more viable than the present and establishing a basis upon which we can individuate ourselves. In this respect, she incarnates an utterly contemporary dimension of ethnicity in American culture, namely the fantasy of de-assimilation.[53]

It may be noted that my reading of Marisa Tomei's ethnic persona highlights particularly the films and public discourses of her career in the early and mid-1990s, a period which now appears to have been the peak phase of her popularity. Yet the fundamental grounding of Marisa Tomei's persona in values of ethnic authenticity is well illustrated in the way that her career in the late 1990s seems to have sputtered due to her casting in roles that don't put those values in play. The 1998 CBS made-for-television movie *Only Love*, specifically separates Tomei from an ethnic identity; in a gesture of contrastive casting, she appears as the American wife of a husband still emotionally tied to his Italian ex-girlfriend. When Tomei's over-the-top sensuality is not given ethnic explanation, it is made pathological, as in *The Slums of Beverly Hills* (1998) where the actress plays a pill-popping nurse. Such examples sustain the point that themes of ethnic vitality and exuberance crucially structure Marisa Tomei's persona. Roles that don't oblige a sense of ethnic nostalgia simply don't play to the fantasy of ethnicity that I have argued stands at the heart of her celebrity.

As her public prominence has receded in recent years, Tomei's name has lived on most actively as a punchline in jokes about her 'illegitimate' Oscar win that maintain a surprising vehemence. As recently as Spring, 2000, Tomei's name was invoked again in a *Saturday Night Live* skit, this time in a satirical advertisement for a series of commemorative plates detailing 'America's Worst Moments.' Along with political scandals of obvious national import such as the mendacious testimony of Colonel Oliver North, and the Clinton impeachment trial, the vignettes to be featured as 'America's most humiliating failures' included both Cher's music video 'If I Could Turn Back Time' and Tomei's Oscar award. In the chapter that follows, I hope to shed further light on the way that comedy such as this originates in a culture where female performativity is often seen as a disruption of national normality.

7

STARDOM, CORPOREALITY AND ETHNIC INDETERMINACY

Cher's disrupted/disruptive body

> In contemporary popular culture, unruly celebrities and riotous
> popular events force our attention and our fascination (if by noth-
> ing other than their sheer ubiquitous presence) over debates con-
> cerning 'appropriate' boundaries of contemporary racial, gendered
> and sexual identities.[1]

In US culture, the ideology of American whiteness is anchored in a narrative of
progression and assimilation, a narrative that the anomalies of Cher's career
serve to disrupt. While Richard Dyer has posited the white body as the denied
body, stardom continuously threatens to disturb this understanding by putting
the celebrity body on display.[2] Cher's star body in particular challenges conventions of whiteness in its high degree of self-awareness. What is particularly
striking about Cher's celebrity is the way that it moves in cycles to undo
moments of assimilation and integration, positioning her ambiguously and continuously as neither fully inside nor outside prevailing categories of identity.

Thus, the singer associated with hippie radicalism and youth culture in the
1960s becomes an icon of family-oriented entertainment in *The Sonny and Cher
Comedy Hour*; the single mother who dates scandalous rock stars becomes an
Academy Award winning actress by 1987; that same film star descends to the
low genres of infomercial and catalogue sales in the 1990s, then returns more
recently to 'artistic' pursuits as an actress once again associated with 'quality'
projects such as an HBO film on abortion.

Cher's star persona has drawn the attention (though mostly in passing) from
a number of feminist critics. In a discussion of *Moonstruck* (1987), Kathleen
Rowe has alluded to Cher's persona as 'unruly woman,' assessing her character
in that film as 'a paradigmatic woman on top, enhanced by the strong unruly
offscreen presence Cher brings to the part.'[3] In her discussion of the politics
of cross-dressing, Marjorie Garber has referred to the star's 'relentless self-
construction.'[4] Most recently, Yvonne Tasker devotes attention to Cher's film
and popular music roles noting some of the ways in which 'Cher repeatedly
comments on her own construction, on her search for perfection and on the
performance of the female body.'[5] While it is beyond the scope of this chapter

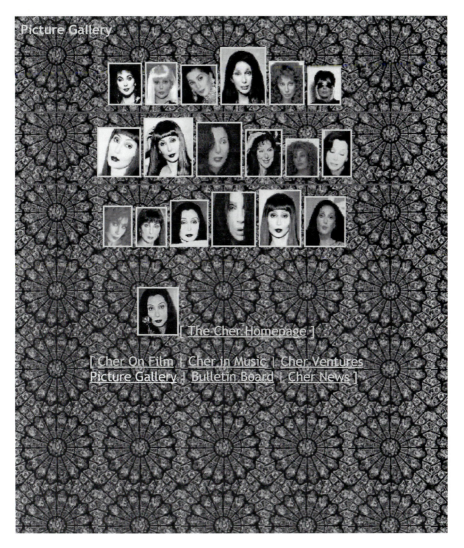

Figure 10 Cher's contemporary persona activates themes of multiplicity and longevity

to deal comprehensively and fully with every facet of Cher's long career and complex persona, I want to isolate certain elements and moments that are particularly communicative of the ways that Cher's star persona both indicates a confusion of gender, class and age distinctions, and problematizes the security of whiteness.[6] P. David Marshall among others has noted that 'The intense focus on the body and its reformulation is central to the construction of the female star.'[7] I will show how Cher's body functions as the sign of her unstable class and ethnic attributes – the marker of her ability to complicate operative distinctions between white and non-white, and high and low cultural forms. I will also suggest that Cher's persona works to thematize ethnic chameleonism by referencing assimilation imperatives that have historically impacted both ethnic immigrants and persons of color. My aim here will be to contrast Cher's body as an object of patriarchal ownership in the 1970s with the triumphantly self-produced body she displays in the 1990s. Positing that in her most recent incarnation she displays a set of meanings that run sharply counter to what George Lipsitz has termed 'the possessive investment in whiteness,'[8] I will link Cher's strong sense of bodily ownership to a perception of unpleasurable chaos in some contexts, and pleasurable multiplicity in others.

Central to such perceptions is a high degree of public knowledge about Cher's tattoos and plastic surgeries. At a time when the performance of celebrity identity and the display of celebrity beauty have become increasingly ironic, this sense of irony is particularly apparent in a website devoted to celebrity plastic surgeries, the 'Plastic People' website.[9] The mission of the website is simple and to the point. It reads, 'This is a listing of famous people who have gone under the knife to undergo magnificent changes into the incredible bodies and faces we see today.' Of the sixty-four celebrities whose surgeries are detailed on the site, Cher holds the distinction of the most numerous procedures, with plastic surgery reportedly performed on her breasts, nose, teeth, cheeks, stomach, butt, and navel as well as liposuction and a face lift. Discourses on Cher's transformable, constructed body have persisted through nearly her entire career, while the current emphasis on the self-produced Cher represents a strong departure from the activations of Cher's body and voice on display in *The Sonny and Cher Comedy Hour* of the early 1970s.

The mainstreaming of hippie culture: Cher, television and social transition

Cher's persona reflects well the transformations in American culture since the white ethnic revival of the 1970s. Conceptualizing ethnic identity as a matter of flexible consent, rather than rigid descent, for many Americans as Mary Waters has observed, 'ethnicity is increasingly a personal choice of whether to be ethnic at all, and, for an increasing majority of people, of which ethnicity to be.'[10] Marilyn Halter has linked such new modes of ethnic identity to a modernized culture in which the vast realm of possibility tied to consumption necessitates emphasis on dynamic, fluid ethnic affiliations. She writes that:

> If modernization is seen as enormous movement from destiny to choice, the change from 'being' to 'becoming' ethnic perfectly exemplifies this shift. It signifies a monumental reorientation in how identity is constructed and expressed. In traditional societies, ethnicity had an ascriptive status in which cultural affinities were an imperative, but with the evolution of modernity, what characterizes ethnicity is its optionality and malleability.[11]

166

If stars such as Marisa Tomei embody a romanticized ethnic authenticity, Cher represents another mode of ethnic selfhood, one which is both multiple and carnivalesque. In the current climate, Cher's multi-ethnicity resonates with a broader pattern in which 'more and more instances of what can be called "blended ethnicity," the amalgamation of two or more ethnic backgrounds, are showing up in the marketplace.'[12] Through the 1970s in her television and popular music stardom, Cher represented a chameleonic sense of multi-ethnicity through bodily display. In the 1980s, she becomes ethnically unmarked, then in the 1990s she reverts back to an ethnic mobility, but on fundamentally more transgressive terms.

Cher's first ethnic point of reference is to Native American culture through her iconographic slim, straight body and long dark hair. Native American identity constitutes a particular form of 'off-white' ethnicity in American culture, operating as a kind of 'white borderland' from forms of European ethnicity. Yet Philip Deloria suggests that 'whenever white Americans have confronted crises of identity, some of them have inevitably turned to Indians.'[13] By selectively and sporadically coding her body as Native American Cher provides one ethnically-based means of rationalizing its decoration. (Her connections to white trash culture provide another interpretive grid as I shall show).

As David Savran has pointed out, white hippies drew the source material for their fashioning of alternate identity paradigms from cultures of color. Self-styled victims of contemporary capitalism, they sought to align themselves with histories of oppression and positions of disenfranchisement that were perceived as enobling. As Savran notes, 'the genocidal history of North American conquest gives the surviving Native Americans possession of a secret knowledge and makes them the source of an imagined authenticity and psychic wholeness lacked by European or African Americans.'[14] Symbolic Indianness was a key value of the communal cultures and antiwar movements of the 1960s and 1970s, and references to Indian culture substantiated and legitimated the tribal consciousness of the youth movement in an era in which, as Deloria has pointed out, 'the meanings of Indianness drifted away from actual Indians more quickly and thoroughly than ever.'[15] The first phase of Cher's intermittent Indian narrative coincided with acclaimed films such as *Little Big Man* (1970) that featured the appropriation of Indianness by a white protagonist (played by Dustin Hoffman) and controversial public events such as Hollywood star Marlon Brando offering up a Native American representative, Sasheen Little Feather, to refuse his Academy Award for *The Godfather* (1973), in an effort to re-direct the energy from a celebrated fictionalized heritage narrative toward the compelling real one that supported the Red Power movement. Thus, Cher's emergence as a popular music and television star took place as images of Indian savagery were giving way to images of American nobility, and this newly positive image was being hijacked by the white counterculture.[16] Presented as both hippie and Native American in the early years of her stardom, Cher was well positioned to reconcile the split between hippie whiteness and Native American exoticism.

In the mid-1960s Sonny Bono and Cher emerged as popular music celebrities largely on the basis of their third single, 'I Got You, Babe.' At the time that they appeared on Milton Berle's vaudeville-inspired weekly variety program *The Hollywood Palace*, in 1965, the couple were clearly presented as representatives of a hippie subculture. Long-haired and outfitted in vests and bell bottoms, they engaged in interaction with Berle that showcased his sense of bemusement and wonder about their appearance and perceived value system. Yet in the later years of the 1960s the couple's ability to speak convincingly as representatives of youth culture receded due to changing musical styles and their oppositional stance toward drugs. Their audiences dwindled, and they could no longer play to that culture through its dominant venue, the concert arena. But television (particularly CBS television in its quest to update programming in the early 1970s) offered an ideal forum for the couple to productively expand their audience base to an older, more conservative audience, somewhat responsive to changing times but unwilling to accept hippie radicalism.

As has been well noted by a number of television historians, the late 1960s were an era in which the industry differentiated its quality demographics from more rural and traditional viewers in an effort to deliver higher-consuming audiences to advertisers.[17] The single clearest example of this trend, of course, was CBS's so-called 'purge' of its high-rated rural comedies in the late 1960s in an effort to improve its audience profile and produce 'quality numbers.' In most accounts of broadcast history, the corollary to this trend is seen to be the advent of the socially-critical sitcom exemplified by Norman Lear's *All in the Family*. New narrative paradigms such as the Lear sitcom are cited as part of the 'new wave' of more socially relevant programming to come in following the ideological decline of such sunny visions of postwar American life as might be found in *Father Knows Best* and *Leave it to Beaver*, and the economic decline of the no-longer demographically desirable rural comedies like *The Beverly Hillbillies*. Often overlooked in accounts of this transition, however, is the variety show, which in some ways belonged neither to the conservative past nor the more progressive present, and for that very reason constitutes an important example of television's need to reconcile socially disparate audiences in the shifting landscape of US culture in the late 1960s and early 1970s.[18] With their narratively fragmented style and emphasis on masquerade, such shows as *Rowan and Martin's Laugh-In*, *The Smothers Brothers Comedy Hour*, and *The Sonny and Cher Comedy Hour* were well suited to reflect and respond to social identities in flux and to stage social contestation in such a way as to re-orient difference as diversity.

Because of its stars' crossover connections to popular music and their status as celebrity couple, *The Sonny and Cher Comedy Hour* was arguably positioned as the variety show with the most direct connections to social experience in this period. In part through their self-consciously ethnic identities (Bono as Italian, and Cher as Native American) the two hosts continuously engaged questions of the status and social role of the outsider. In part a performance of ethnic flexibility and in part a demonstration of the incorporatibility of elements of radical youth cultures, *The Sonny and Cher Comedy Hour* attempted to discursively knit back together an increasingly polarized American culture by mainstreaming its hippie hosts. It did this chiefly by filtering their alterity through the fundamentally conservative discourse of family and the moderately conservative generic discourse of the variety show. Given the *fluidity* of roles in the variety show format, 'hippieness' could be seen as transient, un-serious and put on.

As a showcase for Cher's mutability, *The Sonny and Cher Comedy Hour* also inaugurated two of the most distinctive features of Cher's star persona in this period. It interpreted Cher's French, Armenian and Cherokee ethnic backgrounds as catalysts for a process of ethnic chameleonism and it inscribed her body with a set of meanings conducive to the interests of white patriarchy. In the 1970s Cher exemplified the idealized and governed female body, a fact well illustrated in her role as a blank foil to Sonny Bono, and in comments by designer Bob Mackie, who praised Cher's body as the ideal 'hanger' for his designer costumes on *The Sonny and Cher Comedy Hour*. Indeed, in one telling sketch from the series, Cher and guest star Farah Fawcett-Majors played mannequins whose mute bodies are positioned and adjusted by male workers.

At the same time, the show also displayed a number of strategies for reining in and recuperating Cher's dominance over Sonny both as a vocal performer and as the narratorial 'voice' at work behind songs about love and romance. To a great extent, Cher's presence in the show was constructed in the terms of an enigmatic absence, a fact which Cher herself recognized in the interview for a 1976 *TV Guide* article where she commented, 'Do you know that in the monologues, the openings and closings, I never talked? I said like three words to Sonny's 25, and then only to Son, never to the audience.'[19]

Just as Cher's body was conceptualized as significant only insofar as it showcased the creations of a male fashion designer, her voice was interpreted as a sign of her husband's creativity and virtuosity. On the 1965 album, *Cher*, for instance, the liner notes displace Cher as the record's performer to centralize Sonny's role as producer. Indeed, the liner notes are written not in Cher's voice, but in Sonny's. Most remarkable of all, Cher herself is among the people whom Sonny thanks. Sonny writes, 'Now, at the risk of sounding prejudiced, I must add that I am especially proud of Cher. For each song in this album, I asked her to pour out her heart and her soul – she did. Love, Sonny.'

Despite these kinds of maneuvers, Cher's career in the 1970s is often best remembered today for the sharp and unruly public put-downs she regularly delivered to her husband. Though her speech was more limited than Sonny Bono's, it tended to be blunt and biting. Indeed, the couple's signature repartee on *The Sonny and Cher Comedy Hour* was constructed entirely around a dynamic in which Sonny would set up a joke with a self-flattering observation and Cher would provide the often ego-deflating punchline. So central was the couple's performance of incessant (but warm) marital bickering that once they had separated in 'real life,' the show's formula was no longer viable – when a couple with real marital problems delivered them, the jokes at the heart of the show were no longer very funny.

References to Cher as a comically or transgressively ethnic figure abound during the 1970s. The titles of such hit songs as 'Dark Lady,' 'Gypsies, Tramps and Thieves,' and 'Half Breed' all bespeak a degree of investment in the figure of the ethnic outsider. One regular feature on *The Sonny and Cher Comedy Hour* was a musical number entitled 'Vamp,' a collection of brief sketches in which Cher played a series of historically notorious women, indirectly referencing popular memories of the vamp as a caricature of predatory ethnic femininity. Yet any suggestion that Cher spoke from and for the position of marginalized cultural identities was countered by public knowledge of her ongoing association with a variety of powerful male mentors – Sonny Bono, Bob Mackie, and later mogul David Geffen. Perceptions of her star body as an object of display in their interests and under their control rendered her an exoticized, but often silenced figure.

Cher and the narrative of social incorporation and sponsorship

If Cher's bodily configurations in the 1970s constructed her as an ideal site for the meanings of others, offering her up as a body that could showcase male creativity, Cher's body comes decisively under her own ownership and control in her later career. As the writer of a 1987 *Newsweek* article noted:

> Over the last 10 years or so, Cher has staged a coup – kind of occupied her own life and took over the radio station. She's 41 now. The person she calls 'Cher the Product,' is gone, dead; so deeply buried, it seems, that it would be hard to convince someone born in the 60's (say, one of Cher's boyfriends) that this woman ever stood by Sonny's side and sang Sonny's songs at dates that Sonny booked wearing clothes that Sonny selected.[20]

Through much of the 1980s, in the biographical narrative constructed through press coverage of the star's personal and professional pursuits, and within most of the individual film fictions in which she appeared, Cher is conceptualized as an emancipated and assimilated body. As she supplemented her recording career by building a parallel career as a film actress, Cher was increasingly figured in a discourse of approval.[21] Praised in the mainstream press as hard-working, talented, and humble about her acting ambitions, Cher was also presented as a caring mother (both off and sometimes on screen) and as a woman who exercised appropriate discipline over her body. (Like Jane Fonda, she fought off the aging process through a rigorous program of exercise). Moreover, her film roles de-glamorized her and moved her away from the excessive, spectacular body displayed on *The Sonny and Cher Comedy Hour*. When she departed from this norm, to wear an outrageous costume to the 1986 Academy Awards, Cher was immediately and sharply criticized.

Praise for the new Cher persona was generated in outlets such as *Ms.* magazine, which in 1998 prefaced a short series of articles and testimonials about the star with a rhapsodic introductory piece which noted that 'beneath the glitz lives an authentic feminist hero.'[22] In this period, Cher was also profiled in the *Reaching Your Goals* book series of illustrated inspirational readers for children. Given the same treatment as political and entertainment industry figures including Jesse Jackson, Steven Spielberg and Henry Cisneros whose biographies also appear in the series, Cher's life is detailed in triumphalist terms emphasizing the importance of self-actualization. The account closes with particular stress on Cher's integrity and perseverance:

> For years, Cher worked hard to become a successful singer. Then she worked hard to become an actress. Even when she needed money, she turned down movie roles that weren't right for her. Her goal has always been to be a *good* actress, not just a rich and famous one.[23]

Assimilation in this second phase of Cher's career was associated with a process of ethnic unmarking.[24] If in the first phase of her career, Cher was associated with a stridently ethnic body whose ongoing assimilation was guided and supervised by a variety of male mentors, in this second phase her assimilated status is showcased in her film roles. In large part, this involves displacement of Cher's body by her voice, speaking out in narratives in which she is credited with powerful speech on behalf of others. In this phase of her celebrity, Cher is as associated with unruly speech as she has been in different ways throughout her career, but significantly that forthright speech is largely put to use to secure beneficial treatment for others. Through the 1980s, Cher consistently appeared in film roles where she served as a social intermediary to disenfranchised male characters. Whether interacting with Eric Stoltz's elephantiasis victim in *Mask* (1985), Liam Neeson's mute homeless veteran in *Suspect* (1987), or even Nicolas Cage's socially isolated, semi-freakish baker with a wooden hand in *Moonstruck* (1987), Cher stages social incorporation or redemption implicitly based on her own experience.[25]

This type of advocacy is most explicitly delineated in *Suspect*, a legal thriller in which Cher plays Kathleen Riley, a Washington DC public defender. Historically, stylistically and thematically occupying a kind of middle ground between 1970s conspiracy films like *All the President's Men* (1976) and the serial conspiracies yet to come in 1990s tv dramas like *The X-Files*, *Suspect* thematizes speech as a form of social power. Mounting a vigorous defense on behalf of accused murderer Carl Wayne Anderson (Neeson), Kathleen calls the innocent man 'a frightened, lost human being. Just like you and me.' To exonerate her client, Kathleen recovers an audio cassette in the murder victim's car containing testimony about how a federal judge fixed a case in the late 1960s, and from this point forward she herself is targeted (though, to what extent remains unclear) as a group of powerful men act to conceal their involvement in or knowledge of the corrupt court case and the murder committed to preserve its secrecy.

Kathleen's ally in her efforts to free Carl and bring the corruption to light is Eddie Sanger (Dennis Quaid), a lobbyist for the milk industry. Depicting the world of Capitol Hill as thoroughly sordid and corrupt, the film implies that Eddie has been sexually compromised by his participation in it. At the start of the film we see that his lobbying work reduces him to the status of a gigolo as he sleeps with a Congresswoman to win her vote on a key issue. Called to jury duty for the murder trial of Carl Anderson, Eddie's sharp observations and ability to provide clandestine communication to Kathleen strengthen her case considerably while giving him the opportunity to purify himself in a shared effort to affect legitimate justice. (That Kathleen and Eddie have to subvert the judicial system through jury tampering in order to show how justice has been subverted is a point that the film leaves little room to explore).

Although *Suspect* provides Cher's character with a name that suggests an oblique attempt to confer ethnicity on her (and her hair is styled here into the kind of tight curls that often connote Irish or Jewish identity for Hollywood) the film gives no further information about her, introducing no family members or even much of a private life for a character whose conscientious devotion to work has overshadowed all other concerns. The portrait sketched by the film of an urban single woman, professional though poorly paid and living in a small apartment, balances the All-American looks and affluent demeanor of Dennis Quaid as the two contend against corrupt Deputy Attorney General Paul Gray. What seems most significant is that here as in other Cher films of the 1980s, her character's integrity seems to trigger honest communication and acceptance from those who have either hidden the truth or been prevented from speaking it. (When a combative prosecuting attorney contends that 'Ms. Riley has the gift of speech,' he perhaps says more than he knows). In *Suspect* this pattern is most spectacularly brought to a close in a courtroom finale in which Carl Anderson takes the stand, writing his responses to questions from Kathleen and the prosecuting attorney. As he does so, his words are then articulated by an African-American court clerk who speaks them with increasing emotion, as if she recognizes in his story broader patterns of social silencing and discrimination. Carl relays a poignant story of the wounds he suffered while fighting in Vietnam in a powerful speech act that culminates his involvement in the film.[26] Shortly thereafter, armed with newly unearthed information that enables her to tie up all the strands of the conspiracy to keep the fixed court case silent, Kathleen calls to the stand the presiding judge, Matthew Helms (John Mahoney) in a defiant gesture that critiques the accumulation of power as a shield of silence against social victimization. Kathleen's courtroom performativity accomplishes an act of justice that exonerates Carl, restores a sense of integrity to Eddie, and symbolically overturns a corrupt system. It is a resonant form of closure perhaps not just for the film, but for a phase of Cher's stardom in which celebrations of her agency accumulated in film, print, and other modes of public discourse.

'That Cher was a man:' contemporary figurations of Cher's impossible body[27]

Rather than directly capitalizing on her film and recording successes, Cher was more involved with a variety of sales ventures through most of the 1990s. These included a book on working out, nutrition and weight loss entitled *Forever Fit*, two workout videos, a perfume, a prominent association with the Lori Davis line of hair care products, the launching of her own line of skincare products called Aquasentials by Cher, and a catalogue called *Sanctuary* which enabled consumers to mailorder gothic and medieval accent pieces.[28] Cher's decision to initiate this wide range of business ventures is in keeping with the changing meanings of her body during this period of time. As Cher has aged, her persona has altered to position her not as the result of patriarchal production (the woman whose career was made by Sonny Bono, Bob Mackie, David Geffen, or even Robert Altman, Peter Bogdanovich or Mike Nichols) but as a more transgressive figure involved in her own production efforts on a variety of fronts.

Cher's involvement with a 1997 HBO movie, *If These Walls Could Talk*, as both a director and actress seemed to confirm her flexibility in moving across generic boundaries and traversing distinctions between high and low culture. Nominated for a Golden Globe for her performance as a gynecologist working in a women's abortion clinic, Cher seemed to inaugurate a period of higher profile activity that continued up to the winter and spring of 1998 with significant public attention paid to Cher's eulogy for Sonny Bono at his funeral in February, and her appearance a short time later at the Academy Awards ceremony. Nonetheless through the 1990s it seems that dominant institutions of cinema, television and popular music have struggled to accommodate Cher's impossible (which is to say troublesome, contentious and excessive) body. Consequently, the actress has appeared in very few films in the past eight years, starring only in *Mermaids* (1990) and *Faithful* (1996), providing a cameo appearance in Robert Altman's *Ready to Wear* (1994), and acting as an ensemble member in *Tea with Mussolini* (1999). If there is one cinematic image that indicates the 'problem' of Cher in the 1990s, perhaps it is the promotional poster from the black comedy *Faithful* which features Cher bound and gagged.

By the late 1980s and 1990s, Cher's body had become openly scandalous and subversive. Her association with low culture merchandising, her lack of film parts, and her appearance in music videos such as 'If I Could Turn Back Time,' which triumphantly displays Cher's ever-young body as an ironic fulfillment of the song's lyrical content, all confirmed her as a too-visible image of the female body.[29] While 1980s films such as *Moonstruck* had thematized a turning back the clock process,[30] gesturing toward the transformative dynamics central to Cher's persona such transformations were now perceived to be chaotic.

Figure 11 The problem of Cher in the 1990s

A 1992 concert video, *Cher at the Mirage*, offers evidence of the way that Cher herself calls upon images of the multiple Cher, the constructed Cher. In a performance of the song 'Perfection' that lyrically links 'women's work' to the attainment of bodily perfection, a male transvestite emerges providing counterpoint to Cher as she continues to sing the song. The male performer, John Elsin Kenna, is so remarkable a replica of Cher that we are actually momentarily confused as to which Cher is 'real.' In authorizing her own quotation, Cher acknowledges herself as fictionalized production, and proffers to her audience a pleasurable plurality. In somewhat similar fashion, Cher's performance of the song 'After All' in the same concert video begins with a biographical montage of Cher, her ex-husbands and children, even posters from her films, inviting a reading of the song as a reflection upon Cher's life, and thus putting into circulation a historical Cher and by extension cinematic, televisual, and popular music Chers as well.

Likewise, in a broadcast of *The Rosie O'Donnell Show*, on July 8, 1996, the appearance of Cher as a guest seemed to inspire quotation by both the host and another guest. O'Donnell referenced a sense of bodily performativity associated with Cher by displaying a Cher doll and proposing that she might add tattoos to it. Another guest, television actor Malcolm Gets, appeared on stage wearing a wig of long, straight dark hair, and displaying his midriff. After removing the wig, he placed it on a chair, and addressed it as 'Cher' for the remainder of the segment.[31]

Cher's appearance at the 1998 Academy Awards ceremonies served as a forceful reminder of the impossibilities she represents in the current discursive climate on celebrity bodies. In recent years the boundaries of the Oscar show text have significantly expanded with an increasing emphasis on pre- and post-show commentary. Such coverage attends scrupulously to the hairstyle, makeup and clothing choices of nominees, presenters and guests, and reads their choices as appropriate or inappropriate in relation to perceptions of their star personae and conventional norms of male and female beauty.

In a climate in which celebrity bodies at the Oscars have increasingly been displayed as mannequins for dress and jewelry (and in 1998 even handbag)[32] designers, Cher appeared at the Oscar ceremonies in a costume designed by Bob Mackie that disrupted prevailing modes of bodily display. Clearly replicating the outfit she wore to the 1987 Oscar ceremonies,[33] the costume with its elaborate headdress and scant covering of the star's fifty-two-year-old body was simultaneously an invocation of Native American costume, a sartorial reference to the kinds of costumes Cher performed in on *The Sonny and Cher Comedy Hour*, and a display of the bodily fitness rendered by exercise, diet and plastic surgery. If one of the functions of fashion is to make visible one's membership in a community,[34] Cher's costume subversively announced her separation from the community of performers feting themselves and each other at the Academy Awards.[35] With its vaguely ethnic semiotic, the outfit confused rather than confirmed any sense of clear meaning.

For commentators on the Oscars that year, Cher clearly served as a benchmark for anti-fashion. Variously interpreted as an homage to *Titanic*, an invocation of the Statue of Liberty and an attempt to re-create an ice cream waffle cone, Cher's ensemble inspired confusion and consternation amongst Oscar commentators. Her costume's very indecipherability was an affront to those who read the Oscar text for clues to the way that stardom confirms age, class and gender distinctions. The effect of the costume was to de-naturalize the ensembles worn by other celebrities, the excess of Cher's outfit serving to communicate the performed nature of celebrity appearances at the Oscars and working against the pleasurable perception of reality that inspires such close scrutiny of star bodies and clothing at the event. (We pretend that the Oscars are an occasion to see stars in their real lives.) This, I would argue, was the source of the strong disapproval registered for the outfit by so many Oscar commentators, not the least of whom was Joan Rivers who in her increasingly influential 'Academy Awards Fashion Review' on the E network assembled a panel of experts to evaluate the appearances of stars at the Oscars. The panel reserved their strongest condemnation for Cher, implying that her outfit was semiotically inconsistent with the meanings of the event. In one article another panel of fashion reviewers grading the stars' outfits found fault with Cher's attire. Her cumulative grade was a D, reflecting a total of three Fs one A, and a refusal to grade by one commentator who asserted that the star 'belongs in a league of her own.'[36]

In a year when Oscar commentators praised the meeting of 'Old Hollywood' and 'Young Hollywood,' applauding the good taste, style, simplicity and panache of veterans like Julie Christie and newcomers like Minnie Driver, Cher personified the instability of these distinctions and rendered them less meaningful. For the telecast, she served as a sartorial and corporeal enigma, vehemently criticized for her failure to observe the codes that confer intelligibility on the celebrity body in the context of the Academy Awards.

Where for the Academy Awards telecast, Cher's flamboyant and self-authored body was deemed unruly and inappropriate, it took on more positive connotations in a fourth season episode of the Fox television drama *The X-Files*. 'The Post-modern Prometheus,' an episode broadcast November 30, 1997, emphatically presents Cher's star persona as the marker for transformative empowerment. In the world of everyday grotesquerie conjured up by the episode, Cher's body affirms the power of desire to transcend conditions of disempowerment. Referencing *Frankenstein*, *Mask*, and the films of Tim Burton, 'The Post-modern Prometheus' depicts the work of an evil scientist and 'The Great Mutato,' his deformed, isolated, human creation who searches for a mate. Socially isolated, the deformed boy idolizes Cher; indeed, just prior to discovering him in a basement, FBI agents Mulder and Scully stumble upon a sort of Cher shrine which he has assembled. At the episode's conclusion, Mulder and Scully take the boy to a Cher concert where the star picks him out of the audience and invites him to dance.

Openly using an impersonator, *The X-Files* shoots 'Cher' from the back, inviting speculation as to the extent of the impersonation being rendered. Following the broadcast, such speculation was lively on a number of the websites devoted to *The X-Files*. While a first wave of commentary centered around the question of whether the performer was in fact Cher herself, later participants seemed to concur that it was an impersonator. Moreover, as one fan wrote breathlessly to his fellow discussants, 'Did anyone else notice that Cher was in drag? That's right you heard it here first – that Cher was a man!' Commenting on the intertextual associations to Mary Shelley's novel in an Internet discussion of the episode, one fan observed, 'Of course, in this tale, there was no bride, though Cher does remind me of Franky's Mrs.'[37] Indeed the Great Mutato's search for a mate like himself comes to a fitting endpoint in his encounter with Cher, another created, invented human body.

While Cher's body and image are used in the episode to invoke the possibility of self-transformation, her voice is associated with oblique forms of agency that circumvent patriarchy. Cher songs are prominently featured on the soundtrack during the sexual encounters between the Great Mutato and two local women (Shaineh Berkowitz and Elizabeth Pollidori), encounters that take place in homes enclosed by striped termite tenting. This juxtaposition of sound and image cues our perception that we have entered the realm of carnival where the normal order of things is inverted. Although the Great Mutato has apparently impregnated them without their consent (or knowledge) it would be an oversimplification to describe these incidents as rape, because in both cases it is suggested that they lead to children for women who lack satisfactory partners. Sexual intimacy with an 'other' enables both women to achieve their desire for children through unconventional means while defying marriage (Elizabeth Pollidori's husband has said he does not want to have children and refuses to talk with her about it) and science (Shaineh Berkowitz has had her tubes tied). The incidents thus figure as moments of magical resolution for women whose options under patriarchy would normally be intensely constrained.

The Great Mutato remains nevertheless a figure tinged with ambivalence. His associations with Cher connote both a positive expression of agency, and a negative expression of fearfulness about bodily self-construction. Near the end of the episode, when he is cornered by the agents, and confronted by a mob of angry townspeople, he speaks poignantly about his condition while the camera inspects the faces of those present and finds that many of them do not look fully human. We realize that all bodies are imperfect and engineered, and that assumptions of identity based on bodily normality and stability may need to be called into question. Finally, the episode's interest in thinking through conditions of bodily impossibility is established in large part by centralizing Cher's star body as the paramount repository for these concerns. In this way, the episode capitalizes on the defining features of unruliness, instability, and mobility in Cher's de-assimilated 1990s body. Cher makes spectacularly visible the paradox of social expectations for the female body in late twentieth-century US culture. The bodily impossibility she represents is equivalent to the impossible position of all women's bodies under late capitalism. In its refusal to be assimilated, safely commodified, and stable, Cher's 'impossible' body displays a subversive level of knowledge about the cultural work women's bodies are expected to perform.

The kinds of meanings attached to Cher in 'The Post-Modern Prometheus' typify one strand of discursive response to the star's sexualized, aging body, but the meanings she provokes are not always so sanguine. Current discourses reveal a split between anxious and approving responses to the way that Cher's body registers a sense of ontological uncertainty. Cher frequently emerges as a negatively-coded posthuman body in popular cultural jokes and references; at other times her posthuman status is used to positive and forceful effect. For instance in 1999, Cher's hit single 'Believe' employed a voice-altering 'vocoder' technique to technically morph her voice on certain words in such a way that it appears the singer's human persona easily gives way to and interrelates with a technical manufacturing process.[38] The song, the biggest hit of Cher's career, is musically consistent with those questions raised by her persona in its most recent stage which invites attention to the self-consciously produced nature of Cher's body and voice. At the same time, the structure and style of the song approaches the recycling and sampling style of dance remixes, suggesting a relationship to the past that is particularly resonant and potentially fruitful for reconciling the past and the present in Cher's persona.

At other times, Cher is the subject of derisively humorous references that engage her as a transgressive, synthetic object. The emergent tensions in Cher's aging ethnic persona were nowhere more evident than in a *Saturday Night Live* skit broadcast on March 20, 1999. In the skit Cher (being parodied by the youthful Drew Barrymore) was referred to as being 'half Cherokee, and half rubber.' In the mock news broadcast hosted by Colin Quinn on *Saturday Night Live* of April 10, 1999, Quinn joked that 'the method used to prepare Lenin's body for display is the same as that used to prepare Cher for the 'Believe' video.' In early 2000, a character in the sitcom 'Oh Grow Up' asserted that 'The real and the unreal are blending together – like Cher's face.' Meanwhile, the critic Blackwell has called Cher 'a Hawaiian bar mitzvah,' a resonant phrase that bespeaks a hostile stance toward the indecipherable, variable ethnic status that is at other times a source for productive play within her persona.

Blackwell's jibe illustrates how the ethnic components of Cher's persona seem to operate in the form of a palette, into which she (and others) can selectively delve. As early as *The Sonny and Cher Comedy Hour*, the star's persona has proved flexible in such a way that different ethnic identities can be called upon at various times, a considerable representational strength for the format of the variety show. Outside of that genre, Cher's multiethnicity has registered on more ambivalent terms. In 1993, she was even associated (though temporarily) with an ethnic homeland, as she paid a humanitarian visit to Armenia, when that nation was still endeavoring to recover from a devastating earthquake. Fully covered by a press team that included journalists from *People* magazine and the ABC news program *20/20*, Cher's trip was reported in the form of a travelogue of celebrity tourism, a heritage journey whose most important meanings centered around the star rather than the people she met or the conditions of the country she visited. The article in *People*, for example, closes by recounting how Cher met a stone carver during her trip, learning some of his skills and 'beginning to feel Armenian.'[39]

Another strand of discourse on Cher in the late 1990s and early 2000s connects her to the satisfactions of longevity and domesticity. As home decorating and refuge lifestyling became key trends in the late 1990s, coverage of Cher sometimes showcased her ability to create a home that reflected her personal style. Articles such as a 1996 profile in *Architectural Digest* of the Gothic, Moorish, Spanish and Byzantine styles fused together in Cher's Miami Beach home emphasized an aesthetic founded on the 'ethnic history look – between a temple and a church.'[40] Throughout her career, Cher has been photographed and profiled in her various homes in states of exotic domesticity, yet always with an underlying focus on her itinerant status and changing personal taste. A 1991 article observed that:

> Cher buys houses the way many women buy dresses. She has bought, built and redesigned fourteen houses in the past twenty years, from a Tuscan villa in Bel-Air where she lived with her husband, Sonny Bono, and a lot of period French and Italian furniture, through a contemporary Egyptian temple in Beverly Hills, to what she called a 'prehistoric/ futuristic' New York triplex apartment . . . and, of course, the Deco adobe. Currently, she's planning a new house on the beach in Malibu, which will rise 'shimmering from the sand like something out of the *Arabian Nights*,' says [Cher's decorator] Ron Wilson.[41]

In this way coverage of Cher's homes substantiates both her ethnic mutability and the ongoing operative tension between exceptionalness (in the form of wealth and flamboyance) and typicality (Cher's status as a single mother, her desire for a quiet homelife) sustained by her star persona.[42]

It may seem that if there is any form of whiteness to which Cher can ultimately be most securely attached it is to 'white trash,' that category which Matt Wray and Annalee Newitz contend operates as 'an allegory of identity which is deployed to describe the existence of class antagonism in the US.'[43] Cher's links to unrestrained consumption, her excessive and self-produced body, stated affiliation with Elvis (in her video for 'Walking in Memphis,' Cher impersonates him) and proximity to camp all align her persona with some of the signature elements of white class culture. The *X-Files* episode discussed above seems to understand this as well, in its placement of Cher as presiding deity over a working-class, white trash community. In keeping with the tendencies of white trash, and as part of a late twentieth-century trend in which divadom 'escaped its elite precincts and "descended" to the realm of pop music and culture,'[44] Cher's persona has the ability to unsettle a number of apparently fixed cultural boundaries.

Further, as Gael Sweeney notes, 'It is fascinating that many of the icons of White Trash, from Elvis to Bill Clinton to Loretta Lynn, have acknowledged an Indian heritage, linking themselves at least in spirit to these marginal mixed-race groups.'[45] For Cher, residual traces of Native American identity constitute reference to a form of ethnicity that operates as a 'white borderland,' a peripheral version of whiteness explanatory of her blunt speech, unruly behavior and vacillation between high and low modes of stardom. Nor does her well-publicized wealth necessarily interrupt the narrative of her white trash identity. As Wray and Newitz observe:

> The idea that white trash can have a lot of money and yet still some-how remain 'trash' seems contradictory, particularly when we consider that trash are marked by their position at the bottom of the white socioeconomic ladder. However, 'trash with money' is precisely the way in which white trash have been made accessible to Americans as a kind of cultural group with whom they might like to identify.[46]

Filtering Cher's transgressive body and unruly speech through a discourse of 'white trash' preserves the bond between whiteness and decorous femininity, while conjoining marginal forms of whiteness with class disempowerment.

My purpose in providing this analysis of the corporeal codes of Cher's stardom has been based on the premise that it can tell us something of the complex ways in which we scrutinize the celebrity body at the beginning of the twenty-first century. Anne Cranny-Francis has noted '. . . the dissolution of conservative notions of the body as a coherent and unified identity, defined and regulated by a range of hierarchised dualisms, such as male/female, white/black, mind/body, human/alien, human/machine, human/animal.'[47] Cher, it seems, provides one of the most striking examples of the celebrity body that works on these terms. In the 1990s the meanings of Cher's body-based star persona centered upon ethnic, gender and class ambiguities located decisively in her bodily configurations. Disrupted in the sense that she herself has foregrounded the interventions made upon it, and disruptive to patriarchy and its normative usages of the female body, Cher strenuously resists the proprieties of white femininity. Her connection to the transgressive category of 'white trash' has elicited consternation at times, while recent celebrations of her as a survivor diva seem to be grounded in new identity models that emphasize multiethnicity. Yet as an example of the newly-visible aging female film star, Cher sustains a level of ethnic signification that has been in many ways indigestible to mainstream, conservative culture.

In charting the trajectory of Cher's bodily performativity, it may seem that I have led my reader to a point of closure based entirely on celebrating Cher's current stature as a self-owned and self-produced body. While I do think there is some value in this, I want to heavily qualify any such invitation to celebrate, for in Cher's case the construction of such a body-based sense of identity is founded on highly problematic choices about dietary and surgical interventions on the body. Such 're-writings' of the aging female body clearly perpetuate a climate of body evaluation that is antithetical to the cultural and psychic interests of women, while conducive to the economic interests of others.

At the beginning of the twenty-first century, public commentary on Cher's stardom trades alternately in themes of grotesque hybridity and multi-ethnic validation. For these reasons, her celebrity operates in mixed modes of celebration and combative humor; there are few stars who are as frequently targeted for derisive jokes, yet Cher's spectacular re-emergence in the last years of the twentieth century saw her performing anthems of endurance and survival to great popular approval and being ushered into divadom.[48] In the early twenty-first century, Cher's persona is best classed alongside those of other revived pop icons like Stevie Nicks, Debbie Harry and Tina Turner, as she has re-emerged couched in an approving discourse of survival and longevity. A 2000 *Entertainment Weekly* profile noted warmly:

> Fame is a microscope. The crushing adulation that comes with celebrity has laid low many an unprepared star. But that rubric never applied to Cher. For her, fame was/is/always will be a kaleidoscope. Train your gaze on Cher at any point in her three-decades-plus career, and just as you begin to resolve one spectacular, oversaturated vision of her, she turns your focus just a bit, letting another multihued shard of her personality fall into view.[49]

The emergent thematics of survival and longevity that have been taken into the Cher persona contrast rather sharply with the post-peak careers of other ethnic female stars whose careers are examined here. Clearly Cher incarnates a more complex, dynamic and unruly sense of female identity than has tended to be validated by previous models of female stardom. But before we can fully assume that this shift reflects a more progressive set of social possibilities for women, we should note that Cher has had access to varieties of age-defying technology largely unavailable to stars in earlier eras. Indeed, her celebrity narrative is consistent with a broader cultural narrativization (for me, deeply disturbing) of plastic surgery as empowerment.[50] Yet despite the qualifications these features of her persona introduce, it is evident that Cher's authorship of her own body clearly works to disturb mainstream cultural forums, to threaten cherished patterns of patriarchal ownership, and to de-stabilize some of the more conservative meanings of glamor and stardom.

NOTES

1 HOLLYWOOD FILM AND THE NARRATIVIZATION OF ETHNIC FEMININITY

1 My understanding of the function of popular monuments is derived from points made by Anne O'Byrne in 'Memory, Monuments, and Counter-monuments,' a paper delivered at the 1994 Remapping the Borders: Irish Cultural Studies in the 1990s Conference, University of Texas at Austin.

2 Eakin in *The New York Times*, December 4, 1994, XX p. 22.

3 See Marchetti (1993). Other important work has been done by Sumiko Higashi in Friedman (ed.) (1991).

4 Such work ranges from survey-oriented analyses, such as Woll (1977), or Lopez in *Unspeakable Images*, to more specific investigations of Latino or Latina stars such as Shari Robert's '"The Lady in the Tutti-Frutti Hat:" Carmen Miranda, A Spectacle of Ethnicity,' or Hershfield (2000) or Valdivia's (2000) analysis of 'Latina spitfire' Rosie Perez, a significant predecessor to stars such as Jennifer Lopez. Another collection of writings on Latino representation is Noriega and Lopez (1996).

5 See Bogle (1989), Guerrero (1993) and Winokur's 'Black is White/White is Black: "Passing" as a Strategy of Racial Compatibility in Contemporary Hollywood Comedy,' in Friedman (ed.) (1991).

6 See Basinger (1999).

7 Decker (1997: 207).

8 With the high level of scholarly interest in deconstructing whiteness in recent years, there has emerged a particular emphasis on whiteness and masculinity. Scholarship in this area includes Pfeil (1995), Studlar (1996), Nelson (1998), Savran (1998) and Robinson (2000). My project counterbalances some of this work by linking recent theoretical formulations to the construction of idealized femininities through stardom.

9 Giroux in Clark and O'Donnell (eds) (1999: 230).

10 Dyer (1997).

11 Willis (1997: 3).

12 duCille (1998).

13 Dyer, pp. 42–3.

14 Jacobson (1998: 5).

15 See Berlant (1997: 175–220).

16 Lipsitz (1998: vii).

17 Ibid., p. 99.

18 Hartigan Jr. (1999: 25).

19 Ibid., p. 34.

20 Frankenberg (1993: 231).

21 Ibid., p. 6.
22 Dyer, *Stars* (1979: 30).
23 Mayne (1993: 138).
24 See for instance Perkins in Gledhill (ed.) (1991), Dyer's 'Judy Garland and Gay Men,' in *Heavenly Bodies* (1986) and Mayne's discussion of Bette Davis in 'Star-Gazing' in *Cinema and Spectatorship* (1993).
25 Gaines (1982: 20).
26 King in Kerr (ed.) (1986: 155–6).
27 Studlar (1996: 8–9).
28 McLean in *Journal of Film and Video*, 44(3/4) Fall 1992/Winter 1993, pp. 8–26.
29 Ibid., p. 9.
30 Roberts in *Cinema Journal* 32(3) (Spring, 1993), pp. 3–24.
31 To borrow a phrase from Miller (1994: 6).
32 Koszarski (1990: 195).
33 deCordova (1990: 113).
34 Wolfe in Gledhill (ed.) (1991: 92).
35 And this process becomes even more complex when the ethnic 'outsider' is, in fact, an 'insider' constructed to embody difference but only on the foundation of essential similarity.
36 For an example of this kind of study see Morrison (1998).
37 Indeed, the actress is credited with having 'launched the career of Ernst Lubitsch' in her entry in Barrett and McDonnell (eds) (1994: 206).
38 Higashi in Friedman (ed.) (1991: 7).
39 Hall (1992: 206).
40 Shohat in Friedman (ed.) (1991: 215).
41 Ibid.
42 Marchetti in Friedman (ed.) (1991: 305).
43 Several feminist film historians have generated studies which draw attention to the complexity and significance of negative cinematic images of women. Such 'reclaiming' work has been done, for example by Doane (1991), Staiger (1995) and Jacobs (1991).
44 For a useful discussion of some of the stakes of multiculturalism, see King (2000). King persuasively argues that the restrictive immigration legislation of the 1920s marks a key point of origin for contemporary multicultural debate for it 'introduced distinctions into the US polity that necessarily weakened the assimilationist ideal, devaluing southeastern European immigrants to the benefit of Europeans descended from northwestern countries. The modern upshot is an ambivalence (among groups outside the Anglo-American group) about both assimilation and Americanization, an ambivalence that has provided some of the political support for multiculturalism,' p. 269.
45 Browder (2000: 11).
46 Alba (1990: 295).
47 I discuss one such instance in Slater and Bachman (eds) (2001).
48 Mizejewski (1999).
49 Banet-Weiser (1999: 21).
50 Ibid., p. 29.
51 Ibid., p. 161.
52 Clark in *Cultural Studies*, 1(2) (May, 1987), p. 198.
53 Banta (1987: 91).
54 Indeed, the very choice to group these stars together as products of an apparently monolithic 'Hollywood' might well be called into question. Let me stress my recognition of the fact that the various forms of stardom I discuss here have been generated within very different institutional frameworks that have gone under the same

name (Hollywood) but are clearly in important ways also to be set apart from one another.
55 See 'A Melting Pot for the 21st Century,' *Newsweek*, September 27, 1999, p. 35.
56 Halter (2000).

2 THE WEARING OF THE GREEN

1 Dreiser, 'Hollywood Now,' *McCalls Magazine* September, 1921, p. 15.
2 It is interesting to observe that Irishness seemed to connote something less positive for industry males, whether actors or directors, who if described as Irish, were often associated with quick-temperedness, abusiveness or alcoholism – sometimes all three. I am thinking in particular of director Marshall (Mickey) Neilan, who was cast as a self-destructive Hollywood bad boy who might have had a brilliant career had he not been alcoholic, and of producer John McCormick, who was married to Moore. Their marriage was reputed to be the prototype for the film *What Price Hollywood?* later re-made as *A Star Is Born*. Moore herself was reported to have provided the inspiration behind the famous conclusion of that film by pointedly identifying herself to studio bosses as 'Mrs. John McCormick' at the height of her celebrity.
3 Joseph Curran (1988: 31) observes that the American Film Institute Catalogue lists ninety-one films made during the 1920s that are about the Irish or Irish-Americans (though only a few of these still survive). Of course, the subject matter of films produced is an incomplete index of the prominence of Irish discourses in Hollywood, which would also have been strongly tied to elements such as stardom.
4 Whereas by the 1930s, entire genres would be organized around the tensions between European 'Old World' values and the requirements of Americanization (i.e., the gangster film), in the less consolidated industrial climate of 1920s Hollywood, the meanings of ethnicity and assimilation could be most consistently carried through stardom.
5 Curran, p. 30.
6 Wright in *Motion Picture Magazine*, April, 1914, p. 120.
7 Grabo in *The Dial*, LXVI (1919), p. 541.
8 Ibid., pp. 539–40.
9 Curran, p. 28.
10 Dyer (1986: 2–3).
11 The magazine is unspecified, but the type style and reference to 'Adela' (gossip columnist Adela Rogers St. Johns) suggest it was probably *Photoplay*. Such discursive Irishness was frequently used to situate Moore in blurbs and photo captions. For instance, a photo in the *Chicago Herald-Examiner* on Dec. 17, 1923, appeared as follows: 'Sure, 'an yez know the darlint Colleen Moore? "An the grand boy wid her is her husban", Mr. John McCormick.'
12 Deland's comments are cited in Banta (1987: 61).
13 In setting up this model of Hollywood as an assimilating production line and Moore its product, I in no way discount Moore's agency through participation in and even initiation of such promotional endeavors. However, it is impossible to accurately assess the degree of Moore's self-determination (though in her own accounts of her career, one has the tantalizing sense that she suppresses and disavows her agency at times). My focus remains on the way in which Moore's life, career and achievements were represented to the public, and accordingly her agency is not heavily stressed here.
14 Smith in *Motion Picture* 21, June, 1921, p. 54.
15 Ibid.
16 Gassaway in *Picture Play Magazine*, January, 1920, p. 78.

17 Ibid.
18 Ibid., p. 79.
19 Review of *Little Orphant Annie*, *Variety*, December 6, 1918, p. 39.
20 Gabaccia (1994: 112).
21 Peltret in *Motion Picture Classic*, July, 1922, p. 17.
22 By contrast, other well-known actresses of the period, such as the Canadian-born Mary Pickford, who as Joseph Curran points out was half-Irish, were not publicized in terms of their ethnicity at all, but as purely 'American' products. Curran writes 'Like Colleen Moore, Mary Pickford was half-Irish, her mother being the child of immigrants from Co. Kerry. But despite this fact and her Roman Catholic upbringing, "America's Sweetheart," was not identified as Irish and did not play Irish parts.' p. 29.
23 Colleen Moore, *Silent Star*, Garden City, NY: Doubleday & Co., 1968, p. 25.
24 Spears in *Films in Review*, August–September, 1963, p. 404. The regular emphasis on the involvement of Moore's grandmother in her life served a number of functions. It obliquely furthered Moore's Cinderella image (with Mary Kelly as godmother/grandmother), it disguised Moore's agency by suggesting her career was shaped by others, and it burnished her image of sexual innocence by providing her with a nearly constant guardian of her virtue.
25 Moore in *Chicago Daily News*, Feb. 2, 1968, p. 24.
26 Mitchell, 'The Irish in the Movies,' February, 1923, p. 20. (Source Unknown) Colleen Moore Clippings File, Academy of Motion Picture Arts and Sciences, Margaret Herrick Library, Beverly Hills, California. (Hereafter AMPAS).
27 Saurin in *Photoplay*, March, 1921, p. 31.
28 Gassaway in *Motion Picture Magazine*, June, 1922, p. 40.
29 Uncited clipping dated January 14, 1928, Moore Clippings File, AMPAS.
30 Taylor in *The New York Times*, October 26, 1971.
31 In a miniature version of *This Side of Paradise* for the library of Moore's dollhouse.
32 Taylor *ibid*.
33 Banner (1983: 279–80).
34 Ibid., p. 279.
35 Spears, p. 403.
36 Review of *Irene*, *Variety*, March 3, 1926, p. 34.
37 A town famous for its month-long matchmaking festival.
38 *Come On Over* thus predates *The Quiet Man* (1952) in representing the return of the native son whose achievements in America give him a distinctive height in the local Irish landscape. (Michael's comment recalls John Ford's incessant tight framing on Sean Thornton [John Wayne] in the White O'Morn cottage and the continual attention of the Irish townspeople to Sean Thornton's height). Both films contrast Americanization as height with the low stature of native Irishness.
39 Review of *Irene*, *Los Angeles Times*, December 6, 1925.
40 Kate Price (who also appears in *Come on Over*) and Charlie Murray, the actors playing the roles of Ma and Pa O'Dare, would have been familiar as Irish 'types' to contemporary audiences, being strongly associated with other Irish roles. *Irene* helped to perpetuate such typecasting. Murray, for instance, had played a character named 'Hogan' in Mack Sennett comedies, and would play Irish roles in *McFaden's Flats* in 1926 and *Around the Corner* in 1930. Murray and Price would also play Irish parents again in the best-known of many films of the 1920s which explored Irish-Jewish relations, *The Cohens and the Kellys* series from 1926–1933. For a discussion of these films see Fielder in *Eire-Ireland* 20(3) (1985), pp. 6–18.
41 In a wonderful 'aside,' Irene then runs into a girl on rollerskates who commiserates with her, then immediately takes off one skate and gives it to Irene, and the two skate off arm-in-arm. The moment stands as one of the film's instances of evasive play,

signifying a return to girlish camaraderie at that moment when womanly sexuality is most immediate.

42 This valorization of Irish ethnicity at the expense of 'lesser' ethnic identities is also made plain in a number of passing references to Turks in the context of decadence and social aberration. When Donald tells Madame Lucy he 'has three girls' (to serve as models), the couturier tells him he must be a Turk. Irene at one point jokes that the cigarette she is pretending to smoke is called a 'Turkish Atrocity.'

43 Banner, p. 14.

44 In her autobiography, Moore relates that she reached a point where her 'fan mail came to over ten thousand letters a week. A staff of four secretaries handled the mail, answering each letter with a form letter which appeared to be a personal letter from me, telling about my newest film, asking them to be sure to inquire at their local theatre as to when the picture would be shown there, and signed with my name – all four secretaries could copy my signature perfectly.' p. 170.

45 Koszarski (1990: 262).

46 Johnson in *Classic Images*, 133 (July, 1986), p. 25.

47 On April 26, 1925, for instance, the *Albuquerque Journal* reported that 'Colleen Moore and Mae Marsh Will Sail Soon: Former Going to Ireland While Latter Will Make Picture in London' and observed that 'Colleen could speak only of Ireland and home.' An article in the *Wisconsin Press* of April 15, 1925, quoted Moore as follows: 'We're going to kiss the blarney stone, John and I, and spend a lot of time around County Kilkenny, which is our county.'

48 Scrapbook #5, Colleen Moore's Scrapbooks, AMPAS.

49 'Colleen Moore To Arrive in Dublin on Monday,' *Dublin Evening Herald*, June 13, 1925.

50 'Picture Stories of the Day,' *Dublin Evening Herald*, June 15, 1925.

51 Ibid.

52 'High Jinks Abroad,' *Boston Post*, June 24, 1925.

53 The promotion of tourism appears to have been a key agenda item in the government of the newly-formed Irish Free State, which saw itself as engaging in damage control after several incidents in which tourists were placed in danger during the social and political turmoil of the early 1920s. See 'Tourist Traffic in Ireland,' *Irish Times*, June 23, 1925.

54 See 'Advertising Ireland,' *Irish Times* May 10, 1925.

55 For a discussion of the film that emphasizes its release of flapper energies see Landay in Bean and Negra (eds) (2002).

56 'A Fractious Farce,' *The New York Times*, date not listed.

57 Moore's career dovetailed with an important period of coalescence in the American doll industry. For a discussion of dolls as symbolically nationalized bodies see Formanek-Brunell (1993).

58 Howe in *Photoplay*, 47 (August, 1922), p. 47.

59 Ibid.

60 Collura in *Classic Images* 89 (no date given), p. 15.

61 Anderson in *Philadelphia Inquirer*, February 11, 1968.

62 Accounts of Moore's later life bear this out – unlike the Eastern European vamps who tended to be represented as mourning their lost fame in old age, Moore apparently did not make much of her Hollywood career. When an interviewer screened one of her films for her in the 1960s, Moore reportedly laughed in amazement, not having seen herself in a film since her career had ended. In the chapters to follow I address this phenomenon of residual stardom in more detail.

63 'Colleen Moore, Ultimate Flapper of the Silent Screen, Is Dead at 87.' *The New York Times*, January 27, 1988, p. D23.

64 Moore (1968: 254).

65 Kobal (1985: 33).
66 On the subject of 'the pedophilic gaze' that she argues structured Mary Pickford's celebrity see Studlar in Bean and Negra (eds) (2002).

3 IMMIGRANT STARDOM IN IMPERIAL AMERICA

1 Basinger (1999: 238).
2 Hall (1983: 86).
3 Bruno (1970: 29).
4 Hunt (1987: 37).
5 Erdman (1996).
6 Rosenberg (1982: 42).
7 Ibid., pp. 100–101.
8 LaFeber (1989: 316).
9 Douglas (1995: 189–90).
10 MacKenzie (1986: 5).
11 Rydell (1984: 237).
12 Kaplan in Amy Kaplan and Donald E. Pease (eds) (1993: 4).
13 Ibid., p. 11.
14 Ibid., flyleaf.
15 By 1926, three-quarters of all films shown worldwide were American.
16 Later in 1927 after completing the film *Barbed Wire* Negri married Prince Serge Mdivani, an act which many felt weakened her career. It seems likely that as Paramount worked to invent an 'American' Pola Negri, the establishment of such direct connections to European royalty would have forcefully counteracted that construction.
17 Douglas, p. 305.
18 Anonymous *Photoplay* January, 1924, p. 32.
19 D'Emilio and Freedman (1988: 173).
20 Ibid., p. 201.
21 Ryan in Friedman and Shade (eds) (1976: 301).
22 Rudman in *Film History* 1(4), (1987: 330).
23 Plunkett, unpublished essay.
24 Auerbach (1995: 6).
25 See for instance Ben Blumenthal's letter to Adolph Zukor c/o Famous Players-Lasky Corporation, June 30, 1922, which reads in part 'we think that with Negri and Lubitsch both working in America the financial conditions of the Hamilton will be such that they will soon be able to stand, on their own feet, the same as we know or feel that most American directors would only be too delighted to work with Negri, we are sure the great stars in America would also desire to work under Lubitsch's direction.' Letter in Paramount Files, Margaret Herrick Library, Academy of Motion Picture Arts and Sciences (hereafter AMPAS).
26 Paramount Files, AMPAS.
27 Ibid.
28 A question which had been directly posed by Harrison Haskins in the February, 1921 issue of *Motion Picture Classic*. The article, 'Who is Pola Negri?' recaps Negri's stage and screen achievements, but says virtually nothing about the actress herself.
29 *Screenland* August, 1922, p. 4.
30 Jordan in *Photoplay*, March, 1923, p. 63.
31 Shlusinger in *Motion Picture Classic*, October, 1922, pp. 18–19, 74, 77.
32 Howe in *Photoplay*, November, 1923, p. 38.
33 Vinder in *Photoplay*, May, 1922. This was apparently the first American film magazine article devoted to Negri.

34 Ibid., p. 38.
35 Howe in *Photoplay*, November, 1922, p. 38.
36 Ibid.
37 Ibid., p. 59.
38 Negri made two other American films – *Hi Diddle Diddle* in 1943, and *The Moonspinners* in 1986. In the first film Negri plays opera singer Gegna Smetana, in a send-up of her imperious 1920s persona, and in the second film she plays a small role as a dowager.
39 Plunkett, p. 28.
40 Howe (1923: 37).
41 Negri, 'What is Love?' *Photoplay*, November, 1924, p. 30. Contrast Negri's aggressive, almost military definition of love with that of an altogether different kind of ethnic star, Colleen Moore, quoted in the same piece: 'Love is a song. It is the twittering of the birds in the treetops, an expression of sheer job that remains muted only long enough to let the clouds of a passing shower roll away, certain of the sun behind the gloom,' pp. 29–30.
42 Anonymous, 'A Bit of Europe in Hollywood,' *Photoplay*, May, 1926, p. 81.
43 At the same time that Negri was leaving Germany to make films in America, *The Cabinet of Dr. Caligari* (1919) was inspiring a succession of imitators in the German Expressionist style, among them F.W. Murnau's *Nosferatu* starrring Max Schreck as the vampire.
44 *Carmen* was a popular story in early Hollywood. Among the versions produced was one by William Fox starring vamp prototype Theda Bara.
45 The kind of regionalism many Americans associated with the outbreak of war in Europe, and which differed distinctly from nationalist satisfaction in non-contentious American regional diversity. Brennan (1989).
46 Hall, 'Diary of a Professional Movie Fan,' 1923, Source and precise date of publication unknown, Clipping in the Gladys Hall Collection, AMPAS.
47 Griffith (1970: 70). Bearing in mind Mary Douglas's famous formulation of dirt as 'matter out of place', Negri's 'dirty neck' suggests that she is culturally out of place in the US. See Douglas (1966). It is important to bear in mind that Negri was an inheritor of the diva tradition in theatre of Europeans who 'conquered' America. Linda Mizejewski profiles theatrical star import Anna Held, a woman whose combined Polish/Jewish and French/Catholic backgrounds certainly makes her a comparable figure to Negri. Her discussion of the way that elements of glamour and sordidness were held in operative tension in the Held persona equally explains Pola Negri's appeal. She writes, 'Anna Held's high-profile discourses on Parisian fashion and beauty tips were the standard entrée for the imported female celebrities at the turn of the century, offering the old world as elegant shop. But for Held, these discourses were also loosely layered strata under which the old world lurked with its damp, musky secrets. Anna Held's appeal rested within the liminal space between these two Old Worlds, fashionable and filthy.' Mizejewski (1999: 44).
48 Dyer (1986: 6).
49 Ibid., p. 5.
50 Tentler (1979: 3).
51 In the eyes of some commentators Negri's American career was effectively bounded by moments of such public hysteria attached to the spectacle of ethnicity. Paralleled to the pandemonium generated by *Passion* was the hysteria at Rudolph Valentino's funeral in 1926 in which Pola Negri was a signficant participant. The actress is often remembered for her dramatic grief at Valentino's death, with the majority of commentators suggesting that it was largely manufactured as a publicity stunt. See for instance Vincent Tajiri's account in *Valentino* (1971: 126), or Alexander Walker's

Rudolph Valentino in which he describes Negri 'swooning with exclamations of grief and declarations of love for the dead Valentino whose name had been romantically linked with hers only a few short weeks ago.' (1976: 116).

52 The film was also instrumental in bringing Ernst Lubitsch to Hollywood's notice.
53 Smuts (1971: 45),
54 Peiss (1998).
55 Bruno, p. 36.
56 Howe (1923: 37).
57 Howe (1922: 60).
58 Howe (1923: 38).
59 Dijkstra in *Idols of Perversity* (1986: 343).
60 Vinder, p. 20.
61 Shlusinger, p. 68.
62 St. Johns in *Photoplay*, January, 1926, p. 53.
63 St. Clair, p. 76.
64 Hall in *Photoplay*, December, 1928, p. 29.

4 SONJA HENIE IN HOLLYWOOD

1 Schatz (1997: 226).
2 Carroll in *Coronet*, May, 1944, p. 14.
3 The contemporary association between Scandinavian nationalities and uninhibited female sexuality does not seem to have been operative to any degree during the span of Sonja Henie's career. Though to a contemporary spectator it sometimes appears that in her films Henie overplays her demureness such that it can be read as highly knowledgeable, there is no evidence to suggest that this was an intentionally performed element, and there is no recognition of such a dynamic in any of the commentary that I have reviewed from the period.
4 The casting of Cesar Romero in two of Henie's films, *Happy Landing* and *My Lucky Star* seems to reflect his placement as an ethnic male foil to Henie's whiteness. In *My Lucky Star* Romero (as George Cabot Jr.) impersonates Henie's (as Christina Nielson) uncle, and another character passes a sarcastic remark that the two 'sure look alike.' Romero, a Cuban-American, referred to himself as the 'Latin from Manhattan.' His star biography emphasized that he was the grandson of Jose Marti.
5 Dyer (1997: 122).
6 Notably, the strong and consistent emphasis on Norwegian ethnic identity in Henie's star discourse is modified only occasionally by several references to an Irish grandmother. For instance, an undated publicity photo accounts for the 'non-Norwegian twinkle in the eye' through such a reference, while Gladys Hall describes Henie as being '. . . like an ice flower, warmed and made vivid by, perhaps, the Irish blood in her veins, the Irish blood of her exciting maternal grandmother, who was a "character."' 'Not As Other Girls . . .' Draft Manuscript for *Picture Play*, April 22, 1938, Gladys Hall Special Collection, Academy of Motion Picture Arts and Sciences (hereafter AMPAS). In such constructions Irishness operates as an ideal accessory ethnicity as it has also done more recently for popular music stars such as Mariah Carey and Christina Aguilera, both of whom have announced that they have an Irish ancestor. In Henie's case Irishness is called upon to enliven a potentially stolid Norwegianness, but it serves to moderate the Latino ethnicity of the two contemporary stars.
7 *American Magazine*, 12 April, 1937, p. 98.
8 Hall in *Picture Play*, April 23, 1938, p. 18.
9 Merish in R.G. Thompson (ed.) (1996: 186).
10 Ibid., p. 188.

11 Indeed, Jane Feuer has noted the striking physical similarities between Temple and Henie. In her article 'Nancy and Tony and Sonja: The Figure of the Figure Skater in American Entertainment,' she writes, 'Sonja Henie, for instance, although about twenty-five when she began her US film career, looked far more like Twentieth Century Fox's other major female star of the 1930s, Shirley Temple, than she did an adult movie star.' In *Women on Ice: Feminist Essays on the Tonya Harding/Nancy Kerrigan Spectacle*, Baughman (ed.) (1995: 5).

12 Merish, p. 187.

13 Given that Shirley Temple was the number one box office drawing star between 1935 and 1939, it could easily be argued that Henie's stardom followed upon it as a second stage, engaging themes of romance that would have been out of bounds in the world of a Temple film.

14 Eckert in Gledhill (ed.) (1991: 60).

15 The proximity of the Shirley Temple and Sonja Henie personae in the public imagination would be an interesting question to investigate further. Occasionally, the proximity registers within the Henie films, as for instance, in *Second Fiddle* where publicity agent Jimmy Sutton travels to Minnesota to locate Henie's character Trudi Hovland, and is surrounded by a group of local people clamoring for insider information about their favorite Hollywood stars. To gain attention amidst the rambunctious group, a young girl belts out a strident version of Temple's signature number 'Good Ship Lollipop.'

16 All quoted material from Chapter 10, pp. 2–4 of 'The Life Story of Sonja Henie,' Twentieth Century Fox Studios Publicity, AMPAS.

17 Faller (1987: 157).

18 Sullivan in *Silver Screen*, 7(8) June 1937, p. 22.

19 Review discourses on Henie's films reflect a trajectory of rising critical acceptance of Henie as an actress as well as a featured skater. A *New York Times* review of *My Lucky Star* on September 10, 1938 noted that 'However, ill-equipped she may be for dramatic purposes, she has her skates and they seem to be enough.' p. 20, while a *Variety* reviewer evaluating *Sun Valley Serenade* on July 23, 1941, called the film 'an excellent compound of entertaining ingredients, displaying Sonja Henie as a sparkling comedienne of top rank without necessity of putting on the blades, and displaying box office potentialities of high calibre.'

20 Faller (1987: 151).

21 Guttman (1996: 80).

22 For a discussion of the celebrity of Esther Williams see Williamson in *Camera Obscura*, 38(5) (1996) pp. 5–29. Williamson identifies the Henie films as in many ways a blueprint for the films of Esther Williams.

23 Hail in *Citizen News*, Feb. 16, 1946.

24 Skolsky in *Citizen News*, Sept. 7, 1944.

25 Welky in *Journal of Sport History*, 24(1), p. 42.

26 'When Henie Had an Edge, She Knew How to Maintain It,' *Los Angeles Times*, Feb. 18, 1988.

27 Some commentators have implicated Henie in a volatile race/religious politics. For instance, Henie looms large as a dangerous icon of racial purity in Epstein (1999). The novel fictionalizes a Jewish European refugee who comes to Hollywood and plays a part in the making of *Everything Happens at Night*. Epstein has Henie rant anti-semitically against the Jewish studio executives and performers of Hollywood, comparing them to 'lice.'

28 This reference is an allusion to the National Socialist militia that flourished between 1921 and 1934.

29 *Motion Picture Herald*, Aug. 9, 1941, p. 31.

30 'Cash-Register Champion,' *Look*, May 1, 1945, p. 73.

31 Since Henie would go on to make an additional seven films after this one (four for Twentieth Century Fox) such a culminating narrative might well seem premature. However, the release of *Second Fiddle* does roughly mark the end of the star's peak box office years.

32 And in this way the film is able to shift attention to the musical and dramatic talents of its other stars. This tendency grew more pronounced in some ways in the Henie films, and commentators were increasingly critical of the lengths to which her films would go to rationalize the inclusion of a skating number. Many of the Henie films awkwardly contrive to 'accidentally' discover the skating talent of the characters she plays. With most of its major action taking place in Southern California and with Trudie playing a non-skating character in a movie, *Second Fiddle* suffers particularly from this problem. At one point in the film, a skating number is conjured up purely as a dream sequence.

33 Ueda in Lewis A. Erenberg and Susan E. Hirsch (eds) (1996: 202).

34 Reid in *Silver Screen*, 12(10) August, 1942, 54–5, 86. And Vallee *Silver Screen*, 15(7) May, 1945, p. 43.

35 'Skater Sonja Henie Dies of Leukemia,' *San Francisco Chronicle*, Oct. 13, 1969, p. 2.

36 The conjoinment of the Henie star persona and the Glenn Miller Orchestra made for a powerful cocktail of patriotic elements in *Sun Valley Serenade*. Other Henie films also included popular swing bands, among them *Iceland* (Sammy Kaye and his orchestra) and *Wintertime* (Woody Herman and his orchestra). Swing was an important musical vehicle for giving shape and sound to a unified America in the war years. 'Miller played an especially important role as he created a military version of his sweet swing, all-American band for battle against the Nazis. Under the leadership of a reassuring father figure who had sacrificed profit for duty, the military band smoothly melded civilian values and military goals in a common cause.' Erenberg in Erenberg and Hirsch (1996: 151).

37 Earl Wilson's Column, *Los Angeles Daily News*, May 24, 1953.

38 'Frozen Gift to Ice Star Finds New Home,' *Los Angeles Herald-Examiner*, Dec. 13, 1988.

39 'Hot Stuff on Ice,' *Newsweek*, Oct. 25, 1948, p. 86.

40 Kindem and Sorenssen (1996) provide an account of Henie's fraught national status in Norway.

41 'Letters to Bob Dorian,' *American Movie Classics Magazine*, December, 1994, p. 13.

42 Chisholm in *Journal of Sport and Social Issues*, 23(2) May, 1999, p. 126.

43 Ibid., pp. 134–5.

44 For the most recent academic account of the Harding/Kerrigan rivalry and its mass mediated construction see Daddario (1998: 105–28).

45 Merish, p. 189.

5 ETHNICITY AND THE INTERVENTIONIST IMAGINATION

1 Kilgallen in *The American Weekly*, 3 February 1952, p. 18.

2 Griffith (1970: 37).

3 For a discussion of Lamarr's post-peak television appearances see my article in Thumim (ed.), *Small Screens, Big Ideas: Television in the 1950s* (2001).

4 For instance in a letter from David O. Selznick to his associate Harry Ginsberg, dated 10 August 1938, Selznick writes, 'I think we are going to pass up a fortune if we lose our chance to get Hedy Lamarr for a picture . . . I think the best and almost only opportunity that we have to use her is opposite Colman in "SECOND MEETING" . . . Even if we don't get Lamarr, I should still like to get Colman for "SECOND

MEETING," as there are any number of women who could play the role. I simply think that rush is essential because I feel that Lamarr is worth at last a half a million dollars to the gross of the picture.' Correspondence in the David O. Selznick Collection, Harry Ransom Humanities Research Center, Austin, Texas.

5 From an undated and untitled manuscript in the Gladys Hall Special Collection, Academy of Motion Picture Arts and Sciences (hereafter AMPAS).

6 Ducas in *Sunday Mirror*, 20 November 1938, p. 4.

7 George Weller, 'The Ecstatic Hedy Lamarr,' 27 January 1939, source unknown.

8 Ibid.

9 From an undated and untitled manuscript in the Gladys Hall Special Collection, AMPAS.

10 George Weller, 'The Ecstatic Hedy Lamarr,' 26 January 1939, source unknown. Clearly this comparison is meant to further the distinction between Lamarr and some of the assertive heroines of American films in the 1930s. Given her still rather heavy Austrian accent, it would have been impossible for the actress to play one of the fast-talking heroines of that mode. It is interesting, thus, to consider Lamarr's comparative silence after the assertive, articulate heroines played by stars such as Mae West, Katharine Hepburn and Rosalind Russell.

11 Gladys Hall, 'Has Hedy Lamarr A Corner on the Glamour Market?' Manuscript prepared for *Silver Screen*, date and publication details unknown, Gladys Hall Special Collection, AMPAS.

12 Weller, 'The Ecstatic Hedy Lamarr,' p. 12.

13 Hayes, Barbara in *Photoplay* (April, 1939), p. 18.

14 Later films made productive use of Bennett's construction as the pure, white feminine ideal. In *The Reckless Moment* (1949) for example, she plays an American mother staunchly defending her family from the taint of ethnic criminality and the kind of invasive male ethnicity brilliantly portrayed by James Mason as an Irish gangster.

15 Sidney Skolsky in *Hollywood Citizen News*, 9 February 1950.

16 Despite the postwar revival of the couture centers of Europe, European fashions were often figured as being best worn by American women, rather than European ones.

17 Grantham, *The United States Since 1945* (1976: 3).

18 Goldman, *The Crucial Decade – And After* (1966: 28).

19 The North Atlantic Treaty Organization (NATO) and the South East Asia Treaty Organization (precursors to the Korean and Vietnam wars) testified to the American commitment to engage militarily whenever Russian influence appeared unpropitious.

20 Quigley, *The Ruses for War* (1992: 32).

21 Klunk (1986: viii).

22 Stillman and Pfaff in Bliss and Johnson (eds), *Consensus at the Crossroads* (1972: 201–2).

23 Murray in *Modern Screen*, April, 1939, p. 33.

24 Hopper in *Life*, July 25, 1938.

25 Kilgallen in *The American Weekly*, Feb. 3, 1952, p. 21.

26 Crichton in *Collier's*, November 5, 1928, p. 14.

27 The fact that this self-consciousness about Lamarr's starmaking is expressed through another character with a higher degree of agency is in keeping with Lamarr's broadly static role in the film Charles Affron describes *Ziegfeld Girl* as featuring 'Hedy Lamarr's near-death mask, a figure of stasis (her smile is intrusive to the utter calm of the mask)' in *Cinema and Sentiment* (1983: 141).

28 Banner (1983: 284).

29 Hedy Lamarr eavesdropped by Bob Edison, 'Hubba, Hubba, Hubba . . . It's Hedy!' *New York Times*, Sept. 26, 1971. Even after such cuts were made, the film ran into trouble with some censors. In *Sin and Censorship* (1996: 183), Frank Walsh notes,

'When Hedy Lamarr introduced herself as Tondelayo in the PCA-approved *White Cargo*, the story of a native woman on a rubber plantation who drives men wild with lust, the Legion condemned it until MGM made enough changes to raise it to a B.'

30 Savran (1998: 175).
31 A typical vamp pedigree.
32 Dyer in *Screen* 29(4) 1988, pp. 44–6.
33 Ibid., pp. 53–4.
34 Weller, 'The Ecstatic Hedy Lamarr.'
35 Ibid.
36 Hall, 'Marriage – And Hedy Lamarr,' p. 11.
37 Hamilton in *Photoplay*, October, 1938, p. 74.
38 In 1938 in the context of a great deal of speculation about what sorts of roles Lamarr might play, it was suggested that she might undertake the part of Pocahontas, which seems a tellingly appropriate suggestion, given this character's status as the orginal embodiment of a benign version of ethnic femininity in American national mythology. In 'Hedda Hopper's Hollywood' in the *Chicago Daily News* on July 23, 1938, the gossip columnist wrote, 'the latest report is that this vivid Viennese charmer is going to play an American Indian – Pocahontas. If the Indians hear about it, they'll probably get out their tomahawks and go right into their war dance. Smith will probably rise from his grave and beg to play opposite her!' p. 16.
39 'The Art of Having a Baby,' *Los Angeles Times*, April 15, 1945.
40 'My Neighbor, Lamarr,' p. 3.
41 'The Art of Having a Baby.'
42 See Proctor in *Photoplay*, November, 1942, pp. 45–6, 77.
43 'Hedgerow (Exclusive Color Pictures of the Hilltop Home of Hedy Lamarr and John Loder),' *Motion Picture Magazine*, July, 1944.
44 Skolsky in *Photoplay*, May, 1944, pp. 36–7.
45 See Fleming Meeks, 'I Guess They Just Take and Forget About a Person,' *Forbes*, May 14, 1990, p. 136. While it is unclear whether Lamarr had the scientific and technical knowledge necessary to generate such an idea (though recent accounts do suggest that Lamarr's invention was genuinely hers), it may also be the case that a fan opted to give her co-credit for it, in which case it is also noteworthy that Lamarr was linked to a solution to national defense crises.
46 'Hedy Lamarr Invention Seen as Defense Aid,' *Los Angeles Times*, October 11, 1941.
47 'Hedy Comes Up With Idea for US Defense,' *Hollywood Citizen News*, September 30, 1941. A more complete account of Lamarr's idea (and her collaboration on it with film composer George Antheil) is provided in MacDonald (1992: 319–21).
48 Westbrook in *American Quarterly*, 42(4) (December, 1990), p. 611.
49 The global map is also a privileged element of the mise-en-scene at the Immigration and Naturalization Service in *Lady Without a Passport*, 1950.
50 Reports that Hope (afraid of being upstaged) edited the film to diminish Lamarr's contribution and punctuate his own serve as an interesting extra-textual correlative to the film's denial of Lily Dalbray's contribution to the interventionist mission.
51 Just as Pola Negri's fall from public favor in the US was associated with her reversion to an aristocratic European past, Lamarr's cultivation as an American icon was linked to her wholehearted rejection of aristocratic power.
52 Hopper in *Los Angeles Times*, Nov. 21, 1948.
53 Bergan and Karney (eds) (1988: 173).
54 'Hedda Hopper's Hollywood,' *Chicago Daily News*, July 23, 1938, p. 16.
55 Review discourses on the film suggests that its 'realism' was well-recognized. For instance, a review of the film in the *New York Times* noted that *Lady Without a*

Passport 'undoubtedly . . . is meant as a tribute to the self-effacing stalwarts of the United States Immigration and Naturalization Service.' (August 4, 1950), p. 13.

56 'Hedy Lamarr Enacts "Lady Without Passport,"' *Los Angeles Times*, September 15, 1950.

57 At the close of the film Karczag will tell Marianne Lorress (Lamarr) that with Palinov's 'gift for language, my boss will want to hear him talk,' suggesting that Palinov's criminality is marked by his ability to perform ethnic impersonation.

58 And this reference is brief indeed. Marianne's past is never alluded to again in the film, so it is never clear whether the 'we' she refers to signals Jews in particular or dispossessed people in general.

59 Baker in *New York Times*, February 10, 1996, p. A15.

60 'Hedy Lamarr, Stauffer on Carmel Honeymoon,' *Herald Express*, June 12, 1951.

61 'A Look at Look Mag Turns Hedy Lamarr Livid,' *Variety*, May 9, 1951.

62 Stein in *Hollywood Spectator*, May 23, 1936, p. 14. The recurring issue of Lamarr's 'Jewishness' is noteworthy, though I have read nothing that definitively establishes her religion. Lamarr was described as 'an Austrian Jew' as recently as February, 2000, at the time of her death. See Sauter in *Entertainment Weekly*, 524 (February 4, 2000) p. 76. Rendered Jewish, of course, Lamarr became a more ideal candidate for American interventionist rescue.

63 *Hollywood Citizen*, July 16, 1936.

64 After 1945, known simply as the MPAA, for Motion Picture Association of America.

65 '*Ecstasy* Burned Despite Appeal,' *New York Times*, Aug. 8, 1935.

66 Charles R. Metzzer, Report on *Ecstasy*, July 21, 1936, p. 3. MPAA Production Code Files, AMPAS.

67 Letter from Breen to Smith, May 27, 1937, MPAA Production Code Files, AMPAS.

68 It would appear that *Ecstasy* was one of relatively few films of the period to be judged as thoroughly unacceptable by the Hays Office. A letter from Breen to Francis Harmon dated 4 January, 1938, for instance, observes that 'the only pictures we can think of that may be classified as "off color," and which are currently on exhibition, are the following: *Love Life of a Gorilla, Children of Loneliness, Club de Femmes*, and *Ecstasy*.' MPAA Production Code Files, AMPAS.

69 *Motion Picture Herald*, Feb. 4, 1951, p. 35.

70 MPAA Production Code Files, AMPAS.

71 MPAA Production Code Files, AMPAS.

72 Birmingham in *New York Times*, August 23, 1970, p. D11.

73 Roberts in *Los Angeles Times*, November, 1966, p. 48.

74 See Martin in *Saturday Evening Post*, February 5, 1944, pp. 19–45, and Martin in *Saturday Evening Post*, February 29, 1951, pp. 32–3, 35, 54, 56–9.

75 Kilgallen in *The American Weekly*, Feb. 3, 1952, pp. 18, 21.

76 Prelatsky in *Los Angeles Times*, Mar. 24, 1968.

77 A clear contrast is presented in other celebrity auctions, such as the 1996 event held by Sotheby's to sell off the belongings of Jacqueline Kennedy Onassis. On the one hand, that collection was seen as a limited grouping of items that did not hold strong personal significance for the former First Lady's family, the sale was held by a prestigious auction house, and making a purchase was something that only the very wealthy could do, due to the high prices fetched for even the smallest objects. It may also be that the lack of public opprobrium for that sale is due to the fact that only when an intensely well-known public narrative is in place to lend meaning to the smallest pieces of minutaie, can such an auction be carried off without unpleasurably demystifying a star persona.

78 See for instance *People*, Nov. 11, 1991, Hedy Lamarr Clippings File, AMPAS.

79 Young (1978: 51).

80 'Actress Hedy Lamarr Busted for Shoplifting,' *New York Post*, Aug. 2, 1991, p. 9.

81 The tendency to sensationalize and/or invent narratives of beautiful but emotionally and economically unstable women in Hollywood clearly exceeds these few examples. The tabloid and mainstream press (though that distinction is certainly becoming harder to draw) have zealously covered beautiful female stars who 'crack up' in the form of Frances Farmer, Farrah Fawcett, Margot Kidder and most recently Anne Heche.

82 Moore's seamless transition to private life is a contradiction worth noting given that she was certainly the most consistent box-office draw of the actresses in this study, and that her wealth, social prominence, and active fundraising for the Republican Party after leaving Hollywood gave her a rather high profile. Nevertheless, her identity as a Hollywood star appears to have been largely erased in favor of her role as a wife, stepmother, and what would have been called in the 1950s, a 'clubwoman.'

83 Lamarr's 'unsanctioned retirement' is specifically addressed in Louella Parsons' article 'Hedy Lamarr Reveals She'll Retire From Films,' *Los Angeles Examiner*, Jan. 2, 1951, where the columnist writes, 'Hedy Lamarr yesterday said she is retiring from the screen and gives as her reason her desire to lead a normal private life . . . It is difficult for those of us who know Hedy and how impulsive she is to believe she is serious about retirement.'

84 Lamarr's post-peak stardom also ran in tandem with a cycle of films such as *Sunset Boulevard* (1950) and *Whatever Happened to Baby Jane?* (1962) writing the epitaph for Old Hollywood in the form of the aging female film star. See Brooks in Woodward (ed.) (1999: 232–47).

85 Caption to publicity photo for *Experiment Perilous* (1944), Harry Ransom Center Photography Collection, Austin, Texas.

86 Kobal (1980: 60).

87 See 'A Culture of Outsiders, 1943–1958,' in Crunden (1994).

88 Thanks to Steven Cohan for helping me to articulate this point.

6 MARISA TOMEI AND THE FANTASY OF ETHNICITY

1 Alba (1990: 318–19).

2 Tomei's first appearance in a film was in Garry Marshall's 1984 *The Flamingo Kid* in which she had one line of dialogue.

3 See Laplanche and Pontalis in Kaplan et al. (eds) (1986: 5–27).

4 Burgin in Wright (ed.) (1992: 87).

5 Brown (1993).

6 Wolpin (1991: 1).

7 Ibid.

8 See Miringoff and Miringoff (1999).

9 Crunden (1994: 330–31).

10 A term put to use by Henry Giroux in his essay 'Rewriting the Discourse of Racial Identity: Toward a Pedagogy and Politics of Whiteness,' in Clark and O'Donnell (eds) (1999: 227).

11 Conzen et al. in *Journal of American Ethnic History*, 12(1) (Fall, 1992), p. 13.

12 Schatz in Collins et al. (eds) (1993: 16).

13 In an unpublished essay 'True Value: Technological Hardware and Containment in James Cameron's *True Lies*' Walter Metz has insightfully argued that one recent action film stages the recovery of the family in tandem with a defense of the interests of the national security state.

14 Graham (1994: 189).

15 Iverson in *Harper's Bazaar*, September, 1994, p. 414.

16 *People*, September 18, 1995.

17 *People*, October 25, 1993.
18 Ibid.
19 Gliatto in *People*, May 15, 1995, p. 20.
20 Numerous puns about tailoring as murder seem to suggest that all 'ethnic professions' are potentially criminal.
21 With Poole played by the campy Tim Curry, best known, of course, for his role as a transvestite in the cult classic *The Rocky Horror Picture Show* (1975), it is somewhat difficult to discern whether he is playing straight here. The performance is rather contained, but Curry's mere physical presence in the role suggests that he cannot straightforwardly embody the same kind of conservative white culture associated in the film with the bankers and the federal agents.
22 Kirkwood is played by Ken Howard, whose intertextual associations to whiteness carry through from his best known work as a sympathetic white coach of a black basketball team in the 1970s television series, *The White Shadow*.
23 Gamson (1994: 170–71).
24 'Beauty Watch,' *Glamour* (1996), p. 104.
25 Katz in *Village Voice*, March 31, 1992, p. 66.
26 *US*, January, 1993, p. 57.
27 Engel in *The New York Times*, March 22, 1992, p. H12.
28 Jami Bernard, untitled, *New York Post* (February 12, 1993), 33. In both films and film-related publicity and promotion Latina Rosie Perez suggestively foils Tomei's ethnic whiteness. For a discussion of Perez's celebrity see Valdivia (2000: 89–105).
29 Tepper (1995: 443).
30 Tomei in *Interview*, March, 1993, p. 135.
31 Koffler in *Seventeen*, April 1, 1992, p. 39.
32 Powell in *Redbook* 184(1) November, 1994, pp. 84–7, 126.
33 Lord in *Details*, April, 1992, p. 91.
34 Koffler, p. 39.
35 Silverman in *Cosmopolitan* 217(2) August, 1994, p. 133.
36 Woll and Miller (eds) (1987: 290).
37 Powell, p. 84.
38 Denby in *New York*, May 22, 1995, p. 78.
39 Garcia in *Films in Review*, September, 1995, p. 58.
40 The film features appearances by a number of well-known local New York news personalities to heighten its regional realism. These include Rosanna Scotto, Donna Hanover (then wife of Mayor Rudy Guiliani), Jane Hanson, and Chuck Scarborough.
41 Those in positions of power at *The Sun* tend to be de-ethnicized white (Publisher Graham Keighley, Editor-in-Chief Bernard White, Managing Editor Alicia Clark and Metro Editor Henry Hackett). Those in supporting positions (columnists, reporters) are ethnic with names such as Carmen, Carmine, and McDougal.
42 Glenn Close's casting in the part is significant, activating a set of intertextual association to her prior roles as hyper-empowered, marauding WASP women in such films as *Fatal Attraction* (1987) and *Dangerous Liaisons* (1989).
43 Henry's choice is further complicated by his status as the fitting replacement to the ailing patriarch at *The Sun* – we learn that Bernie White is suffering from prostate cancer.
44 A not altogether incidental question, as one of the stylistic means by which the film contrasts Marti's vibrant ethnicity with Alicia's sterile WASP identity is costume. While Glenn Close appears in severely styled pantsuits and other professional attire, Tomei wears long, floral-patterned dresses. When Henry asks what she is wearing at this particular moment, then, the question may be seen as a verification that she is helping to advance his professional agenda, rather than fostering her own.
45 Halter (2000: 12).

46 Bradshaw (1988).
47 In an earlier era, emblematic Europeans such as Pola Negri were expected to be cosmopolitan and not regional. Yet Tomei's emblematic European-American status is crucially grounded in regionalism.
48 The most successful romantic comedy of 1995, for example, *While You Were Sleeping*, presents an orphaned heroine whose real romance is with the hero's family.
49 Freud (1959). In his essay in Gledhill (ed.) (1987: 255–67) Richard deCordova discusses Freud's inattention to the extra-familial elements that help to support the family romance. He argues that Freud's focus on issues of the family tends to foreclose analysis of other important and related factors, for 'the family romance draws upon material that exceeds and contradicts the terms of a purely private drama.' (260).
50 Harvey in *Los Angeles Times*, March 23, 1995, Marisa Tomei Clippings File, Academy of Motion Picture Arts and Sciences, Beverly Hills, CA.
51 'The Backlot: Cinephile,' *Variety*, April 5, 1994.
52 Whether she is being actively managed as a potential 'loose cannon' figure in films such like *My Cousin Vinny* and *Oscar* or celebrated as an icon of ethnic and regional authenticity, Tomei's stardom holds her energies in check in a particularly de-legitimating fashion to suggest that she does not need to perform, she can just simply be herself on screen. In contrast to a star like Meryl Streep whose perceived non-ethnic whiteness leads her ethnic roles to be celebrated for their artistry, Tomei is seen as an actress whose work is only an extension of her 'real self.' This feature of her celebrity may also have contributed to the indignation expressed (openly and covertly) at her winning the Academy Award.
53 I consider the 1990s heritage quest narrative as one category of response to this de-assimilationist impulse in my chapter 'Romance And/As Tourism: Heritage Whiteness and the (Inter) National Imaginary in Recent Film,' in Villarejo and Tinkcom (eds) 2001.

7 STARDOM, CORPOREALITY AND ETHNIC DETERMINACY

1 Banet-Weiser (1999: 2).
2 Dyer (1997).
3 Rowe (1995: 204).
4 Garber (1992: 117).
5 Tasker (1998: 193).
6 Although I do not have room here to talk about subcultural appropriations of her persona, it should be clear that Cher's presentation of her own invented body makes her a potent figure of identification for gay men and others who perceive the need to invent themselves in opposition to dominant culture.
7 Gamson (1994: 266–7) (Chapter 4, Footnote 40).
8 A phrase which provides the foundation for a wide-ranging discussion in Lipsitz's trenchant (1998) book.
9 The website address is http://www.geocities.com/Hollywood/7990/plastic.html.
10 Waters (1990: 147).
11 Halter (2000: 194).
12 Ibid., p. 186.
13 Deloria (1998: 156).
14 David Savran (1998: 119).
15 Deloria, p. 159.
16 A public service announcement of the period, part of the 'Keep America Beautiful' campaign, famously used an image of Indian nobility to speak for broader cultural interests, by depicting an Indian chief weeping at the desecration of the American landscape by litter.

17 For one example see Marc (1984).

18 Two critics have addressed the social and institutional frame of the 'The Smothers Brothers Comedy Hour,' one of the most volatile television texts in this genre. See Steven Alan Carr in *Cinema Journal* 31(4) (Summer, 1992) 3–24, and Aniko Bodroghkozy in Lynn Spigel and Michael Curtin (eds) 1997, pp. 200–19.

19 'Cher Gets Her Heads Together,' *TV Guide*, Oct. 16, 1976, p. 10.

20 Leerhsen in *Newsweek*, Nov. 30, 1987, p. 66.

21 Sometimes this approval was granted by the directors and stars who worked with Cher. Robert Altman *(Come Back to the Five and Dime, Jimmy Dean, Jimmy Dean)*, Jack Nicholson *(The Witches of Eastwick)* and Meryl Streep *(Silkwood)* all praised Cher's talent and professionalism on the set.

22 'Cheers for Cher,' *Ms.* July, 1988, p. 53.

23 Petrucelli, Vero Beach, FL: Rourke Enterprises, p. 21.

24 Significantly, Cher doesn't play an ethnic character until *Moonstruck*, a film that seems to have been lauded in part for its ability to generate a coherent heritage framework for the star's ethnicity. *Moonstruck* replaces ethnic chameleonism with the stability of a single Italian ethnic identity.

25 This argument might also encompass *Silkwood* (1984), in which Dolly Pelliker (Cher)'s lesbianism has the effect of rendering protagonist Karen Silkwood (Meryl Streep)'s political commitment and alternately sexual identity (she chooses to remain unmarried to her male companion) more mainstream to secure necessary viewer identification with such an unconventional protagonist.

26 Interestingly, once 'assimilated' himself, the Northern Ireland-born Neeson would play the role of cultural and linguistic interpreter to Jodie Foster's Nell in the 1994 film of that name.

27 Thanks are due to Chris Holmlund for furthering my conception of the 'impossibility' of Cher's star body through our discussions as co-panelists at the 1998 Society for Cinema Studies Conference.

28 In an important intertextual reference, a *Sanctuary* catalogue was glimpsed in the hands of Roseanne Connor on the sitcom 'Roseanne' at a time when the Connor family had recently won the lottery. The choice to reference Cher merchandising in relation to white nouveau riche culture conveys something of the perceived paradox of wealth linked to lower-class taste. The reference also indirectly links Cher to Roseanne, both unruly 'white trash' women.

29 Public perceptions of Cher's age-denying body seemed to be at the heart of rumors that circulated several years ago that a small weight gain by the actress was attributable to pregnancy when in fact she was going through menopause.

30 The premise of the ethnic comedy in which Cher's character, Loretta Castorini, falls in love with a young baker named Ronny Camereri, seemed to be uncannily replicated in tabloid accounts that emerged not long after the film was released touting Cher's real-life romance with Rob Camelleti, a young New York bagel-maker.

31 This action was also replicated in an episode of the NBC sitcom *Will and Grace*, broadcast on November 16, 2000 centered upon the hyperbolically gay Jack (one of the show's four featured characters) whose idolatry of Cher is directed at a Cher doll, until the star herself shows up. Jack mistakes Cher for an impersonator, until she sings a line from 'If I Could Turn Back Time.' In this instance, Cher is linked to a vocal authenticity that verifies identity when her body cannot do so.

32 In 1999, a Joan Rivers' program on E, the 'Academy Awards Fashion Review,' featured an extended sequence on the making of a Titanic-themed handbag for nominee Gloria Stuart. A segment was also devoted to accessories for the first time, with scrupulous attention given even to such minute items as the stars' hairpins.

33 A well-remembered costume which was placed third in the *TV Guide Book of Lists'* 'top ten most outrageous fashion statements at the Oscars.'

34 See Barnard (1996).

35 And the manner in which she did so re-activated residual ethnic and class elements in her persona through a costume whose excesses were classically 'unruly' and obliquely Native American in style.

36 Pener in *Entertainment Weekly*, April 3, 1998, p. 41.

37 These two observations come respectively from postings by *X-Files* fans Eddie Cabot on Dec. 2, 1997, and J.T. Thomas on December 1, 1997.

38 In an episode of the WB drama *Buffy the Vampire Slayer*, broadcast in Spring, 2000 Buffy believes her new college roommate isn't human, in part, because she incessantly plays 'Believe' in their dorm room. This use of the song capitalizes on Cher's current status as an 'easy mark' for a variety of jokes about her musical skill and career longevity, but also implicitly turns on the single's 'posthuman' sound and the implication that Cher's combination of youthfulness and age is somehow illicit. As it turns out, Buffy is right; her roommate is a centuries-old vampire engaging in a masquerade of youth.

39 Cheever in *People* 39(19) May 17, 1993, p. 41.

40 Klein in *Architectural Digest* 53(10) October, 1996, p. 156.

41 Cheever in *Architectural Digest* 48 November, 1991, p. 128.

42 In her discussion of the interrelations between fetishized homes and fetishized stars, Marjorie Garber cites Cher as 'by far the queen of celebrity real estate savvy.' See Garber (2000: 138).

43 'Introduction' in Wray and Newitz (eds) (1997: 8).

44 Leonard and Pope (1996: 22). The authors further write that the diva 'by virtue of her social positioning as the exception to feminine silence and powerlessness and by the fact that she performs both femininity and masculinity – unsettles gender oppositions,' p. 21.

45 Sweeney in Wray and Newitz (eds) (1997: 253).

46 Newitz and Wray in Hill (ed.) (1997: 178).

47 Cranny-Francis (1995: 113).

48 In May, 1999 Cher appeared as a featured performer on VH-1's 'Divas Live '99,' alongside Tina Turner, Chaka Khan, and others. *Jet* magazine reported that the concert 'was seen by a record 9.5 million viewers, making it the highest-rated program in VH-1's history.' 'Whitney, Tina and Brandy Sizzle on "Divas Live '99,"' *Jet* 95(22) May 3, 1999, pp. 58–61.

49 *Entertainment Weekly* 'Fab 400 Entertainers.' For more moderately adulatory discussions of Cher's longevity see Stephen Holden, 'Queen of the Comeback, Cher Tries Yet Again,' *New York Times* June 30, 1996, p. 24, and Strauss in *New York Times* March 11, 1999, pp. B1 and B6. Both articles open by citing an unflattering joke that proposes Cher and cockroaches as the only likely survivors of a nuclear apocalypse.

50 Kathryn Pauly Morgan has written that 'In any culture that defines femininity in terms of submission to men, that makes the achievement of femininity (however culturally specific) in appearances, gesture, movement, voice, bodily contours, aspirations, values, and political behavior obligatory of any woman who will be allowed to be loved or hired or promoted or elected or simply allowed to live, and in any culture that increasingly requires women to purchase femininity through submission to cosmetic surgeons and their magic knives, refusal and revolt exact a high price,' in *Hypatia* 6(3) (Fall, 1991), p. 47.

BIBLIOGRAPHY

Affron, Charles, *Cinema and Sentiment*, Chicago: University of Chicago Press, 1982.

Alba, Richard D., *Ethnic Identity: The Transformation of White America*, New Haven: Yale University Press, 1990.

Auerbach, Nina, *Woman and the Demon: The Life of a Victorian Myth*, Cambridge: Harvard University Press, 1982.

—— *Our Vampires, Ourselves*, Chicago: University of Chicago Press, 1995.

Baker, William J., *Sports in the Western World*, Urbana: University of Illinois Press, 1988, Rev. Ed.

Bakhtin, M.M., *The Dialogic Imagination: Four Essays*, Austin: University of Texas Press, 1981, trans. Caryl Emerson & Michael Holquist.

Balio, Tino, *Grand Design: Hollywood as a Modern Business Enterprise 1930–1939*, New York: Charles Scribner's Sons, 1993.

Banet-Weiser, Sarah, *The Most Beautiful Girl in the World: Beauty Pageants and National Identity*, Berkeley: University of California Press, 1999.

Banner, Lois W., *American Beauty*, New York: Alfred A. Knopf, 1983.

—— *In Full Flower: Aging Women, Power, and Sexuality*, New York: Alfred A. Knopf, 1992.

Banta, Martha, *Imaging American Women: Ideas and Ideals in Cultural History*, New York: Columbia University Press, 1987.

Barber, Paul, *Vampires, Burial, and Death: Folklore and Reality*, New York: Yale University Press, 1988.

Barnard, Malcolm, *Fashion as Communication*, London: Routledge, 1996.

Barnouw, Erik, *Tube of Plenty: The Evolution of American Television*, 2nd Ed. New York: Oxford University Press, 1990.

Barrett, Judy and Judith McDonnell (eds) *European Women in the United States: A Biographical Dictionary*, New York: Garland Publishing, 1994.

Basinger, Jeanine, *Silent Stars*, New York: Alfred A. Knopf, 1999.

Baughman, Cynthia (ed.) *Women On Ice: Feminist Responses to the Tonya Harding–Nancy Kerrigan Spectacle*, New York: Routledge, 1995.

Bean, Jennifer and Diane Negra (eds) *A Feminist Reader in Early Cinema*, Durham: Duke University Press, 2002.

Bergan, Ronald and Robyn Karney (eds) *The Holt Foreign Film Guide*, New York: Henry Holt & Co., 1988.

Berlant, Lauren, 'The Face of America and the State of Emergency,' in *The Queen of America Goes to Washington City: Essays on Sex and Citizenship*, Durham: Duke University Press, 1997, pp. 175–220.

Bernard, Malcolm, *Fashion as Communication*, London: Routledge, 1996.

Bhabha, Homi K., 'The Other Question – the Stereotype and Colonial Discourse.' *Screen* 24(6), 1983, pp. 18–36.

——— 'Of Mimicry and Man: The Ambivalence of Colonial Discourse.' *October* 28, Spring, 1984, pp. 125–33.

Blessing, Patrick J., 'The Irish.' *Harvard Encyclopedia of American Ethnic Groups*, Stephan Thernstrom (ed.), Cambridge: Harvard University Press, 1980, pp. 524–45.

Bogle, Donald, *Toms, Coons, Mulattoes, Mammies and Bucks: An Interpretive History of Blacks in American Film*, New York: Continuum, 1989.

Bordo, Susan, *Unbearable Weight: Feminism, Western Culture, and the Body*, Berkeley: University of California Press, 1993.

——— *Twilight Zones: The Hidden Life of Cultural Images from Plato to O.J.*, Berkeley: University of California Press, 1997.

Bordwell, David, Janet Staiger and Kristin Thompson, *The Classical Hollywood Cinema: Film Style and Mode of Production to 1960*, New York: Columbia University Press, 1985.

Boylan, James, *The World and the 20's: The Golden Years of New York's Legendary Newspaper*, New York: Dial Press, 1973.

Brennan, Timothy, *Salman Rushdie and the Third World*, New York: St. Martin's Press, 1989.

Bradshaw, Michael, *Regions and Regionalism in the United States*, Jackson: University of Mississippi Press, 1988.

Brooks, Jodi, 'Performing Aging/Performance Crisis,' in *Figuring Age: Women, Bodies, Generations*, Kathleen Woodward (ed.), Bloomington: Indiana University Press, 1999, 232–47.

Brooks, Peter, *Body Work: Objects of Desire in Modern Narrative*, Cambridge: Harvard University Press, 1993.

Browder, Laura, *Slippery Characters: Ethnic Impersonators and American Identities*, Chapel Hill: University of North Carolina Press, 2000.

Bruno, Michael, *Venus in Hollywood: The Continental Enchantress from Garbo to Loren*, New York: Lyle Stuart, 1970.

Carr, Steven Alan, 'On the Edge of Tastelessness: CBS, the Smothers Brothers, and the Struggle for Control,' *Cinema Journal* 31(4) (Summer, 1992), 3–24.

Chisholm, Ann, 'Defending the Nation: National Bodies, US Borders, and the 1996 US Olympic Women's Gymnastics Team,' *Journal of Sport & Social Issues*, 23(2), (May, 1999), pp. 126–39.

Clark, Ann K., 'The Girl: A Rhetoric of Desire.' *Cultural Studies* 1(2) (May, 1987), pp. 195–203.

Clark, Christine and James O'Donnell (eds) *Becoming and Unbecoming White: Owning and Disowning a Racial Identity*, Westport, CT: Bergin & Garvey, 1999.

Collins, Jim, 'Genericity in the Nineties: Eclectic Irony and the New Sincerity,' in *Film Theory Goes to the Movies*, Jim Collins, Hilary Radner, and Ava Preacher Collins (eds), London: Routledge, 1993, 242–63.

Conzen, Kathleen Neils, David A. Gerber, Ewa Morawska, George E. Pozzetta and Rudoph J. Vecoli, 'The Invention of Ethnicity: A Perspective from the U.S.A.' *Journal of American Ethnic History*, 12(1) (Fall, 1992), pp. 3–41.

Coontz, Stephanie, *The Social Origins of Private Life: A History of American Families 1600–1900*, London: Verso, 1988.

Corner, John and Sylvia Harvey, 'Mediating Tradition and Modernity: The Heritage/ Enterprise Couplet.' in *Enterprise and Heritage: Crosscurrents of National Culture*, John Corner and Sylvia Harvey (eds), London: Routledge, 1991, pp. 45–75.

Cranny-Francis, Anne, *The Body in the Text*, Melbourne: Melbourne University Press, 1995.

Crunden, Robert M., *A Brief History of American Culture*, New York: Paragon House, 1994.

Curle, J.H., *To-Day and To-Morrow: The Testing Period of the White Race*, London: Methuen, 1926.

Curran, Joseph, *Hibernian Green On the Silver Screen: The Irish and American Movies*, New York: Westport Press, 1989.

Curry, Ramona, *Too Much of a Good Thing: Mae West as Cultural Icon*, Minneapolis: University of Minnesota Press, 1996.

Curtis, L. Perry Jr, *Apes and Angels: The Irishman in Victorian Caricature*, Washington: Smithsonian Institution Press, 1971.

Da, Lottie and Jan Alexander, *Bad Girls of the Silver Screen*, New York: Carroll & Graf, 1989.

Daddario, Gina, *Women's Sport and Spectacle: Gendered Television Coverage and the Olympic Games*, Westport, CT: Praeger, 1998.

Dathorne, O.R., *In Europe's Image: The Need for American Multiculturalism*, Westport, CT: Bergin & Garvey, 1994.

Davis, Natalie Zemon, 'Women on Top,' in *Society and Culture in Early Modern France*, Stanford: Stanford University Press, 1975, 124–51.

Davis, Tracy C., *Actresses as Working Women: Their Social Identity in Victorian Culture*, London: Routledge, 1991.

Dearborn, Mary, *Pocahontas's Daughters: Gender and Ethnicity in American Culture*, Oxford: Oxford University Press, 1986.

Decker, Jeffrey Louis, *Made in America: Self-Styled Success from Horatio Alger to Oprah Winfrey*, Minneapolis: University of Minnesota Press, 1997.

De Cordova, Richard, 'A Case of Mistaken Legitimacy: Class and Generational Difference in Three Family Melodramas,' in *Home is Where the Heart Is: Studies in Melodrama and the Woman's Film*, Christine Gledhill (ed.), London: BFI, 1987, pp. 255–67.

—— *Picture Personalities: The Emergence of the Star System in America*, Urbana: University of Illinois Press, 1990.

Deloria, Philip, *Playing Indian*, New Haven: Yale University Press, 1998.

D'Emilio, John and Estelle B. Freedman, *Intimate Matters: A History of Sexuality in America*, New York: Harper & Row, 1988.

Dijkstra, Bram, 'Metamorphoses of the Vampire: Dracula and His Daughters,' in *Idols of Perversity: Fantasies of Feminine Evil in Fin-de-Siecle Culture*, Oxford: Oxford University Press, 1986, pp. 333–51.

Dittmar, Linda, 'Beyond Gender and Within It: The Social Construction of Female Desire.' *Wide Angle* 8(3/4) (1986), pp. 79–88.

Doane, Mary Ann, *Femmes Fatales: Feminism, Film Theory, Psychoanalysis*, New York: Routledge, 1991.

Douglas, Ann, *Terrible Honesty: Mongrel Manhattan in the 1920s*, New York: Farrar, Straus and Giroux, 1995.

Douglas, Mary, *Purity and Danger: An Analysis of Concepts of Pollution and Taboo*, New York: Praeger, 1966.

Doyerson, Mark, *Making the American Team: Sport, Culture and the Olympic Experience*, Urbana: University of Illinois Press, 1981.

Dreiser, Theodore, 'Hollywood Now.' *McCalls Magazine*, September, 1921, pp. 15, 18, 54.

DuCille, Ann, 'The Shirley Temple of My Familiar ' *Transition* (The White Issue), 73 (1998) Durham: Duke University Press.

Dyer, Richard, *Stars*, London: BFI, 1979.

—— *Heavenly Bodies: Film Stars and Society*, New York: St. Martin's Press, 1986.

—— 'Heritage Cinema in Europe.' *Encyclopedia of European Cinema*, London: BFI, 1995, pp. 204–05.

—— *White*, London and New York: Routledge, 1997.

Eakin, Julie Sinclair, 'The Silver Screen's Street of Dreams,' *The New York Times* December 4, 1994, XX p. 22.

Epstein, Leslie, *Ice Fire Water*, New York: W.W. Norton & Co., 1999.

Erdman, Andrew, 'The World, the City, and Bigtime Vaudeville: Negotiations in American Culture, 1880–1917.' Paper Presented at the 1996 Society for Cinema Studies Conference, Dallas, Texas.

Erenberg, Lewis A. and Susan E. Hirsch (eds) *The War in American Culture: Society and Consciousness During World War II*, Chicago: University of Chicago Press, 1996.

Ewen, Elizabeth, 'City Lights: Immigrant Women and the Rise of the Movies.' *Signs: Journal of Women in Culture in Society*, 5(3) (1980), pp. 545–65.

Falk, Pasi, *The Consuming Body*, London: Sage, 1994.

Faller, Greg S., *The Function of Star-Image and Performance In the Hollywood Musical: Sonja Henie, Esther Williams, and Eleanor Powell*, PhD Dissertation, Northwestern University, 1987.

Feldman, Egal, 'Prostitution, the Alien Woman and the Progressive Imagination, 1910–1015,' *American Quarterly* XIX, (Summer, 1967), pp. 192–206.

Fielder, Mari Kathleen, 'Fatal Attraction: Irish-Jewish Romance in Early Film and Drama,' *Eire-Ireland* 20(3) (1985), 6–18.

Fine, Michelle, Lois Weis, Linda C. Powell and L. Mun Wong, *Off White: Readings on Race, Power and Society*, New York: Routledge, 1997.

Flamini, Roland, *Thalberg: The Last Tycoon and the World of MGM*, New York: Crown Publishers, 1994.

Formanek-Brunell, Miriam, *Made to Play House: Dolls and the Commercialization of American Girlhood 1830–1930*, Baltimore: The Johns Hopkins University Press, 1993.

Foucault, Michel, *The History of Sexuality: An Introduction Vol. I*, New York: Random House, 1978, trans. Robert Hurley.

Frankenberg, Ruth, *White Women, Race Matters: The Social Construction of Whiteness*, Minneapolis: University of Minnesota Press, 1993.

Freud, Sigmund, 'Family Romances,' in *Psychological Works of Sigmund Freud*, Vol. IX, London: Hogarth Press, 1959, trans. James Strachey.

Friedman, Lester (ed.) *Unspeakable Images: Ethnicity and the American Cinema*, Urbana: University of Illinois Press, 1991.

Gabaccia, Donna, *From the Other Side: Women, Gender, and Immigrant Life in the US 1820–1990* Bloomington: Indiana University Press, 1994.

Gaines, Jane, *The Popular Icon as Commodity and Sign: The Circulation of Betty Grable, 1941–1945*, PhD Dissertation, Northwestern University, 1982.

Gamson, Joshua, *Claims to Fame: Celebrity in Contemporary America*, Berkeley: University of California Press, 1994.

Garber, Marjorie, *Vested Interests: Cross-Dressing and Cultural Anxiety*, London: Routledge, 1992.

—— *Sex and Real Estate: Why We Love Houses*, New York: Pantheon, 2000.

Gelley, Alexander, *Unruly Examples: On The Rhetoric of Exemplarity*, Stanford: Stanford University Press, 1995.

Gitlin, Todd, *The Twilight of Common Dreams: Why America Is Wracked By Culture Wars*, New York: Henry Holt & Co., 1995.

Gledhill, Christine (ed.) *Stardom: Industry of Desire*, London: Routledge, 1991.

Goldman, Eric F., *The Crucial Decade – And After*, New York: Vintage Books, 1966.

Grabo, Carl H., 'Americanizing the Immigrants,' *The Dial* LXVI (1919), p. 541.

Grantham, Dewey W., *The United States Since 1945*, New York: McGraw-Hill, 1976.

Griffith, Richard, *The Movie Stars.* Garden City, NY: Doubleday & Co., 1970.

Guback, Thomas H., 'Hollywood's International Market,' in *The American Film Industry*, Tino Balio (ed.), Madison: University of Wisconsin Press, 1976, pp. 387–409.

Guttman, Allen, 'Erotic Athleticism and Popular Culture,' in *The Erotic in Sports*, New York: Columbia University Press, 1996.

Hake, Sabine, *Passions and Deceptions: The Early Films of Ernst Lubitsch*, Princeton: Princeton University Press, 1992.

Hall, Carolyn, *The Twenties in Vogue*, New York: Harmony Books, 1983.

Hall, Catherine, *Male and Middle Class: Explorations In Feminism and History*, New York: Routledge, 1992.

Haller Jr, John S., 'From Maidenhood to Menopause: Sex Education for Women in Victorian America.' *Journal of Popular Culture* XI, (Summer, 1972), pp. 49–69.

Halter, Marilyn, *Shopping for Identity: The Marketing of Ethnicity*, New York: Schocken Books, 2000.

Hartigan Jr, John, *Racial Situations: Class Predicaments of Whiteness in Detroit*, Princeton: Princeton University Press, 1999.

Haskell, Molly, *From Reverence to Rape: The Treatment of Women in the Movies*, New York: Penguin, 1974.

Heath, Stephen, 'Questions of Property: Film and Nationhood,' in *Explorations in Film Theory: Selected Essays From Cine-Tracts*, Ron Burnett (ed.), Bloomington: Indiana University Press, 1991, pp. 180–90.

Hershfield, Joanne, *The Invention of Dolores Del Rio*, Minneapolis: University of Minnesota Press, 2000.

Hewison, Robert, *The Heritage Industry: Britain in a Climate of Decline*, London: Methuen, 1987.

Higashi, Sumiko, *Virgins, Vamps, and Flappers: The American Silent Movie Heroine*, New York: St. Albans, 1978.

—— *Cecil B. DeMille and American Culture: The Silent Era*, Berkeley: University of California Press, 1994.

Higham, John, *Strangers in the Land: Patterns of American Nativism 1860–1925*, New Brunswick, NJ: Rutgers University Press, 1988.

Higson, Andrew, 'Re-presenting the National Past: Nostalgia and Pastiche in the Heritage Film,' in *Fires Were Started: British Cinema and Thatcherism*, Lester Friedman (ed.), Minneapolis: University of Minnesota Press, 1993, 109–29.

Hollinghurst, Alan, 'Suppressive Nostalgia.' *Times Literary Supplement*, Nov. 6, 1987, 1225.

Hunt, Michael H., *Ideology and US Foreign Policy*, New Haven: Yale University Press, 1987.

Hutchinson, Tom, *Screen Goddesses*, New York: Exeter Books, 1984.

Jacobs, Lea, *The Wages of Sin: Censorship and the Fallen Woman Film 1928–1942*, Madison: University of Wisconsin Press, 1991.

Jacobson, Matthew Frye, *Whiteness of a Different Color: European Immigrants and the Alchemy of Race*, Cambridge: Harvard University Press, 1998.

Jeffords, Susan, 'The Big Switch: Hollywood Masculinity in the Nineties,' in *Film Theory Goes to the Movies*, Jim Collins, Hilary Radner, and Ava Preacher Collins (eds), London: Routledge, 1993, 196–208.

Jones, Amelia, 'She Was Bad News: Male Paranoia and the Contemporary New Woman.' *Camera Obscura* 25/26, (January/May, 1991), pp. 296–320.

Kaplan, Amy and Donald E. Pease (eds) *Cultures of United States Imperialism*, Durham: Duke University Press, 1993.

Kaplan, E. Ann, *Motherhood and Representation: The Mother in Popular Culture and Melodrama*, London: Routledge, 1992.

Kincheloe, Joe L., Shirley R. Steinberg, Nelson M. Rodriguez and Ronald E. Channault (eds) *White Reign: Deploying Whiteness in America*, New York: St. Martin's Press, 1998.

Kindem, Gorham, 'Hollywood's Movie Star System: A Historical Overview,' in *The American Movie Industry*, Carbondale: Southern Illinois University Press, 1982, 79–93.

Kindem, Gorham and Bjorn Sorenssen, 'A Documentary History of Stardom and a Contemporary Document of Norwegian National Culture: Edvard Hambro's "Sonja Henie, Queen of the Ice,"' unpublished essay.

King, Barry, 'Stardom as an Occupation,' in *The Hollywood Film Industry*, P. Kerr (ed.), London: Routledge & Kegan Paul, 1986.

King, Desmond, *Making Americans: Immigration, Race, and the Origins of the Diverse Democracy*, Cambridge: Harvard University Press, 2000.

Kirshenblatt-Gimblett, Barbara, *Destination Culture: Tourism, Museums, and Heritage*, Berkeley: University of California Press, 1998.

Klunk, Brian, *Consensus and the American Mission*, New York: University Press of America, 1986.

Kobal, John, *Hollywood Color Portraits*, New York: William Morrow & Co., 1980.

Kobal, John, *People Will Talk*, New York: Alfred A. Knopf, 1985.

Koszarski, Richard, *An Evening's Entertainment: The Age of the Silent Feature Picture 1915–1928*, New York: Scribner's, 1990.

LaFeber, Walter, *The American Age: United States Foreign Policy at Home and Abroad since 1750*, New York: W.W. Norton & Co., 1989.

Landay, Lori, *Madcaps, Screwballs, and Con Women: The Female Trickster in American Culture*, Philadelphia: University of Pennsylvania Press, 1998.

Laplanche, Jean and Jean-Baptiste Pontalis, 'Fantasy and the Origins of Sexuality,' in *Formations of Fantasy*, Cora Kaplan et al. (eds), London and New York: Methuen, 1986, pp. 5–27.

Lapsley, Robert and Michael Westlake, 'From *Casablanca* to *Pretty Woman*: The Politics of Romance.' *Screen* 33(1), (Spring, 1992), pp. 27–49.

Lenskyj, Helen, *Out of Bounds: Women, Sport and Sexuality*, Toronto: The Women's Press, 1986.

Leonard, Susan J. and Rebecca A. Pope, *The Diva's Mouth: Body, Voice, Prima Donna Politics*, New Brunswick: Rutgers University Press, 1996.

Lipsitz, George, *The Possessive Investment in Whiteness: How White People Profit from Identity Politics*, Philadelphia: Temple University Press, 1998.

Litoff, Judy Barrett and Judith McDonnell (eds) *European Immigrant Women in the United States: A Biographical Dictionary*, New York: Garland Publishing, 1994.

MacAloon, John J., 'Double Visions: Olympic Games and American Culture,' *Kenyon Review*, 4 (Winter) 1982.

Mackenzie, John (ed.) *Imperialism and Popular Culture*, Manchester: Manchester University Press, 1986.

Marc, David, *Demographic Vistas: Television in American Culture*, Philadelphia: University of Pennsylvania Press, 1984.

Mayne, Judith, 'Immigrants and Spectators,' *Wide Angle* 5(2), (1982), pp. 32–41.

—— 'Star-Gazing,' in *Cinema and Spectatorship*, London: Routledge, 1993, pp. 123–41.

Marchetti, Gina, *Romance and the 'Yellow Peril': Race, Sex, and Discursive Strategies in Hollywood Fiction*, Berkeley: University of California Press, 1993.

McClintock, Anne, *Imperial Leather: Race, Gender and Sexuality in the Colonial Contest*, New York: Routledge, 1995.

McCormick, Thomas, 'Every System Needs a Center Sometimes: An Essay on Hegemony and Modern American Foreign Policy,' in *Redefining the Past: Essays in Diplomatic History in Honor of William Appleman Williams*, Corvallis: Oregon State University Press, 1986, pp. 195–220.

McDonald, Anne L., *Feminine Ingenuity: Women and Invention in America*, New York: Ballantine Books, 1992.

McLean, Adrienne L., 'The Construction of Rita Hayworth,' *Journal of Film and Video*, 44(3/4) Fall 1992/Winter 1993, pp. 8–26.

Merish, Lori, 'Cuteness and Commodity Aesthetics: Tom Thumb and Shirley Temple,' in *Freakery: Cultural Spectacles of the Extraordinary Body*, Rosemarie Garland Thompson (ed.), New York: New York University Press, 1996, pp. 185–203.

Miller, Mark Stuart, *Promoting Movies in the Late 1930s: Pressbooks at Warner Bros.* PhD dissertation, University of Texas at Austin, 1994.

Miringoff, Marc and Marque-Luisa Miringoff, *The Social Health of the Nation: How America Is Really Doing*, New York/Oxford: Oxford University Press, 1999.

Mizejewski, Linda, *Ziegfeld Girl: Image and Icon in Culture and Cinema*, Durham: Duke University Press, 1999.

Modleski, Tania, *Loving with a Vengeance: Mass-Produced Fantasies for Women*, London: Routledge, 1982.

Moore, Colleen, *Silent Star*, Garden City, NY: Doubleday & Co., 1968.

Morgan, Kathyrn Pauly, 'Women and the Knife: Cosmetic Surgery and the Colonization of Women's Bodies,' *Hypatia* 6(3) (Fall, 1991), 25–53.

Morrison, James, *Passport to Hollywood: Hollywood Films, European Directors*, Albany, NY. SUNY Press, 1998.

Mullin, Molly, 'Representations of History, Irish Feminism, and the Politics of Difference,' *Feminist Studies* 17(1) (Spring, 1991), pp. 29–50.

Mulvey, Laura, 'Pandora: Topographies of the Mask and Curiosity,' in *Sexuality and Space*, Beatriz Colomina (ed.), New York: Princeton Architectural Press, 1992, 54–71.

Murphy, Paul L., 'Sources and Nature of Intolerance in the 1920s,' in *The 1920s: Problems and Paradoxes*, Milton Plesur (ed.), Boston: Allyn & Bacon, 1969, pp. 165–83.

Negra, Diane, 'Romance And/As Tourism: Heritage Whiteness and the (Inter)National Imaginary in Recent Film,' in *Keyframes: Popular Film and Cultural Studies*, Amy Villarejo and Matthew Tinkcom (eds), London: Routledge, 2001.

—— 'Re-Made for Television: Hedy Lamarr's Postwar Star Textuality,' in *Small Screens, Big Ideas: Television in the 1950s*, Janet Thumim (ed.), London: I.B. Tauris, 2001.

—— 'The Fictionalized Ethnic Biography: Nita Naldi and the Crisis of Assimilation,' in *A Slightly Different Light: Exploring Marginalized Issues and Forces in American Silent Film*, Thomas J. Slater and Gregg Bachman (eds), Carbondale: Southern Illinois University Press, 2001.

Nelson, Dana, *National Manhood: Capitalist Citizenship and the Imagined Fraternity of White Men*, Durham: Duke University Press, 1998.

Newitz, Annalee and Matthew Wray, 'What Is "White Trash?:" Stereotypes and Economic Conditions of Poor Whites in the United States,' in *Whiteness: A Critical Reader*, Mike Hill (ed.), New York: New York University Press, 1997, 168–84.

Noriega, Chan and Ana Lopez, *The Ethnic Eye: Latino Media Arts*, Minneapolis: University of Minnesota Press, 1996.

O'Byrne, Anne, 'Memory, Monuments, and Counter-monuments,' Paper delivered at 1994 Remapping the Borders: Irish Cultural Studies in the 1990s Conference, University of Texas at Austin.

Parker, Andrew, *Nationalisms and Sexualities*, New York: Routledge, 1992.

Peiss, Kathy, *Hope in a Jar: The Making of America's Beauty Culture*, New York: Metropolitan Books, 1998.

Pfeil, Fred, *White Guys: Studies in Postmodern Domination and Difference*, New York and London: Verso, 1995.

Plunkett, Helen, *Theodosia, Theda, and the Vamp: Sex and Identity*, unpublished essay.

Quigley, John, *The Ruses for War: American Interventionism Since World War II*, Buffalo: Prometheus Books, 1992.

Radner, Hilary, 'Pretty Is as Pretty Does: Free Enterprise and the Marriage Plot,' in *Film Theory Goes to the Movies*, Jim Collins, Hilary Radner and Ava Preacher Collins (eds), London: Routledge, 1993, 56–76.

Ragan, David, *Who's Who In Hollywood: The Largest Cast of International Film Personalities Ever Assembled*, New York: Facts on File, 1992.

Ringer, Benjamin B. and Elinor R. Lawless, *Race-Ethnicity and Society*, New York: Routledge, 1989.

Roberts, Kenneth L., *Why Europe Leaves Home*, New York: Bobbs-Merrill Company, 1922.

Roberts, Shari, 'The Lady in the Tutti Frutti Hat: Carmen Miranda, A Spectacle of Ethnicity,' *Cinema Journal* 32 (Spring, 1993), pp. 3–23.

Robinson, Sally, *Marked Men: White Masculinity in Crisis*, New York: Columbia University Press, 2000.

Rony, Fatimah Tobing, *The Third Eye: Race, Cinema, and Ethnographic Spectacle*, Durham: Duke University Press, 1996.

Rogin, Michael, *Blackface, White Noise: Jewish Immigrants in the Hollywood Melting Pot*, Berkeley: University of California Press, 1998.

Rose Peter, *They and We: Racial and Ethnic Relations in the United States*, New York: Random House, 1981, 3rd Ed.

Rosen, Marjorie, 'Old Mores for New,' in *Popcorn Venus: Women, Movies and the American Dream*, New York: Avon, 1973, 59–71.

Rosenberg, Emily S., *Spreading the American Dream: American Economic and Cultural Expansion 1890–1945*, New York: Hill & Wang, 1982.

Ross, Steven J., *Working-Class Hollywood: Silent Film and the Shaping of Class in America*, Princeton: Princeton University Press, 1998.

Rowe, Kathleen Karlyn, *The Unruly Woman: Gender and the Genres of Laughter*, Austin: University of Texas Press, 1995.

Rudman, Lisa L., 'Marriage – The Ideal and the Reel: Or, The Cinematic Marriage Manual,' *Film History* 1(4) (1987).

Russell, Douglas A., *Costume, History and Style*, Englewood Cliffs, NJ: Prentice-Hall, 1983.

Ryan, Mary P., 'The Projection of a New Womanhood: The Movie Moderns in the 1920s,' in *Our American Sisters*, Jean Friedman and William Shade (eds), Boston: Allyn & Bacon, 1976, 500–18.

Rydell, Robert W., *All the World's a Fair: Visions of Empire at American International Expositions 1876–1916*, Chicago: University of Chicago Press, 1984.

Savran, David, *Taking It Like A Man: White Masculinity, Masochism, and Contemporary American Culture*, Princeton: Princeton University Press, 1998.

Schatz, Thomas, 'The New Hollywood,' in *Film Theory Goes to the Movies*, Jim Collins, Hilary Radner and Ava Preacher Collins (eds), London: Routledge, 1993, pp. 8–36.

—— *Boom and Bust: The American Cinema in the 1940s*, New York: Charles Scribner's Sons, 1997.

Shulman, Irving, *Valentino*, New York: Trident, 1967.

Sklar, Robert, *Movie-Made America: A Cultural History of American Movies*, New York: Vintage Books, 1975.

Slide, Anthony, *The Cinema and Ireland*, Jefferson, NC: McFarland & Co., 1988.

Smuts, Robert W., *Women and Work in America*, New York: Schocken Books, 1971.

Sowell, Thomas, *Ethnic America: A History*, New York: Basic Books, 1981.

Spigel, Lynn and Michael Curtin, *The Revolution Wasn't Televised: Sixties Television and Social Conflict*, New York: Routledge, 1997.

Stacey, Jackie, *Star Gazing: Hollywood Cinema and Female Spectatorship*, London: Routledge, 1994.

Staiger, Janet, *Bad Women: Regulating Sexuality in Early American Cinema*, Minneapolis: University of Minnesota Press, 1995.

Stein, Howard F. and Robert F. Hill, *The Ethnic Imperative: Examining the New White Ethnic Movement*, University Park, PA: Pennsylvania State University Press, 1977.

Stillman, Edmund and William Pfaff, 'Towards a New Foreign Policy,' in *Consensus at the Crossroads: Dialogues in American Foreign Policy*, New York: Dodd, Mead & Co., 1972, pp. 200–17.

Strait, Raymond and Leif Henie, *Queen of Ice Queen of Shadows: The Unsuspected Life of Sonja Henie*, Chelsea, MI: Scarborough House, 1985.

Studlar, Gaylyn, *This Mad Masquerade: Stardom and Masculinity in the Jazz Age*, New York: Columbia University Press, 1996.

Tajiri, Vincent, *Valentino: The True Life Story*, London: Bantam Books, 1977.

Tasker, Yvonne, *Working Girls: Gender and Sexuality in Popular Cinema*, London: Routledge, 1998.

Tentler, Leslie Woodcock, *Wage-Earning Women: Industrial Work and Family Life in the United States 1900–1930*, New York: Oxford University Press, 1979.

Tepper, Kirby, *Magill's Cinema Annual, 1995: A Survey of the Films of 1994*, Detroit: Gale Research, 14th Ed., 1996.

Terry, Jennifer and Jacqueline Urla, *Deviant Bodies: Critical Perspectives on Difference in Science and Popular Culture*, Bloomington: Indiana University Press, 1995.

Thernstrom, Stephan (ed.) *Harvard Encyclopedia of American Ethnic Groups*, Cambridge: Harvard University Press, 1980.

Urry, John, *The Tourist Gaze: Leisure and Travel in Contemporary Societies*, London: Sage, 1990.

Valdivia, Angharad N., *A Latina in the Land of Hollywood: and Other Essays on Media Culture*, Tucson: University of Arizona Press, 2000.

Vermilye, Jerry, *The Films of the Twenties*, Secaucus, NJ: Citadel Press, 1985.

Villarejo, Amy and Matthew Tinkcom (eds) *Keyframes: Popular Cinema and Cultural Studies*, London: Routledge, 2001.

Walker, Alexander, *Rudolph Valentino*, New York: Stein & Day, 1976.

Walkowitz, Judith R., *City of Dreadful Delight: Narratives of Sexual Danger in Late-Victorian London*, London: Virago, 1992.

Walsh, Frank, *Sin and Censorship: The Catholic Church and the Motion Picture Industry*, New Haven: Yale University Press, 1996.

Waters, Mary, *Ethnic Options: Choosing Identities in America*, Berkeley: University of California Press, 1990.

Welky, D.B., 'Viking Girls, Mermaids, and Little Brown Men: US Journalism and the 1932 Olympics,' *Journal of Sport History*, 24(1), pp. 24–46.

Welter, Barbara, 'The Cult of True Womanhood 1820–1860,' *American Quarterly* 18 (Summer, 1966) 151–74.

Westbrook, Robert B., 'I Want a Girl, Just Like the Girl That Married Harry James: American Women and the Problem of Political Obligation in World War II,' *American Quarterly*, 42(4) (December, 1990), pp. 587–614.

Wexman, Virginia Wright, *Creating the Couple: Love, Marriage, and Hollywood Performance*, Princeton: Princeton University Press, 1993.

White, Mimi, 'Representing Romance: Reading/Writing/Fantasy and the "Liberated" Heroine of Recent Hollywood Films,' *Cinema Journal*, 8(3) (Spring, 1989), 41–56.

Whittemore, Don and Philip Alan Cecchettini, *Passport to Hollywood: Film Immigrants Anthology*, New York: McGraw-Hill, 1976.

Williams, Linda, 'Film Body: An Implantation of Perversions,' in *Explorations in Film Theory: Selected Essays From Cine-Tracts*, Ron Burnett (ed.), Bloomington, Indiana University Press, 1991.

Williamson, Catherine, 'Swimming Pools, Movie Stars: The Celebrity Body in the Postwar Marketplace,' in *Camera Obscura*, 38(5), 1996, pp. 5–29.

Willis, Sharon, *High Contrast: Race and Gender in Contemporary Hollywood Film*, Durham: Duke University Press, 1997.

Wilson, Elizabeth, *The Sphinx in the City: Urban Life, the Control of Disorder, and Women*, London: Virago, 1991.

Winokur, Mark, *American Laughter: Immigrants, Ethnicity, and 1930s Hollywood Film Comedy*, New York: St. Martin's Press, 1996.

Woll, Allen L., *The Latin Image in American Film*, Los Angeles: Latin American Center, University of California Press, 1977.

Woll, Allen L. and Randall M. Miller, *Ethnic and Racial Images in American Film and Television: Historical Essays and Bibliography*, New York: Garland Publishing, 1987.

Wolpin, Miles D., *America Insecure: Arms Transfers, Global Interventionism, and the Erosion of National Security*, Jefferson, NC: McFarland & Co., 1991.

Wollstein, Hans J., *Strangers in Hollywood: The History of Scandinavian Actors in American Films from 1910 to World War II.*, Lanham, MD: Scarecrow Press, 1994.

Wray, Matt and Annalee Newitz, *White Trash: Race and Class in America*, New York: Routledge, 1997.

Wright, Elizabeth (ed.) *Feminism and Psychoanalysis: A Critical Dictionary*, Oxford: Blackwell, 1992.

Wright, William Lord, 'Motion Pictures and Young America,' *Motion Picture Magazine*, (April, 1914), pp. 120, 156.

Young, Christopher, *The Films of Hedy Lamarr*, Secaucus, NJ: Citadel Press, 1978.

'The Experience of Immigrants: Some Suggestions for Scenarios on Americanization,' (From an Address by Hon. Franklin H. Lane before the National Association of the Motion Picture Industry at the Waldorf-Astoria, Jan. 11, 1920), Published by the Inter-Racial Council, New York.

'Revamping the Vampires,' *The Nation*, 113(2927), (August 10, 1921), p. 140.

This Fabulous Century, Vol. II 1910–1920, New York: Time-Life, 1969.

PUBLICITY AND PRESS SOURCES FOR COLLEEN MOORE

Albert, Katherine, 'Charm? No! No! You Must Have Glamour,' *Photoplay*, (September, 1931), pp. 186–7, p. 341.

Anderson, Jon, 'Book News,' *Philadelphia Inquirer*, February 11, 1968, page not cited.

Boone, Arabella, 'One's Blue, and One's Brown,' *Photoplay*, 50 (February, 1919).

Collura, Joe, 'Star Shines at Cinefest! Colleen Moore,' *Classic Images* #89 14 (no date listed).

Gassaway, Gordon, 'Everybody's Little Sister,' *Picture Play Magazine*, (January, 1920), pp. 78–9.

—— 'With a Dash of Green,' *Motion Picture Magazine*, (June, 1922), p. 40.

Hall, Mordaunt, 'It Must Be Love,' *New York Times*, 20(2), October 4, 1926.

—— 'A Fractious Farce,' *New York Times*, 23(2) June 7, 1926,

Howe, Herbert, 'A Hollywood Girl,' *Photoplay*, 47 (August, 1922).

Johnson, Scott, 'Colleen Moore: The Silent Star Shines at the Fargo Theatre,' *Classic Images*, 133 (July, 1986), p. 25.

Mitchell, George, 'The Irish in the Movies,' February, 1923, p. 20 (Source Unknown) Colleen Moore Clippings Film, Academy of Motion Picture Arts and Sciences, Margaret Herrick Library, Beverly Hills, California.

Moore, Colleen, 'Up From the Extra Ranks,' in Charles Reed Jones (ed.) *Breaking Into the Movies*, New York: Unicorn Press, 1927, rpt. in *The Stars Appear*, Richard Dyer, McAnn (ed.), Metuchen, NJ: Scarecrow Press, 1992, pp. 247–50.

Moore, Colleen, 'My Career and My Doll's House,' *Ladies Home Journal*, 44:14 (August, 1927).

Moore, Patricia, 'The Glory Days of Fair Colleen,' *Chicago Daily News*, Feb. 2, 1968, p. 24.

Peltret, Elizabeth, 'The Celtic Strain,' *Motion Picture Classic*, (July, 1922), pp. 16–17, p. 82.

Saurin, Clodagh, 'The Wearing of the Green,' *Photoplay*, (March, 1921), p. 31, p. 76.

Smith, Frederick James, 'The Unsophisticated Colleen,' *Motion Picture*, 21 (June, 1921) pp. 54–5, p. 95.

Spears, Jack, 'Colleen Moore,' *Films in Review*, (August–September, 1963), pp. 403–24.

Spensley, Dorothy, 'The Cinderella Girl,' *Photoplay*, 30-3:30 (August, 1926).

Tapert, Annette, 'Colleen Moore: The Original Flapper in Bel-Air,' *Architectural Digest*, (April, 1996), pp. 216–21, p. 294.

Taylor, Angela, 'This Flapper Altered Fashion's Course,' *New York Times*, Oct. 26, 1971.

Uselton, Roi A., 'The Wampas Baby Stars,' *Films in Review*, (February, 1970) XXI(?) pp. 73–8.

Watters, James, 'Colleen Moore,' in *Return Engagement: Faces to Remember – Then and Now*, New York: Crown Publishers, 1984, pp. 32–3.

'Colleen Moore, Ultimate Flapper of the Silent Screen, Is Dead at 87,' *New York Times*, January 27, 1988, D23.

Review of *Little Orphant Annie*, *Variety*, December 6, 1918, p. 39.

Review of *Irene*, *Variety*, Mar. 3, 1926, p. 34.

PUBLICITY AND PRESS SOURCES FOR POLA NEGRI

Anonymous, 'An Amazing Revelation: The Autobiography of Pola Negri,' *Photoplay*, (January, 1924), p. 32.

Bruno, Michael, 'Pola Negri: Or Passion's Pulsating Plaything,' in *Venus in Hollywood: The Continental Enchantress from Garbo to Loren*, New York: Lyle Stuart, 1970, pp. 29–39.

Frazer, Robert W., 'Favorite Sweethearts of the Screen – Pola Negri,' *Photoplay*, (July, 1924), p. 31.

Hall, Leonard, 'The Passing of Pola,' *Photoplay*, (December, 1928), p. 29.

Haskins, Harrison, 'Who is Pola Negri?' *Motion Picture Classic*, (February, 1921), p. 43, p. 78.

Howe, Herbert, 'The Real Pola Negri,' *Photoplay*, (November, 1922), p. 59.

—— 'The Loves of Pola Negri,' *Photoplay*, (November, 1923), p. 37.

Jordan, Joan, 'You Can't Hurry Pola,' *Photoplay*, (March, 1923), p. 63.

Lyon, Ben, 'Vampires I Have Known,' *Photoplay*, (February, 1925), p. 28.

Negri, Pola, 'What is Love?' *Photoplay*, (November, 1924), p. 30.

—— *Memoirs of a Star*, Garden City, NY: Doubleday, 1970.

Quirk, James R., 'The Autobiography of Pola Negri Part I,' *Photoplay*, (February, 1924), p. 51.

—— 'The Autobiography of Pola Negri Part II,' *Photoplay*, (March, 1924), p. 56.

—— 'Close-Ups and Long Shots,' *Photoplay*, (July, 1927) p. 27, p. 74.

St. Johns, Ivan, 'How Pola Was Tamed,' *Photoplay*, (January, 1926), p. 53.

Shlusinger, Rose, 'The Uncertainty of Certainty,' *Motion Picture Classic*, (October, 1922), pp. 18–19, p. 74, p. 77.

Valletin, Antonina, 'Film Stars in Germany,' *Shadowland*, (February, 1921), p. 48.

Vinder, Maximilian, 'She Delivered the Goods,' *Photoplay*, (May, 1922), p. 20.

'As We Go to Press,' *Photoplay*, (June, 1927), p. 6.

Review, 'Loves of an Actress,' *Variety*, August 1, 1928.

PUBLICITY AND PRESS SOURCES FOR SONJA HENIE

Carrol, Sidney, 'Sonja Henie: Spice on Ice,' *Coronet*, (May, 1944), pp. 14–17.

Cheatham, M., 'Still Laughing at Love,' *Silver Screen*, 10(3), (January 1940), p. 37.

Hail, Florabel Muir, 'Sonja Henie, Combination of Beauty and Brains,' *Citizen News* February 16, 1946.

Hall, Gladys, 'Not As Other Girls . . . ,' *Picture Play*, April 23, 1938, (Manuscript in the Gladys Hall Collection, Academy of Motion Picture Arts and Sciences).

McEvoy, J.P., 'She Happens On Ice,' *Reader's Digest*, 39, (November, 1941), pp. 41–4.

Reid, James, 'Busy as a B-25!' *Silver Screen*, 12(10), (August, 1942), pp. 54–5, p. 86.

Rhea, Marian, 'Sonja Henie's New Prince Charming,' *Photoplay*, 53(3), (March, 1939), pp. 28–9, p. 78.

Sharpe, Howard, 'Skating Through Life,' *Photoplay*, (in three installments) 51(11), (November, 1937), pp. 14–15, pp. 80–83, 51(12), (December, 1937), pp. 30–31, pp. 88–9, and 52(1), (January, 1938), pp. 62–3, p. 86.

Skolsky, Sidney, 'Tintypes,' *Citizen News*, September 7, 1944.

Sullivan, Ed, 'Champions Vs. The Screen,' *Silver Screen*, 7(8), (June, 1937) pp. 22–3, p. 63.

Vallee, William Lynch, 'Other Side of Sonja,' *Silver Screen*, 15(7), (May, 1945), pp. 42–3, pp. 80–85.

'Skating: Sonja Henie Whirls and Spins in Paris Dresses,' *Newsweek*, 3 March 17, 1934, p. 24.

'Astaire on Ice,' *Time*, 27, March 30, 1936, p. 57.

'One in a Million,' *Life*, January 23, 1939.

'How She Keeps Her Feet in Trim,' *Life*, January 23, 1939.

'Gee-Whizzer,' *Time* 34(3), July 17, 1939, pp. 51–4.

'Fabulous Sonja Henie,' *Newsweek*, 15 January 29, 1940, pp. 72–3.

'Cash-Register Champion,' *Look*, May 1, 1945, pp. 72–3.

'Hot Stuff on Ice,' *Newsweek* 32, October 25, 1948, p. 86.

'Ice Queen,' *Time*, 51, February 2, 1948, pp. 51–4.

'Hot Feud for Icy Gold,' *Life*, 32, February 4, 1952, pp. 46–7.

'Marriage Go-Round,' *Time* 77, January 6, 1961, p. 44.

'Where Are They Now?' *Newsweek* 63, February 10, 1964, p. 14.

'When Henie Had an Edge, She Knew How to Maintain It,' *Los Angeles Times* February 18, 1988.

PUBLICITY AND PRESS SOURCES FOR HEDY LAMARR

Anonymous, 'Hedy Comes Up With Idea for US Defense,' *Hollywood Citizen*, September 30, 1941.

Anonymous, 'Hedy Lamarr Invention Seen as Defense Aid,' *Los Angeles Times*, October 11, 1941.

Anonymous, 'A Look at Look Mag Turns Hedy Lamarr Livid,' *Variety*, May 9, 1951.

Anonymous, 'Hedy Lamar, Stauffer On Carmel Honeymoon,' *Herald Express*, June 12, 1951.

Baker, Russell, 'Movie Fan Tells All,' *New York Times*, February 10, 1996, A15.

Birmingham, Stephen, 'Would You Believe I Was Once a Famous Star? It's the Truth!' *New York Times*, August 23, 1970, D11.

Crichton, Kyle, 'Escape to Hollywood,' *Colliers*, November 5, 1928, p. 14, p. 46.

Ducas, Dorothy, 'Hollywood Bows to Exotic Allure of Hedy Lamarr,' November 20, 1938, p. 4.

Hall, Gladys, 'Luxurious Lamarr,' for *Motion Picture*, undated manuscript in the Gladys Hall Special Collection, AMPAS.

—— 'Marriage – And Hedy Lamarr,' for *Silver Screen*, manuscript dated April 24, 1939, in the Gladys Hall Special Collection, AMPAS (Subsequently appeared in *Silver Screen*, July, 1939).

Hamilton, Sara, 'Hedy Wine,' *Photoplay*, October, 1938, p. 23, p. 74.

Hayes, Barbara, 'Hedy Lamarr Vs. Joan Bennett: And Other Dangerous Hollywood Feuds,' *Photoplay*, (April, 1939), p. 18.

Hopper, Hedda, 'Hedda Hopper's Hollywood,' *Chicago Daily News* July 23, 1938, p. 16.

—— 'The Ecstasy Girl Wins Cheers From Hollywood,' *Life*, July 25, 1938.

—— 'Top Siren of Screen is Really Homebody,' *Los Angeles Times*, November 21, 1948.

Kilgallen, Dorothy, 'You're Wrong About Hedy Lamarr,' *The American Weekly*, Feb. 3, 1952, p. 18, p. 21.

Lamarr, Hedy, 'The Curse of Beauty,' *Look*, June 5, 1951, pp. 72–9.

—— *Ecstasy and Me: My Life as a Woman*, Greenwich, CT: Fawcett, 1966.

Liepmann, Hienz, 'Vienna Farewell,' *Photoplay*, April, 1939, p. 36, p. 89.

Martin, Pete, 'I Go Shopping with Hedy,' *Saturday Evening Post*, February 5, 1944, p. 19, p. 45.

—— 'Hedy Sells Her Past,' *Saturday Evening Post*, February 29, 1951, pp. 32–3, p. 35, p. 54, pp. 56–9.

Meeks, Fleming, 'I Guess They Just Take and Forget about A Person,' *Forbes*, 145(10) (May 14, 1990), pp. 136–8.

Morris, Mary, 'Hedy on Nurse's Day Off,' *PM*, December 9, 1945, m8–m10.

Murray, Lon, 'Hedy Lamarr Has Had Too Much Ecstasy!' *Modern Screen*, (April, 1939), pp. 32–3, p. 38.

Parsons, Louella, 'The Strange Case of Hedy Lamarr,' *Photoplay*, September, 1947, pp. 36–7, pp. 94–5.

Prelatsky, Burt, 'Hedy . . . Going, Going, Gone!' *Los Angeles Times*, March 24, 1968.

Proctor, Kay, 'Play Truth or Consequences with Hedy Lamarr,' *Photoplay*, November, 1942, pp. 45–6, p. 77.

Roberts, Myron, 'Dishonored Lady, or Autobiography Computer Style,' *Los Angeles Times*, November, 1966, pp. 47–9.

Skolsky, Sidney, 'Handbook on Hedy,' *Photoplay*, May, 1944, pp. 36–7, p. 73.

—— 'Hollywood Is My Beat,' *Hollywood Citizen News*, February 9, 1950, page not cited.

Stein, Fred, 'New York Spectacle,' *Hollywood Spectator*, 11(4), May 23, 1936, pp. 14–15.

Weller, George, 'The Ecstatic Hedy Lamarr,' January 26, 1939, source unknown.

West, Rosemary, 'Right About Love,' *Photoplay*, June, 1942, pp. 30–31, p. 85.

Young, Christopher, *The Films of Hedy Lamarr*, Secaucus, NJ: Citadel Press, 1978.

'Hedgerow (Exclusive Color Pictures of the Hilltop Home of Hedy Lamarr and John Loder),' *Motion Picture Magazine* July, 1944.

'Hedy Lamarr Enacts "Lady Without Passport,"' *Los Angeles Times*, September 15, 1950.

'Actress Hedy Lamarr Busted for Shoplifting at 77,' *New York Post*, August 2, 1991, p. 9.

PUBLICITY AND PRESS SOURCES FOR MARISA TOMEI

Brown, Georgia, 'Truly, Madly, Deeply,' *Village Voice*, February 16, 1993, p. 54.

Collins, G., 'Actress' Challenge in Change of Pace and Diction,' *New York Times*, August 10, 1992, 141: C13.

Denby, David, 'I Like To Be in America,' *New York*, May 22, 1995, p. 78.

Engel, J., 'She's Straight Out of Brooklyn,' *New York Times*, March 22, 1992, pp. 141: 12.

Fellingham, Christine, 'Beauty Watch,' *Glamour*, March, 1996, p. 104.

Gerstel, Judy, 'Tomei Rides Fast Track to Stardom,' *Hartford Courant*, February 28, 1993.

Graham, Lamar, 'The Hunger,' *GQ* June, 1994, p. 189.

Handleman, David, 'Women in Waiting,' *Vogue*, March, 1993, p. 206.

Harvey, Steve, 'Only in L.A.,' *Los Angeles Times*, March 23, 1995, page not cited.

Iverson, Annemarie, 'Making Up Marisa,' *Harper's Bazaar*, September, 1994, p. 414, p. 416.

Katz, Alyssa, 'Snap Queen,' *Village Voice*, March 31, 1992.

Koffler, Kevin, 'Marisa Tomei,' *Seventeen*, April 1, 1992, p. 39.

Lord, Lance, 'Marisa Tomei,' *Details*, April, 1992, p. 91.

Powell, Joanna, 'Marisa Grows Up,' *Redbook*, 184(1), (November, 1994), pp. 84–7, 126.

Silverman, Jeff, 'Marisa the Magnificent,' *Cosmopolitan*, 217(2), (August, 1994), pp. 130–33.

Tomei, Marisa, 'The Riveting Rosie Perez,' *Interview*, March, 1993, p. 135.

Van Ogtrop, Kristin, 'Marisa's Moment,' *Vogue*, May, 1994.

'The Backlot: Cinephile,' *Variety*, April 5, 1994.

PUBLICITY AND PRESS SOURCES FOR CHER

Barber, Rowland, 'What Happens When a Couple of Ex-Rock Freaks Join the Establishment,' *TV Guide*, July 14–20, 1973, pp. 2–23.

Cheever, Susan, 'Architectural Digest Visits Cher,' 48, November, 1991.

—— 'In A Broken Land,' *People*, 39(19), May 17, 1993, pp. 36–41.

De Jonge, Peter, 'The Magical Misery Tour: Cher in Armenia,' *Harper's Bazaar*, 3381 August, 1993, pp. 164–7.

Holden, Stephen, 'Queen of the Comeback, Cher Tries Yet Again,' *The New York Times* June 30, 1996, p. 24.

Jerome, Jim, 'Being Cher,' *People*, 49(20), May 25, 1998, pp. 84–92.

Klein, Roberta, 'Architectural Digest Visits Cher,' *Architectural Digest*, 53(10), October, 1996, pp. 150–7, pp. 244–5.

Leerhsen, Charles, 'The Many Faces of Cher,' *Newsweek*, November 30, 1987, pp. 66–72.

Pener, Degen, 'The Fashions,' *Entertainment Weekly*, April 3, 1998, pp. 40–45.

Petrucelli, Rita, *Cher: Singer and Actress*, Vero Beach, FL: Rourke Enterprises, 1989.

Slezek, Michael, 'Cher,' *Celebrity Style*, May, 1999, pp. 44–51.

Strauss, Neil, 'Cher Resurrected, Again, By A Hit,' *The New York Times*, March 11, 1999, B1, B6.

'Cher Gets Her Heads Together,' *TV Guide*, Oct. 16, 1976, pp. 10–11.

'Cheers For Cher,' *MS.*, July, 1988, pp. 53–8.

'Swept Away,' *People*, 49(13) April 6, 1998, 40.

INDEX